Desk Reference on
the Presidency

BOOKS IN THE DESK REFERENCE SERIES

CQ's Desk Reference on American Courts

CQ's Desk Reference on American Criminal Justice

CQ's Desk Reference on American Government,
Second Edition

CQ's Desk Reference on the Economy

CQ's Desk Reference on the Federal Budget

CQ's Desk Reference on the States

CONGRESSIONAL QUARTERLY'S

Desk Reference on
the Presidency

BRUCE WETTERAU

CQ PRESS

A Division of Congressional Quarterly Inc.
Washington, D.C.

CQ Press
A Division of Congressional Quarterly Inc.
1414 22nd Street, N.W.
Washington, D.C. 20037

(202) 822-1475; (800) 638-1710

www.cqpress.com

Printed and bound in the United States of America

04 03 02 01 00   5 4 3 2 1

Designed and typeset by Picas Rule, Baltimore, Maryland
Cover: Dennis Anderson

⊗ The paper used in this publication meets the minimum requirements of the American National Standard for Information Sciences—Permance of Paper for Printed Library Materials, ANSI Z39.48-1992.

Library of Congress Cataloging-in-Publication Data

Wetterau, Bruce.
    Congressional Quarterly's desk reference on the Presidency / Bruce Wetterau.
        p.   cm.— (Desk reference series)
    Includes bibliographical references and index.
    ISBN 1-56802-589-0 (cloth)
    1. Presidents—United States—Handbooks, manuals, etc. 2. Executive power—
    United States—Handbooks, manuals, etc. I. Title. II. Series.

JK516.W44 2000
973'.09'9—dc21   00-063024

CONTENTS

PREFACE

Were any presidents actually born in log cabins? What is an executive order? Are there limits on the president's power to order a nuclear attack? Which presidents vetoed the most and fewest bills? Who was the first president's wife to be called first lady? These are just a few of the many wide-ranging questions answered in CQ's *Desk Reference on the Presidency,* the sixth in CQ's series of seven question-and-answer reference books on government.

The five-hundred-plus questions in this new *Desk Reference* have been selected to provide an uncomplicated look at the whole of the American presidency—and vice presidency. Readers will find information on the presidents' and vice presidents' lives, the history and organization of their respective offices, and the means presidents use to exercise their powers. Chapters feature the presidents and their families, the president's and vice president's powers and duties, the campaigns and elections that brought them to office, highlights of presidential administrations, and the organization of the White House and executive branch.

All the material in the book has been selected and written to be accessible to the general reader—the text is designed to answer frequently asked questions, as well as to provide extensive additional reference information on the presidency. To that end, answers to questions present many useful facts and figures, as well as historic firsts and other interesting sidelights on the presidency. Lists appended to selected entries provide such basic reference information as birth and death dates for the presidents and vice presidents, election statistics, and a list of offices within the Executive Office of the President.

The question-and-answer format presents a wealth of information that can be easily understood, even by someone with little knowledge of the presidency. And, as in other books in the series, readers can use this *Desk Reference* in two ways: they can look up a specific fact, figure, procedure, term, event, or other piece of information relating to the presidency; or they can read through questions sequentially in a chapter and get a quick introduction to presidential powers and duties, presidential campaign history, and the like.

The many cross-references included in the *Desk Reference* are another important feature, because they help readers find specific information and lead them to entries on related subjects quickly and easily. In addition to the cross-references to related questions that follow many of the answers in this book, there are also free-standing cross-references that alert readers to questions that appear in another section, but that might have been included under the current heading as well. The extensive index makes it easy to locate specific information—such as definitions, important firsts, and key events. The alphabetically arranged index headings identify the number of the appropriate question, allowing the reader to turn directly to the desired information.

In many cases, readers will not need to go beyond the pages of this book to find answers to their questions on the presidency. But when further research becomes necessary, the "For Further Information" section at the end of each chapter provides lists of other recently published books. Included are those that provide amplifying information on the topics covered in the chapter, plus a few good encyclopedic works on the presidency that are repeated in all the chapter lists. Taken together, these sections serve as a basic guide to the wide range of books on the presidency.

Finally, mention must be made of all those who helped produce this book in such a timely fashion. My editor, Dave Tarr, deserves special thanks for his help at every stage of production; he has been very generous with his time, even when he had little to spare. Copy editor Sabra Bissette Ledent aimed her blue pencil at every nook and cranny of the manuscript, tightened copy, checked facts, and constantly questioned possible inconsistencies. Belinda Josey took the manuscript through the final phases of production, sorting out the myriad problems that inevitably arise when a manuscript is transformed into a printed book. Freelancers Cindy Poots Remington and Jon Rice provided valuable help with research and compiling lists during the manuscript stage. And, as always, the Alderman and Clemons libraries at the University of Virginia proved an invaluable resource. Among those on Alderman's Government Documents staff who deserve special mention for helping to resolve knotty research problems are Walter Newsome, government information librarian, and his assistant, Carol Hunter, and Haynes Earnhardt, library assistant at Alderman. Warner Grenade, assistant librarian at Clemons Library, also provided a helping hand on numerous occasions.

—Bruce Wetterau

THE OFFICE OF THE PRESIDENT

IN GENERAL

Q **1. Which president gave us the expression "bully pulpit"?**

A Theodore Roosevelt, whose activism set the tone for future presidents, popularized the notion of using the presidency as a "bully pulpit" in the early 1900s. Much more than earlier presidents, Roosevelt realized that he, as the central figure in the government, could command the public's attention when he spoke on an issue. That gave him the power to shape public opinion and push legislation through Congress.

As one who believed the president should "be as big a man as he can," Roosevelt did not hesitate to take advantage of the bully pulpit (*bully* in his day meant great or fantastic). During his administration, he became a champion of progressive reforms, including enactment of the Pure Food and Drug Act (1906), creation of the national park system, and aggressive enforcement of antitrust laws.

(See 29 Do presidents talk more today? 235 Can presidents sway Congress by appealing directly to the public? 261 How do the media and the president interact?)

Q **2. When was "Hail to the Chief" first played?**

A Now traditionally played in honor of the president at ceremonial functions, "Hail to the Chief" has been associated with the president in one way or another for about 170 years. The song was first played in the presence of President John Quincy Adams during a ceremony at the Chesapeake and Ohio Canal in 1828, and it made its debut at a presidential inauguration on March 4, 1837, when Martin Van Buren took office. First Lady Julia Tyler had it played for her husband, President John Tyler, during his administration, and the song was performed regularly in the late 1840s under President James K. Polk.

Chester A. Arthur, who served from 1881 to 1885, did not like "Hail to the Chief," however, and replaced it with "Presidential Polonaise." William McKinley revived

"Hail to the Chief" during his tenure in the late 1890s—with the addition of the musical ruffles and flourishes that are a familiar part of the modern version. "Hail to the Chief" has been played for presidents ever since.

The song's lyrics are from the poem "The Lady of the Lake," written by Sir Walter Scott in 1810. The composer of the melody is not known, but the song appeared in print in America in 1812.

Q 3. Who gave the title "president" to the chief executive?

A Delegates to the 1787 Constitutional Convention wrestled with the problem of just how to structure the office of the chief executive. Should the executive be strong or weak? How long should that official serve? Should there be one or several? At the time they resorted to working titles like governor, supreme executive, and national executive. An important concern was that there be no hint of the monarchical or tyrannical powers in the title.

"President" was not an unfamiliar term, however. Under the Articles of Confederation, Congress had a president, and George Washington was the president of the Constitutional Convention. South Carolina delegate Charles Pinckney had even submitted a plan for organizing the government that proposed naming the chief executive "president." The Convention's Committee of Detail finally settled the matter on August 6, 1787, when it borrowed the title "president" from Pinckney's plan.

Q 4. Which presidents are counted among the Founding Fathers?

A Two future presidents—George Washington and James Madison—were among the fifty-five delegates to the convention that drafted the Constitution in 1787. Both Washington and Madison signed the document, but not all of the delegates—who are considered the Founding Fathers—did. Some left Philadelphia before the document had been completed, and, of those present, three had enough reservations that they refused to sign. Two other future presidents, Thomas Jefferson and John Adams, were not at the convention because they were serving as ambassadors to France and England, respectively.

Today, the term *Founding Fathers* has fallen out of favor. The delegates to the Constitutional Convention are now usually called the *Framers* of the Constitution.

5. Who was the first president to use a presidential seal?

A The first known use of a seal was by Millard Fillmore, who had one made in 1850 by engraver Edward Stabler. No impressions of this first seal survive, but a second one—the first to bear the image of an eagle—was used by President Rutherford B. Hayes soon after his inauguration in 1877. The eagle on this new seal looked leftward while holding its wings upraised, and it clutched thirteen arrows in one claw. Theodore Roosevelt added the encircling legend, "Seal of the President of the United States," in 1903. Harry S. Truman ordered changes in 1945—the eagle's head was turned to face right instead of left (to conform with heraldic custom), and the eagle was encircled by forty-eight stars, one for each of the states. Dwight D. Eisenhower added stars in 1959 and 1960 after Alaska and Hawaii were admitted as states.

Q **6. Which vice president redesigned the vice-presidential seal?**

A Vice President Nelson A. Rockefeller, who won various new perks for the vice presidency, pushed for and got a more imposing image on the vice-presidential seal. The old seal featured an eagle at rest with a single arrow in its claw, but in 1975 Rockefeller had the eagle enlarged and shown with its wings spread upward, as if in flight. The new eagle also featured a starburst at its head and a cluster of arrows in its claw.

Among the other perks Rockefeller secured for the vice presidency were the first official residence and a better plane to use as *Air Force Two*.

(See 219 Do modern vice presidents have more responsibility? 346 When did the vice president get an official residence?)

Q **7. What purpose did the presidential flag originally serve?**

A The American flag served as the first presidential flag. In 1865 Navy Secretary Gideon Welles ordered it flown atop a ship's mainmast whenever President Abraham Lincoln was aboard and on deck. Later, in 1882, the navy designed the first original presidential flag. Emblazoned with the U.S. coat of arms on a blue background, it was to be flown whenever the president was aboard a ship. The army followed suit in 1898, except that its version had a large blue star on a scarlet background.

President Woodrow Wilson approved the design for a presidential flag for all occasions in 1916 (four white stars on a blue field). The present-day design was adopted in 1945, under President Harry S. Truman. The dark blue flag bore the presidential coat of arms surrounded by forty-eight white stars (two other stars were added after Alaska and Hawaii became states in 1959).

Q **8. Which president created the now-famous Oval Office?**

A The first oval-shaped office for the president was built in 1909, during the Taft administration, but there is no evidence that William Howard Taft had a hand in creating the office. The office was located in the West Wing of the White House, which housed the president's staff. Architect Nathan C. Wyeth, who designed the room, may well have been inspired by the Blue Room, an oval-shaped state room in the White House proper. Taft used his new office, but not for ceremonial functions. It fell to President Woodrow Wilson to sign the first bill there in 1914.

Taft's oval office was demolished in 1934 when President Franklin D. Roosevelt expanded the West Wing. The present-day Oval Office was then built, but in a different location in the West Wing—at the southeast corner, adjacent to the Rose Garden. Architect Eric Guler designed the office, which has remained essentially unchanged since then.

Q **9. How many presidents have there been?**

A Although forty-one presidents have held the office, President Bill Clinton is designated the forty-second president. Why? Because of a quirk in the numbering system, any president who serves nonconsecutive terms is numbered twice. Only one president, Grover Cleveland, has done so, and he has the distinction of being both the twenty-second (1885–1889) and twenty-fourth (1893–1897) presidents of the United States.

(See 286 Has any president served nonconsecutive terms? 348 When did the presidents and vice presidents serve?)

Q **10. Was anyone president before George Washington?**

A No. Peyton Randolph, a Virginia statesman, was the first American to be called president, but he was the first president of the Continental Congress, a post he held for a time in 1774 and 1775. In those early years of the Republic, before the Constitution had been written and ratified, Congress was the national government's only branch—the executive branch did not even exist. As such, Randolph's powers as president were nothing like those Washington and his successors had under the Constitution. Both John Hancock and John Jay, among others, also served as president of the Continental Congress. George Washington had the distinction of being the first president to serve under the Constitution.

(See 17 Did the Constitution establish a strong or a weak chief executive?)

Q 11. Who can become president? Vice president?

A The Constitution set forth very few qualifications for holding the office of president and vice president. The candidate for either office must be at least thirty-five years old, must be a native-born citizen, and must have resided in the United States for at least fourteen years. Also, anyone who has been twice elected to the office cannot serve for a third term (Twenty-second Amendment, 1951). In addition to the constitutionally mandated qualifications, presidential candidates also generally must have the experience, political skills, and personal appeal needed to win enough votes to become president—requirements that narrow the field considerably.

Originally the Constitution mentioned no specific qualifications for the vice president because it was assumed they would be the same as the president. But the Twelfth Amendment (1804), which established separate electoral college votes for president and vice president, states outright that the president and vice president are subject to the same qualifications. Experience and other factors also help to determine who becomes vice president, and candidates often are selected in part to help balance the ticket (such as geographically, ideologically).

(See 397 When did the practice of ticket balancing start?)

Q 12. What is the president's oath of office? The vice president's?

A The president's oath is set forth in the Constitution and consists of the following few words: "I do solemnly swear (or affirm) that I will faithfully execute the Office of President of the United States, and will to the best of my Ability, preserve, protect and defend the Constitution of the United States." President Franklin Pierce was the only president to use the optional "affirm" in 1853; his religious beliefs prohibited his use of the word *swear*.

George Washington began an inaugural tradition by taking the oath with his right hand raised and his left hand on the Bible. He ended his oath by adding the words "so help me God," another tradition that survives today.

While taking the oath with a Bible was common practice in Britain and America, there is no record that a Bible was used again in a presidential swearing-in ceremony until 1845, when James K. Polk took the oath of office. Records show Bibles were then used for every swearing-in from President James Buchanan's (1857) onward, except for Theodore Roosevelt's ceremony in 1901. Hastening to swear Roosevelt in after President William McKinley's assassination, officials omitted the Bible.

The vice president's oath does not appear in the Constitution, but it is the same one taken by all federal officials except the president: "I, [name], do solemnly swear (or affirm) that I will support and defend the Constitution of the United States against all enemies, foreign and domestic; that I will bear true faith and allegiance to the same; that I take this obligation freely, without any mental reservation or purpose of evasion; and that I will well and faithfully discharge the duties of the office on which I am about to enter. So help me God."

Q 13. Who is the only president to have been sworn in by a woman?

A Lyndon B. Johnson was the first and to date the only president sworn in by a woman. He is also the only president to be sworn in aboard *Air Force One*. Soon after President John F. Kennedy's assassination in Dallas, Texas, in 1963, Vice President Johnson boarded *Air Force One* to return to Washington to take over the reins of government. Sarah Tilghman Hughes, a federal district judge, administered the oath of office aboard the plane before it left the airport in Dallas.

Under normal circumstances, the chief justice of the United States administers the oath to the president, and a justice administers it to the vice president. In 1989 Dan Quayle became the first vice president sworn in by a woman. She was Sandra Day O'Connor, the first woman named to the nation's highest court.

Q 14. Which president's image appears on the $100,000 bill?

A President Woodrow Wilson's portrait is printed on the $100,000 bill. Wilson is not the only former president featured on big bills though—James Madison appears on the $5,000 note, Grover Cleveland on the $1,000, and William McKinley on the $500. Presidents also are featured on small bills. George Washington's likeness appears on the $1 bill, Abraham Lincoln's on the $5, Andrew Jackson's on the $20, and Ulysses S. Grant's on the $50. The $2 bills featuring President Thomas Jefferson's portrait are hard to come by, unless you happen to take the tour of his home, Monticello, at Charlottesville, Virginia, where they are given out as change.

Presidents are represented on coins as well. The Lincoln penny first appeared in 1909, the Washington quarter in 1932, the Jefferson nickel in 1938, the Franklin D. Roosevelt dime in 1946, the John F. Kennedy half-dollar in 1964, and the Dwight D. Eisenhower dollar in 1971. Specially minted commemorative coins also often feature the likenesses of presidents.

(See 174 Why did Congress wait so long before authorizing construction of the Washington Monument? 175 Which four presidents are represented on Mount Rushmore?)

Q **15. On how many postage stamps has President George Washington appeared?**

A President Washington's likeness has been portrayed on eighty different stamps, more than that of any other individual. The U.S. Post Office printed the first Washington stamp in 1847—and it was just the second adhesive stamp ever issued in the United States. Some other presidents who have been frequently commemorated on stamps are Thomas Jefferson, Andrew Jackson, Abraham Lincoln, Theodore Roosevelt, and Franklin D. Roosevelt.

Dead presidents are routinely remembered on at least one U.S. stamp (an 1866 law made it illegal to commemorate any living person on a stamp). This commemoration stems largely from the efforts of President Franklin Roosevelt, an avid stamp collector, who convinced the Post Office to issue a special series of presidential stamps in 1938 that featured all twenty-nine then-deceased presidents. A new series released in 1986 included the more recently deceased presidents.

Four first ladies also have had their own stamps—Martha Washington, Abigail Adams, Dolley Madison, and Eleanor Roosevelt—and so have fourteen vice presidents.

Q **16. How many state capitals are named after presidents?**

A Presidents have lent their names to just four state capitals—Jefferson City, Missouri; Madison, Wisconsin; Jackson, Mississippi; and Lincoln, Nebraska. No state capital is named after George Washington, but Washington, D.C., and the state of Washington are. Thirty-one states also have Washington Counties.

(See 174 Why did Congress wait so long before authorizing construction of the Washington Monument? 175 Which four presidents are represented on Mount Rushmore?)

THE PRESIDENCY AND THE CONSTITUTION

▶ *Which future presidents signed the U.S. Constitution? See 4 Which presidents are counted among the Founding Fathers?*

Q **17. Did the Constitution establish a strong or a weak chief executive?**

A Although delegates to the Constitution had at first wanted a president subservient to Congress, they ultimately created a government with a strong chief executive. After the Revolution, the American people understandably feared a return to the oppression suffered under the British monarchy, but by 1787 their attempt to create (under the Articles of Confederation) a national government run by a legislature had failed. Clearly, then, the young country needed a strong chief executive, but delegates to the Constitutional Convention in 1787 had no model on which to pattern the new office of chief executive. By degrees, however, the presidency took shape as a single, independent executive officer, elected by the people (not Congress) through the electoral college and empowered with a veto to check Congress's legislative powers. In addition, the delegates assigned the president other specific, enumerated powers that further strengthened the chief executive's office.

(See 20 What are the enumerated powers of the presidency? 226 Who has the power to make laws, Congress or the president? 227 What is a veto?)

Q 18. What other proposals for structuring the chief executive did delegates to the Constitutional Convention consider?

A One thorny problem confronting the Framers of the Constitution was how to structure the post of chief executive. They considered, among the many proposals, a three-person executive (each from a different region), an executive and a council, and a single executive with a life term. Once they decided on a single executive, they faced the issue of selection. Would the president be picked by Congress, state governors, electors, or the people? They chose electors, but had to decide whether the electors would be chosen by state legislatures or the people (they left it up to the state legislatures). The Framers also asked themselves whether the president should serve a life term, a single fixed term, or be eligible for reelection. Ultimately, they settled on a four-year term and the right to reelection. At the convention, debate, consideration, and final decisions often remained fluid throughout the deliberations, with decisions being made and unmade right up to the end.

Q 19. What does the executive branch do?

A To prevent abuses of power, the Framers of the Constitution relied on the basic principle of separation of powers—that is, they divided powers among the three branches of government: the legislative, executive, and judicial. Under this system, the executive branch, headed by the president, is responsible for carrying out and enforcing the laws enacted by the legislative branch. (The judicial branch rules on cases in which laws have been broken or the constitutionality of laws is in question.)

In fulfilling their executive branch duties, presidents are aided by the bureaucracy under their control. The vast size of the bureaucracy and of the federal budget indicate just how large the task of running the government has become. The many hundreds of federal programs and agencies run the gamut from school lunch programs to space exploration.

(See 22 Does the Constitution impose checks and balances on presidential powers? 42 How does government spending today now compare with that for the government's first year of operation? 43 When did the rapid growth of the executive branch begin? 460 What does the Executive Office of the President do?)

Q 20. What are the enumerated powers of the presidency?

A Delegates to the Constitutional Convention were reluctant to write specific powers for the executive (and the other branches) into the Constitution, but they were just as reluctant to resort to a general grant of powers. In the end, they enumerated all the president's powers in Article II of the Constitution, except for the presidential veto power, which appears in Article I. For certain of the enumerated powers, however, they left room for interpretation, allowing presidents to wield wider authority than any delegate might have imagined (these are sometimes called implied powers). Under the Constitution presidents have the power to:

— run the executive branch (executive power)
— appoint government officials
— enforce the laws
— command military forces, including state militias
— veto legislation (president's signature required to enact legislation)
— convene emergency sessions of Congress
— inquire and investigate, extending to all executive departments
— pardon criminals and others
— make treaties
— send and receive ambassadors
— commission officers.

Q 21. Which two constitutional provisions have provided the main justifications for expanding presidential powers?

A The Framers of the Constitution wrote the Constitution in a way that defined the duties and powers of each branch of government, but allowed room for interpretation and contingencies they could not foresee. Article II, which enumerates the president's powers, is more ambiguous than Article I, which grants Congress its powers. But two clauses in Article II, especially, have been used as a basis for expanding the president's powers: section 1, "the executive Power shall be vested in a President...," and section 3, the president "shall take Care that the Laws be faithfully executed..."

Section 3, for example, states clearly that the president is responsible for upholding the law, but just how far can a president go? Grover Cleveland used a broad interpretation of the clause to justify sending federal troops to break up a railroad laborers' strike in 1894 (the Pullman strike). Similarly, Dwight D. Eisenhower used troops in 1957 to enforce a court order to integrate Little Rock, Arkansas, public schools.

Q 22. Does the Constitution impose checks and balances on presidential powers?

A By design, the Constitution sets up a government composed of three independent branches—executive, legislative, and judicial—but has built-in constraints, called "checks and balances," to prevent any one branch from gaining too much power.

The Constitution grants presidents sweeping powers. They are in charge of administering federal agencies and laws and so direct a massive organization capable of drastically influencing society. But Congress has charge of creating and funding the agencies, and it can change them, shut them down, or remove them from the president's direction (if enough members are willing to vote for the changes). Congress's power to investigate executive branch agencies provides another check on the president's executive powers. And if need be, Congress has the power to impeach and remove the president. One way the president controls the executive branch is through his power to appoint the officials who head its agencies. That power is limited, however, by the Senate's power to confirm or reject appointments.

The Senate also shares the president's treaty powers—it must approve any treaties with foreign countries the president signs. (Executive agreements are another matter.) And, although the president is the commander in chief of the armed forces—and can commit American forces to combat in an emergency—he cannot declare war. Only Congress has that power.

The federal courts, particularly the Supreme Court, provide another check on the president's powers. Though the Court has been reluctant to do so, it has ruled against presidents from time to time for overstepping the limits of presidential authority. For example, in 1952 the Court blocked Harry S. Truman's attempt to seize steel mills during the Korean War. Truman had hoped to prevent a strike that would affect production of war materiel.

(See 210 Who declares war, the president or Congress? 241 Did the Supreme Court rule against expansion of presidential powers in the last century? 255 Does the Constitution grant the president or Congress greater powers to conduct foreign affairs? 259 Why have executive agreements become so important?)

Q 23. What checks on powers of the other branches does the president have?

A The power to veto legislation is among the president's strongest checks on Congress's power to pass laws. Congress can override a presidential veto, but that occurs only rarely because it requires a two-thirds vote of each house. The president also influences the legislative agenda by introducing bills, and modern presidents have used direct appeals to voters to push Congress toward favored legislation. Moreover, presidents can call Congress into emergency session and, within limits, also control how the agencies and programs Congress creates are run.

The president's powers include checks on the judicial branch as well. Court rulings have no effect unless the president enforces them, and his willingness to do so has sometimes affected rulings. Through the president's power to appoint judges (who Congress must either confirm or reject), the executive branch is able to exercise some control over the direction of legal opinion. The president also can work with Congress to pass legislation or a constitutional amendment that reverses a Supreme Court ruling. For example, the Twenty-sixth Amendment (1971) replaced an earlier law establishing the income tax, which the Court had ruled unconstitutional.

(See 226 Who has the power to make laws, Congress or the president? 247 Which presidents have had the greatest success in using appointments to influence the direction of Supreme Court rulings? 255 Does the Constitution grant the president or Congress greater powers to conduct foreign affairs?)

Q 24. What is the source of the president's law enforcement powers?

A Actually, the president's power to enforce the law flows from three sources—the Constitution, laws enacted by Congress, and decisions made by the Supreme Court. Article II, section 3, of the Constitution provides a firm foundation for the president's law enforcement powers by stating that the president "shall take Care that the Laws be faithfully executed." Section 2 names the president as commander in chief of the military, while Article IV, section 4 authorizes the president to use force to quell domestic violence when states ask for help. The president's power to appoint officials (Article II, section 1) is also important because it provides a way to influence the machinery of law enforcement. The president's power to pardon (Article II, section 2) offers yet another avenue of control.

In the twentieth century especially, Congress greatly expanded the president's law enforcement powers, widened the areas of federal regulatory control, and provided funding for the larger law enforcement bureaucracy that was needed. Although the expansion did not begin with President Franklin D. Roosevelt's New Deal, the 1930s saw federal regulatory control expand rapidly to many sectors of society, including banking, civilian aviation, the stock market, and working conditions. Later Congresses recognized the need for still more federal regulation in areas ranging from consumer credit to the environment. With each expansion of regulation, of course, the president's power and responsibilities increased.

Although Congress legislated much of the growth in law enforcement powers, the courts also added to them. For example, when the Supreme Court ruled against segregation in 1954 (*Brown v. Board of Education of Topeka*), the president and the executive branch became responsible for enforcing integration. Presidents Dwight D. Eisenhower and John F. Kennedy both resorted to using federal troops to enforce Court-ordered integration in the South.

(See 205 How does the president control law enforcement policy? 206 Can the president pardon criminals?)

▶ *What does the Constitution say about electing the president? See 380 Do we elect the president and vice president directly? 381 How does the electoral college work?*

Q **25. How did the vice presidency come about?**

A The vice presidency was almost an afterthought—a matter handled during the closing weeks of the Constitutional Convention in 1787 that provided a convenient way to tie up some loose ends. The idea of having a vice president was not new—five states had lieutenant governors, and, interestingly, New York's lieutenant governor served as the state senate president (with the power to break tie votes).

The first problem the vice presidency solved was electoral college voting procedures. Each elector would cast two votes for president (one had to be for a candidate from outside the elector's home state). The candidate receiving the most votes would serve as president, the one receiving the second most votes would serve as vice president. (This system was later changed. *See 437 What went wrong in the presidential election of 1800?*)

Another loose end involved filling the post of president of the Senate. Delegates reasoned that someone in the Senate would have to have the authority to break tie votes—a situation likely to occur with some frequency because the body was composed of two senators from each state. Making a senator president of the Senate would mean his state would have an extra vote. So delegates settled that duty on the vice president, even though the arrangement blurred the separation between the executive and legislative branches.

Finally, the vice presidency solved another problem—that of who would succeed a president in the event of his resignation, death, or disability. Delegates had balked at plans to draw a successor from the Senate, the Supreme Court, and even a President's Council.

(See 54 What happens if the president dies or is disabled while in office? 56 When was the current line of succession fixed by law? 57 Who was the first acting president?)

Q **26. Which amendments to the Constitution deal with the presidency?**

A Of the amendments passed since the Bill of Rights (the first ten), only four deal directly with the presidency or vice presidency. The Twelfth Amendment (1804) changed voting procedures in the electoral college, mandating separate votes for president and vice president (to prevent a repeat of the 1800 electoral debacle in which both the presidential candidate, Thomas Jefferson, and the vice-presidential candidate, Aaron Burr, received the same number of votes). The Twelfth Amendment also set the qualifications for vice president (same as for the president). The Twentieth Amendment (1933), known as the Lame Duck Amendment, changed inauguration day from March 4 to January 20, so that the president-elect would take office sooner after the November elections. It also stipulated that the vice president-elect would succeed if the president-elect was disqualified or died. The Twenty-second Amendment (1951) limited presidents to two terms, and the Twenty-fifth (1967) clarified succession of the vice president to the presidency, filling of vacancies in the vice presidency, and procedures for dealing with presidential disability.

(See 54 What happens if the president dies or is disabled while in office? 56 When was the current line of succession fixed by law? 60 Has the office of the vice president ever been vacant? 437 What went wrong in the presidential election of 1800?)

27. Have other constitutional amendments on the presidency been proposed?

A Congress has not approved any additional constitutional amendments on the presidency for ratification by the states, but amendments—some radical—have been suggested. They include: doing away with the electoral college and electing the president directly, limiting the president to a single six-year term, repealing the two-term limit, giving the president a line-item veto, making the vice presidency an appointive office, doing away with the vice presidency and using special elections to fill vacancies in the presidency, allowing Congress to remove the current president (and Congress) by a "no confidence" vote, and allowing members of Congress to serve in the cabinet while retaining a seat in Congress.

THE PRESIDENCY, THEN AND NOW

Q **28. Where did presidents stay before the White House?**

A When the government was organized under the Constitution in 1789, New York City served as the nation's first capital. After his inauguration, President George Washington and First Lady Martha Washington spent the first months of his term at the Walter Franklin House on Cherry Street in lower Manhattan. They soon found larger quarters at the Macomb Mansion on Broadway and moved there in February 1790, but not for long. By August of that year the Washingtons were heading for the new—though also temporary—national capital at Philadelphia. There, they took up lodgings at a house owned by Robert Morris, a wealthy banker who had helped finance the American Revolution. The president and first lady lived in Morris's house for the remainder of his presidency, paying $3,000 a year in rent. Because at the end of Washington's second term in 1797 the nation's new capital at Washington, D.C., was still under construction, Washington's successor, John Adams, also stayed at the Robert Morris House.

(See 290 Who was the first president to live in the White House?)

Q **29. Do presidents talk more today?**

A Being or becoming a president in the early years of the Republic did not include making a lot of speeches—in fact, presidential candidates did not even give campaign speeches until the 1840s. By one count, the presidents who served between 1789 and 1900 together delivered only about one thousand speeches. That was about two hundred fewer than Gerald R. Ford gave in his two-and-a-half-year presidency during the 1970s.

Radio, and later television, certainly increased the impact of the president's words, and twentieth-century presidents did not hesitate to take advantage of the new media to make major policy pronouncements. For example, President Calvin Coolidge, nicknamed "Silent Cal," was not so silent—he delivered twenty-four major addresses while in office from 1923 to 1929 and held an average of eighty news conferences a year. Among recent presidents delivering twenty or more major addresses per term were Dwight D. Eisenhower (both terms), Richard M. Nixon (first term), and Ronald Reagan (both terms). Presidents also get out more these days. Bill Clinton tops the list for public appearances of all kinds in a single term (except political appearances). He made 1,371 during his first term.

(See 1 Which president gave us the expression "bully pulpit"? 262 Which modern presidents have been effective communicators? 268 Which president held the most news conferences? 335 How have the mass media helped presidents shape public opinion? 444 When did presidential candidates first give speeches in their own behalf?)

Q 30. How has the president's staff grown?

A Large presidential staffs are a fairly recent innovation. Herbert Hoover, for example, was aided by just four presidential assistants about forty clerks and typists, as well as an assortment of naval and military attachés. Since the 1930s, however, the size and complexity of the federal government have grown, along with the job of running it. Modern presidents have come to rely on the inner circle of advisers and assistants who make up the White House Office. The actual size of the staff varies from one president to the next. For example, Bill Clinton's White House Office numbered 389 employees in the mid-1990s.

(See 35 Which president got the first publicly funded staff assistant? 455 How is the White House staff organized?)

Q 31. Where did early presidents find their assistants?

A For many years presidents were expected to hire any assistants they needed at their own expense. George Washington, for example, hired his nephew to do clerical work and paid him $300 a year out of his own pocket. Later presidents appointed both relatives and political cronies.

Presidents did have other resources at their disposal, however. For policy advice they relied more heavily on their cabinet appointees than modern presidents do. In addition, they could count on borrowing staffers from the executive branch departments (including the military) for work in the White House. Sometimes presidents carried this process, called detailing, a step further by appointing political advisers to posts in cabinet departments, even though they planned to use them full time for White House duties.

In the 1800s especially, the menial work staffers were assigned, their low pay, and political cronyism sometimes resulted in the appointment of presidential staffers who were inadequate or just plain corrupt. In the 1870s, for example, President Ulysses S. Grant's personal secretary, Gen. Orville E. Babcock, became a major embarrassment to the Grant administration when his role in the Whiskey Ring scandal came to light.

(See 370 What happened in the Whiskey Ring scandal?)

Q **32. How has the cabinet grown since President Washington's administration?**

A During the first year of his administration in 1789, George Washington had just three cabinet departments—State, Treasury, and War. Over the years, however, the role of the federal government expanded enormously and Congress saw fit to approve new departments to meet the government's needs. In addition to the original three departments (the War Department was reorganized and renamed the Department of Defense in 1947), another eleven are in place today. The cabinet departments in order of their creation are:

Department	Year Created
State	1789
Treasury	1789
War	1789
Interior	1849
Justice	1870
Agriculture	1889
Commerce (originally Commerce and Labor, established in 1903)	1913
Labor	1913
Health, Education, and Welfare (reorganized and renamed Health and Human Services in 1979)	1953
Housing and Urban Development	1965
Transportation	1966
Energy	1977

Department	Year Created
Education	1980
Veterans Affairs	1989

(See 464 What does the president's cabinet do?)

Q 33. How has American military power grown over the years?

A Until the twentieth century, the United States maintained only a small standing army, preferring to rely on state militias that could be federalized when war threatened. The country did not even have a navy when the Constitution was ratified in 1789 (warships from the Revolution had been sold off). Congress created the U.S. Navy in 1794, when it authorized the building of the U.S.S. *Constitution* and other frigates, but at the outset of the War of 1812, the Navy had only sixteen seagoing warships. The army at that time was in even worse shape. Composed of volunteers and raw militia, it was poorly equipped and lacked experienced commanders.

During the next century and a half, U.S. military strength expanded and contracted to meet emergencies as they arose, but from World War II on, the country, now one of the world's leading military powers, committed itself to maintaining a large standing army. The Korean and Vietnam Wars, the need to provide military forces should allied nations be attacked, and competition with the Soviet Union during the cold war, were additional reasons for having a strong military.

Although the army was its largest at the close of World War II (eight million men), it still numbered about two million in 1990, when the cold war ended. At that time the navy had 546 ships (including 15 aircraft carriers and 31 nuclear subs), the air force had 24 fighter wings, and the country's nuclear arsenal included 1,600 intercontinental ballistic missiles.

Q 34. In the early 1800s, where did most people employed by the federal government work?

A When President George Washington took office in 1789, the federal government was making do with just a few hundred employees. By 1816 that number had grown to 4,800, but only about 500 of them could be found working in the nation's capital. At that time the Post Office Department, created as a federal agency in 1792, was employing the lion's share of federal workers in post offices around the country, and it continued to be the largest employer in the federal government well into the twentieth century.

35. Which president got the first publicly funded staff assistant?

A Congress first appropriated money for a presidential assistant in 1857, at the start of James Buchanan's term, but funding for staffers remained limited well into the twentieth century. For example, President Herbert Hoover created a small sensation when he increased the number of his administrative assistants from two to four.

(See 30 How has the president's staff grown? 31 Where did early presidents find their assistants?)

Q **36. When did presidents begin to rely on press secretaries to handle the media?**

A President Herbert Hoover appointed the first press secretary in 1930, a reporter named George Akerson. But by the late 1800s, presidents already had begun to rely on aides to deal with news reporters. During Theodore Roosevelt's administration in the early 1900s, the importance of media relations increased considerably.

The position of press secretary began evolving during the administration of Woodrow Wilson and culminated in the formal creation of the post by Hoover. President Franklin D. Roosevelt's press aide, Associated Press reporter Stephen T. Early, was the first press secretary to become known nationally as the president's spokesman, however. Former *New York Times* reporter James C. Hagerty, press secretary to Dwight D. Eisenhower, established the organizational and operational techniques adopted by his successors.

(See 261 How do the media and the president interact?)

Q **37. Has the president always been responsible for preparing a proposed federal budget?**

A Until the early 1900s Congress handled its responsibility for the nation's finances without even preparing a budget. Government departments and agencies within the government simply submitted their budget requests directly to Congress, and presidents had little to say about spending levels. After all, in those days federal spending remained below $800 million. During World War I, however, federal spending shot up to billions of dollars a year. In response, Congress decided to give the president the job of preparing an annual budget proposal. With the 1921 Budget and Accounting Act, Congress created the Bureau of the Budget within the executive branch and required the president to submit budget requests to Congress. In late 1921 President

Warren G. Harding sent Congress the first formal budget request. Some fifty years later, the Bureau of the Budget became the Office of Management and Budget during the Nixon administration.

Q 38. Has the first lady always had her own White House office?

A No, the first vestiges of a staff and office for the first lady did not appear until the beginning of the twentieth century. In 1901 President Theodore Roosevelt's wife Edith brought in the first staffer to act as her social secretary—a clerk named Isabella Hagner detailed to the White House by the War Department. Hagner worked out of Mrs. Roosevelt's bedroom until 1902, when she was given a desk in the West Hall. Arrangements for the staffs of subsequent first ladies remained informal until the 1940s, although demands on them and their staff continued to grow. In 1942 First Lady Eleanor Roosevelt finally got an office of her own in the newly completed East Wing of the White House, and the first lady's staff has been headquartered there ever since.

(See 180 What does the first lady do? 458 What is detailing?)

Q 39. Why was the Executive Office of the President established?

A During the 1930s, when President Franklin D. Roosevelt created dozens of New Deal agencies to combat the depression, the government simply became too big to manage with a small White House staff. Roosevelt appointed a blue-ribbon committee headed by Louis D. Brownlow, a public administration scholar, to look into the matter, and in 1939 Congress agreed to many of the Brownlow Commission's recommendations, including funding for six presidential assistants and creation of the Executive Office of the President (EOP). Roosevelt issued Executive Order 8248 on September 8, 1939, to effect the reorganization.

Under Roosevelt, the EOP was made up of just five units, including the Bureau of the Budget and the White House Office, organized to help the president set policy and better manage the sprawling government bureaucracy. But later presidents, and Congress, have added various other councils, boards, and offices to the EOP, including the Council of Economic Advisers and the National Security Council.

(See 460 What does the Executive Office of the President do?)

Q 40. What are the major parts of the executive branch?

A The president and his closest advisers in the White House Office form the nucleus of the executive branch. Outside this inner circle is another, larger staff that also serves the president. It is known as the Executive Office of the President (EOP). The EOP advises the president and helps him to manage the vast bureaucracy that makes up the executive branch.

The fourteen cabinet departments—Treasury, State, Defense, Commerce, and others—constitute the next level in executive branch organization. As the major operating divisions of the executive branch, they carry out programs and policies, monitor the performance of programs, and gather and disseminate information.

Operating outside the cabinet departments are the executive agencies and commissions, many of which have a quasi-independent status. They include the Central Intelligence Agency and National Aeronautics and Space Administration. Government corporations, such as Amtrak and the Tennessee Valley Authority, are another type of executive agency.

Regulatory commissions set and monitor standards for businesses and others in various economic sectors. They may be located within cabinet departments (such as the Food and Drug Administration located in the Department of Health and Human Services) or operate as independent agencies (for example, the Federal Trade Commission and Consumer Product Safety Commission).

Q 41. Which cabinet department occupies the world's largest office building?

A The Department of Defense has its headquarters in the Pentagon, a five-sided building located just outside Washington, D.C., in Virginia. The Pentagon has three times the floor space of New York City's Empire State Building and is said to be the world's largest office building. Completed in 1943 for $83 million, it was designed to serve as headquarters for all branches of the military. Some 26,000 military and civilian personnel work in the Pentagon, which has seventeen and a half miles of corridors, 150 stairways, 7,748 windows, and 15,000 light fixtures. The Pentagon is the only departmental headquarters situated outside the District of Columbia.

(See 476 When was the Defense Department created?)

Q 42. How does government spending today compare with that for the government's first year of operation?

A By today's standards, federal spending in 1789 was a mere drop in the ocean—$639,000 that year compared with some $1.8 trillion in 2001. The government now spends that $639,000 about every eleven seconds or less, day in and day out, all year-round. But in George Washington's day there were no public retirement or health plans like Social Security and Medicaid, no federally funded highway systems, and nothing like the military forces the United States can muster today.

(See 33 How has American military power grown over the years?)

Q 43. When did the rapid growth of the executive branch begin?

A Expansion of the federal workforce began during the troubled depression era of the 1930s, when President Franklin D. Roosevelt created many New Deal programs to help ease the crisis and reform sectors of the economy. Between 1930 and 1940 federal employment roughly doubled to 699,000 civilian workers (excluding the U.S. Post Office). World War II brought another growth spurt—civilian federal workers topped 3.3 million in 1945. With the return to peacetime, federal employment fell to just under 1.5 million by 1950. During the mid-1960s, which saw the advent of Great Society programs under President Lyndon B. Johnson, employment rose to over 2 million, where it remained until the downsizing of the 1990s. Civilian (nonpostal) employment dropped below 2 million again in 1996.

Q 44. How many people work for the departments and agencies now?

A Total civilian employment in the executive branch, excluding the quasi-independent U.S. Postal Service, was about 1.86 million in 1998. (That number rises to 2.7 million when postal workers are included.) The 693,000 civilian employees of the Defense Department form the single largest bloc within the executive branch, excluding postal workers. Veterans Affairs ranks second (240,000 employees), followed by the Treasury Department (141,000), Health and Human Services (130,000), and Justice (123,000).

45. Why does government spending rise year after year?

A Surpluses in recent years have made it possible for the government to take in more money than it spends, but that does not mean spending has gone down. Federal spending has continued to grow for several reasons. For one thing, agencies and programs run by the government can and do provide people with useful, worthwhile services, and so many of them are popular with voters. That popularity gives politicians in turn an incentive to widen the benefits offered, to help more people, and therefore to garner more votes—even though the costs increase too. Thus spending rises, and politicians resist cutbacks in popular programs.

The type of program also matters. Entitlement programs guarantee benefits to anyone who meets certain qualifications of need. Medicaid, for example, provides health care to the poor, and as more needy people require medical help, spending for the program rises automatically, by law.

Another reason federal spending rises is institutional. Agencies, once established, tend to want to grow and expand their budgets by at least a small amount each year. And the economy comes into play as well. At times of high inflation, the cost of everything rises and government spending increases along with it.

Q **46. Did the Clinton administration succeed in cutting the size of government?**

A After the administration's 1993 National Performance Review, headed by Vice President Al Gore, President Bill Clinton set in motion a plan to cut some 252,000 federal jobs and save more than $100 billion over five years. In addition to planned spending reductions and efforts to promote greater efficiency, Clinton's program sought to reduce the 2.9 million workforce (including postal workers) through early retirement, buyouts, and attrition. A year later, in 1994, the administration said it had eliminated 70,000 jobs and saved $47 billion. Federal employment then continued to decline, falling to about 1.86 million (excluding postal workers) in the executive branch in 1998, down from almost 2.16 million in 1993. The reduction in the executive branch alone was impressive—over 300,000—but nearly two-thirds of that was achieved by downsizing civilian employment at the Defense Department, which was being cut back anyway because the cold war had ended. Although the cuts undoubtedly saved the government millions, federal spending continued to grow larger each year throughout the 1990s.

(See 43 When did the rapid growth of the executive branch begin? 500 What was the National Performance Review all about?)

▶ *See also After the Presidency in Chapter 2, and Campaigns and Elections in Chapter 6.*

Q **47. Where was the first inauguration held?**

A The nation's capital was located in New York City when George Washington took the oath of office on April 30, 1789. Washington encountered cheering crowds along his route from his home in Virginia to New York, as well as outside Federal Hall on Wall Street, where he took the oath of office. (Since 1817 the oath traditionally has been administered outdoors.) Washington then went inside to deliver the first inaugural address to the Senate, and later that day he attended the first inaugural ball. He did so, however, without his wife, Martha, who was still en route from Virginia. Washington's second inauguration and John Adams's only inauguration were held at Philadelphia's Congress Hall. The nation's capital was located in Philadelphia from 1790 to 1800.

In 1801 Thomas Jefferson became the first president to be inaugurated in the newly constructed national capital at Washington, D.C. Inaugurations are traditionally held at the Capitol. Among the other inaugural facts are:

First news of an inaugural carried by telegraph: Samuel Morse, inventor of the telegraph, personally transmitted a description of James K. Polk's ceremony in 1845.

First inaugural address broadcast by radio: Calvin Coolidge's in 1925.

First inauguration recorded on film: Herbert Hoover's in 1929.

Regular live television broadcasts of inaugural addresses: Began with Harry S. Truman's inauguration in 1949.

(See 12 What is the president's oath of office? The vice president's? 49 Who had the first inaugural parade?)

Q **48. Have any outgoing presidents refused to attend their successors' inaugurations?**

A Particularly after a hotly contested election, relations between the outgoing president and the president-elect on inauguration day may not always be the best. Only three presidents, however, have refused to attend their successors' inaugurations. John

Adams, an ardent Federalist and in 1801 the outgoing president, boycotted the inauguration of Thomas Jefferson, leader of the Democratic-Republicans who had defeated Adams's reelection bid. John Quincy Adams, who had earned Andrew Jackson's wrath in 1824 by winning an election decided in the House of Representatives, decided against attending Jackson's 1829 inauguration. And President Andrew Johnson boycotted Ulysses S. Grant's inaugural in 1869 after Grant refused to ride in the same carriage with him.

(See 438 How many presidential elections have been decided by the House?)

Q 49. Who had the first inaugural parade?

A President James Madison's inauguration in 1809 featured the first organized inaugural parade. It proceeded from the White House to the Capitol for Madison's swearing-in ceremony. Inaugural parades have changed considerably since then, though. Today the parade begins after the president takes the oath of office and proceeds from the Capitol down Pennsylvania Avenue back to the White House. Bands, floats, and thousands of marchers take part, and costs have soared—Bill Clinton's inaugural parade cost an estimated $36 million, about two-thirds of which was recouped through the sale of broadcast rights, tickets, and souvenirs. Only three parades were cancelled in the twentieth century: Warren G. Harding's in 1921 (disagreement over costs), Franklin D. Roosevelt's fourth inaugural in 1945 (disagreement over costs), and Ronald Reagan's second in 1985 (severely cold weather). Breaking with tradition, Jimmy Carter walked almost the entire parade route in 1977; George Bush and Bill Clinton also walked part of the way.

Q 50. How did President Andrew Jackson's inaugural differ from earlier ones?

A Having campaigned as a man of the people, President Andrew Jackson threw open the White House doors for his inaugural, allowing people free run of the place. Unfortunately for Jackson, thousands took advantage of the opportunity and in the raucous merrymaking did considerable damage inside the White House.

Q 51. Which inauguration featured the first multiple inaugural balls?

A Dwight D. Eisenhower's inaugural committee organized the first multiple inaugural balls in 1953 to accommodate a growing guest list for this prestigious social event. Since the two Eisenhower balls, the number has grown considerably—White House newcomers Bill and Hillary Clinton visited eleven separate inaugural balls in 1993.

Q 52. When was January 20 set as inauguration day?

A With ratification of the Twentieth (so-called Lame Duck) Amendment in 1933, January 20 became the date for the president's inauguration. The amendment pushed the date back from March 4 so that newly elected presidents would not have to wait nearly four months after the November election before taking office (and outgoing lame duck presidents could return home sooner). Congress had set the original March 4 inauguration date in 1792.

(See 179 What is a lame duck president?)

Q 53. Which president gave the longest inauguration speech?

A Undaunted by driving rain, President William Henry Harrison gave a two-hour inaugural speech that rambled on for almost 8,500 words and still ranks as the longest on record. Unfortunately for Harrison, the combination of his long speech and the rain proved deadly—the new president caught cold and died of pneumonia on April 4, 1841, having served just thirty-one days in office. His term was the shortest of any president's.

George Washington holds the record for the shortest inaugural speech—135 words—delivered at the start of his second term in 1793.

Q 54. What happens if the president dies or is disabled while in office?

A The Constitution stipulates that if the president dies, resigns, is removed from office, or becomes disabled, the vice president assumes the powers and duties of the presidency. Originally it was silent about whether the vice president would actually succeed to the presidency or only serve as an acting president. Vice President John Tyler settled that question, however, soon after President William Henry Harrison died in 1841; he simply announced his plan to serve out Harrison's term and moved into the White House. With the precedent set, the right of succession to the remainder of a dead president's term went unquestioned until the Twenty-fifth Amendment, ratified in 1967, spelled out the procedure.

The Twenty-fifth Amendment also established procedures for filling vacancies in the vice presidency, whether by death, resignation, or succession to the presidency. Whenever a vacancy occurs, the president nominates a new vice president, and Congress confirms or rejects the nominee by a majority vote of both houses.

The amendment also dealt with situations in which presidents were unable to perform their duties, even temporarily. Prior to 1967 eleven presidents had been disabled for some part of their term, notably James A. Garfield and Woodrow Wilson, both of whom were incapacitated for months (Garfield eventually died).) But the Constitution offered no clear guidelines on when power should be transferred. Especially during the cold war years, when nuclear war could have broken out in minutes, the president had to be able to make command decisions at all times.

Thus the Twenty-fifth Amendment set up procedures for the temporary transfer of the president's powers to the vice president, who then becomes the acting president. Presidents can declare their inability to perform their duties (which President Ronald Reagan did before undergoing cancer surgery in 1985), or the vice president and a majority of the cabinet officers can declare the president disabled, as in the case of illness or mental instability.

(See 57 Who was the first acting president? 154 Did President Garfield's doctors contribute to his death from an assasin's bullet? 157 What medical condition left President Wilson incapacitated for several months? 220 Can the vice president declare the president unfit to perform the presidential duties? 221 What precedent did Vice President John Tyler set in 1841?)

Q 55. **Which presidents died in office?**

A The following eight presidents died before the end of their terms, and in each case the vice president succeeded to the presidency:

William Henry Harrison died on April 4, 1841, one month after catching cold during his inauguration. Harrison had delivered the longest inaugural speech on record while standing outside in a heavy rain. John Tyler became the first vice president to succeed to the presidency.

Zachary Taylor died on July 9, 1850, having served only sixteen months. He had become ill and died after overeating at a long, hot outdoor ceremony celebrating the Fourth of July at the Washington Monument. Vice President Millard Fillmore succeeded him.

Abraham Lincoln died on April 15, 1865, the day after being shot by actor John Wilkes Booth. Lincoln was killed a little over a month after starting his second term. Vice President Andrew Johnson succeeded him.

James A. Garfield was shot in a Washington, D.C., railroad station by Charles J. Guiteau, a disgruntled office-seeker, on July 2, 1881, and died two and a half months later from his wounds (September 19). In all, Garfield served just over six months in office. Vice President Chester A. Arthur succeeded him.

William McKinley was shot on September 6, 1901, by anarchist Leon Czolgosz at the Pan-American Exposition in Buffalo, New York. He died of gangrene eight days later, on September 14. Vice President Theodore Roosevelt succeeded him.

Warren G. Harding died of unknown natural causes (possibly from the aftereffects of a heart attack) on August 2, 1923. Because the Teapot Dome scandal involving his administration came to light shortly after his death, some speculated that Harding had committed suicide or had been poisoned, but no evidence supporting either theory was found. Vice President Calvin Coolidge succeeded him.

Franklin D. Roosevelt died of a cerebral hemorrhage on April 12, 1945, early in his fourth term as president. Roosevelt had been weakened by the demands of running the country during World War II. Vice President Harry S. Truman succeeded him.

John F. Kennedy was shot and killed on November 22, 1963, while traveling in a motorcade in Dallas, Texas. Kennedy's assassin was Lee Harvey Oswald, a misfit who had defected to the Soviet Union for a time. Oswald was himself assassinated by a Dallas nightclub owner, Jack Ruby. Vice President Lyndon B. Johnson succeeded Kennedy.

(See 221 What precedent did Vice President John Tyler set in 1841? 296 Which presidents were assassinated?)

Q 56. When was the current line of succession fixed by law?

A While the Constitution was silent on who would succeed in the event both the president and vice president died, it did empower Congress to pass legislation on the matter. The current law on presidential succession was enacted in 1947 to address President Harry S. Truman's concerns that elected, not appointed, officials be closest to the top of the line. The order of succession as it stands today is: vice president, Speaker of the House, president pro tempore of the Senate, secretary of state, secretary of the Treasury, secretary of defense, attorney general, and then the secretaries of interior, agriculture, commerce, labor, health and human services, housing and urban development, transportation, energy, education, and veterans affairs (the secretaries are listed in the order of their department's creation). This order of succession also applies in the event the president-elect, or the president-elect and vice president-elect, dies or fails to qualify before inauguration day.

Congress's first succession law, passed in 1792, called for a special election if both the president and vice president died. In 1886 a line of succession based on the president's cabinet was established, starting with the secretary of state.

(See 60 Has the office of the vice president ever been vacant? 401 What happens if a party's presidential candidate dies before the election?)

Q 57. Who was the first acting president?

A Vice President George Bush became the first acting president on July 13, 1985, while President Ronald Reagan was undergoing cancer surgery. The Twenty-fifth Amendment (1967) established the procedure of making the vice president acting president whenever the president is temporarily unable to carry out his presidential duties. Following procedures established by the amendment, President Reagan sent letters to the Speaker of the House of Representatives and the president pro tempore of the Senate before entering surgery, and so formally transferred power on a temporary basis to acting president Bush. Eight hours later, after completion of the surgery, President Reagan sent two more letters announcing that he was again able to discharge the duties of his office. For his part, Bush played tennis and downplayed his temporary change in status out of respect for President Reagan.

(See 54 What happens if the president dies or is disabled while in office?)

Q 58. Which president resigned from office?

A Only one president, Richard M. Nixon, resigned from office before completing his full term. He was forced to resign on August 9, 1974—part way through his second term—to avoid being impeached and removed from office for his part in attempts to cover up the Watergate scandal.

Nixon had vehemently denied having any role in the scandal, which first came to light in 1972, after White House operatives were caught trying to burglarize the Democratic Party's headquarters in the Watergate office and apartment complex in Washington, D.C. But investigations by newspaper reporters, the Senate, and by a special government prosecutor led to a series of revelations about abuses of power and White House attempts to cover them up. In late 1973 the special prosecutor subpoenaed tapes the president had made of conversations in his White House Oval Office, but Nixon refused to release them, citing executive privilege. The Supreme Court finally ordered the president to turn over the tapes, which showed he had in fact been deeply involved in the cover-up.

With impeachment all but certain, President Nixon announced his resignation on August 8, 1974, and left the White House by helicopter the next day. Vice President Gerald R. Ford was sworn in as president the same day that Nixon left.

(See 55 Which presidents died in office? 59 Have any vice presidents resigned from office? 63 How many presidents have been impeached? 373 What happened in the Watergate scandal?)

Q 59. Have any vice presidents resigned from office?

A Two vice presidents have resigned from office—one intent on greener pastures and the other forced to step down because of corruption charges. President Andrew Jackson's vice president, John C. Calhoun, stepped down in December 1832 when South Carolina promised him a seat in the U.S. Senate. Calhoun had wanted to stay in position for a run at the presidency, but he had fallen out with Jackson and had been dumped from the ticket for Jackson's 1832 reelection bid. Because of that, he found South Carolina's offer too good to pass up. He sent a short letter of resignation to the secretary of state.

Vice President Spiro T. Agnew had troubles of a different sort. Prosecutors filed criminal charges against him in mid-1973 after a federal investigation into bribes he allegedly took from contractors and others while serving in various state government posts in Maryland—including his years as governor. Agnew denied the charges, but two months later pleaded no contest to one count of income tax evasion. He resigned from the vice presidency on October 10, 1973. In return, prosecutors dropped the more serious charges, and Agnew was sentenced to only a $10,000 fine and three years' probation.

Q 60. Has the office of the vice president ever been vacant?

A Before 1967, no mechanism existed to fill the vacancy created when the vice president died, resigned, or succeeded to the presidency. The office remained vacant sixteen times before 1967 (eighteen times to date) for periods ranging from under two months to nearly four years. Since 1789, seven vacancies have occurred because the vice president died while in office, nine because the vice president succeeded to the presidency, and two because of resignation. The shortest vacancy was 57 days from October to December 1973, following Spiro T. Agnew's resignation. The longest was three years and 332 days, after Vice President John Tyler succeeded to office in 1841.

The Twenty-fifth Amendment, ratified in 1967, established the system under which presidents were allowed to appoint a new vice president (with congressional confirmation) to fill vacancies. So far, two vice presidents (Gerald R. Ford and Nelson A. Rockefeller) have been appointed to the office. The following vice presidents died, resigned their office, or succeeded to the presidency.

George Clinton died on April 20, 1812, becoming the first vice president to die in office and leaving President James Madison without a vice president until the end of his first term, March 4, 1813.

Elbridge Gerry died on November 23, 1814, leaving Madison without a vice president until the end of his second term, March 4, 1817.

John C. Calhoun resigned on December 28, 1832, leaving President Andrew Jackson without a vice president until March 4, 1833. Jackson had dumped Calhoun from his reelection ticket and Calhoun resigned to take a seat in the U.S. Senate.

John Tyler became the first vice president to succeed to the presidency on April 6, 1841, following William Henry Harrison's death. The vice presidency remained vacant for the remainder of Harrison's term, which ended on March 4, 1845.

Millard Fillmore succeeded to the presidency on July 10, 1850, following President Zachary Taylor's death. The vice presidency remained vacant until March 4, 1853.

William R. King died on April 18, 1853, just weeks after taking office. President Franklin Pierce was left without a vice president until the end of his term, March 4, 1857.

Andrew Johnson succeeded to the presidency on April 15, 1865, following Abraham Lincoln's assassination. Johnson served with no vice president until the end of his term, March 4, 1869.

Henry Wilson died on November 22, 1875. President Ulysses S. Grant served without a vice president until the end of his second term, March 4, 1877.

Chester A. Arthur succeeded to the presidency on September 20, 1881, following James A. Garfield's assassination. The vice presidency remained vacant until the end of Arthur's term, March 4, 1885.

Thomas A. Hendricks died in office on November 25, 1885. President Grover Cleveland served without a vice president until the end of his term, March 4, 1889.

Garret A. Hobart died in office on November 21, 1899. President William McKinley served without a vice president until the end of his term, March 4, 1901.

Theodore Roosevelt succeeded to the presidency on September 14, 1901, following William McKinley's assassination. The vice presidency remained vacant for almost a full four years, until March 4, 1905, when Roosevelt was reelected.

James S. Sherman died in office on October 30, 1912. The vice presidency remained vacant until the end of President William Howard Taft's term, March 4, 1913.

Calvin Coolidge succeeded to the presidency on August 3, 1923, following Warren G. Harding's death. The vacancy went unfilled until the end of Coolidge's first term, March 4, 1925.

Harry S. Truman succeeded to the presidency on April 12, 1945, following Franklin D. Roosevelt's death. The vice presidency remained vacant for nearly four full years, until January 20, 1949.

Lyndon B. Johnson succeeded to the presidency on November 22, 1963, following John F. Kennedy's death. Johnson served without a vice president until January 20, 1965.

Spiro T. Agnew resigned on October 10, 1973, following allegations he had taken bribes while serving as a state official in Maryland. President Richard M. Nixon served without a vice president until Gerald R. Ford, the first appointed vice president, was sworn in on December 6, 1973.

Gerald R. Ford succeeded to the presidency on August 9, 1974, following Richard M. Nixon's resignation over the Watergate scandal. President Ford served without a vice president until vice-presidential appointee Nelson A. Rockefeller was sworn in on December 19, 1974.

(See 54 What happens if the president dies or is disabled while in office? 55 Which presidents died in office?)

Q 61. Can the president be removed from office?

A The president, vice president, and for that matter any other civilian federal government official can be impeached and removed from office. But because impeachment is controversial and politically very difficult to do—it requires a two-thirds of the Senate—it is rarely used.

One source of controversy in the impeachment process is just what constitutes an impeachable offense. The Constitution specifies that treason, bribery, and "other high crimes and misdemeanors" are impeachable offenses, but does not say exactly what offenses constitute high crimes and misdemeanors. The question has long been a source of debate. In 1970, for example, Republican Gerald R. Ford, then a member of the House of Representatives, supported a broad interpretation, saying that "an impeachable offense is whatever a majority of the House of Representatives considers it to be." Those who favor a narrow interpretation believe that only indictable crimes under the U.S. criminal code are impeachable offenses.

(See 64 Why was President Andrew Johnson impeached? 65 What brought about President Bill Clinton's impeachment?)

Q **62. What is the procedure for impeaching the president?**

A Article I, sections 2 and 3, of the Constitution grant Congress the power to impeach the president, vice president, and other federal government officials. Broadly speaking, the House is empowered to bring charges of impeachment, and the Senate has the responsibility for conducting a trial on the charges. Thus impeachment is only the first step; it is the bringing of charges against the president or other officials. Removal from office occurs only after the Senate has held a trial and two-thirds of the members have voted to convict.

The House has no set procedure for starting the impeachment process, but in recent times it has begun with a hearing by the House Judiciary Committee. If warranted, the committee drafts an impeachment resolution listing the "articles of impeachment" (specific offenses). The full House then decides whether to approve or disapprove the articles by a majority vote. If any article is approved, the House selects "managers" to present the case at the Senate trial.

The trial usually resembles a criminal proceeding, with House managers and the accused's defense team presenting evidence and witnesses. When the president is on trial, the chief justice of the United States presides (for other officials the vice president or president pro tempore presides). After both sides have been heard, the Senate debates and votes on each article of impeachment. If all articles fail, the president is acquitted. But if the Senate approves even one by the required two-thirds vote, the president is convicted. The Senate has the right to vote separately for removal from office and to disqualify the defendant from ever holding public office again.

Q 63. How many presidents have been impeached?

A The House of Representatives has voted articles of impeachment against only two presidents, Andrew Johnson in 1868 and Bill Clinton in 1999. President Richard M. Nixon resigned from office in 1974 to escape almost certain impeachment on charges stemming from the Watergate scandal.

(See 58 Which president resigned from office? 373 What happened in the Watergate scandal?)

Q 64. Why was President Andrew Johnson impeached?

A President Johnson's difficulties stemmed from his opposition to the Radical Republicans in Congress who wanted to impose harsh terms on the South after the Civil War. Lincoln, a Republican, had chosen Johnson, a Democrat from Tennessee, as his vice president because Johnson had opposed Tennessee's secession from the Union. After he succeeded Lincoln, who was assassinated, Johnson frequently resorted to his veto to block legislation passed by the Radical Republicans. But Republicans had the votes to override, which they did in the case of the Tenure of Office Act of 1867. The act required Senate approval before the president could fire appointed officials. Johnson chose to force the issue by firing Secretary of War Edwin Stanton, a supporter of the Radical Republicans, and claiming that the Tenure of Office Act was unconstitutional. Outraged, House Republicans voted eleven articles of impeachment in February 1868, but by May the Senate had narrowly voted down three articles and abandoned the rest.

Q 65. What brought about President Bill Clinton's impeachment?

A President Clinton, a Democrat from Arkansas, faced a Republican-dominated Congress much of the time he was in office. By the late 1990s, battles over the budget and other legislative priorities had created considerable partisan rancor on both sides of the aisle in Congress. Then in early 1998, news broke that President Clinton had been having an affair with a young White House intern, Monica Lewinsky—a relationship that Clinton adamantly denied publicly and privately. He also denied the affair in testimony taken for a lawsuit filed by Paula Jones, a former Arkansas civil servant. In her civil suit, Jones charged that Clinton, while governor of Arkansas, had sexually harassed her.

Independent prosecutor Kenneth Starr began investigating the Lewinsky scandal in early 1998, and some months later Clinton was forced to admit publicly that he had lied about the relationship with Lewinsky. Starr's report to Congress on the Lewinsky scandal included lurid details of the affair and charged that there were grounds for impeachment, including alleged perjury and obstruction of justice by the president.

Voting largely along party lines, the House approved two articles of impeachment on December 19, 1998. Clinton's supporters argued that the president's acts were not impeachable offenses, and by the time of the Senate trial, public support had swung in their favor. After an abbreviated five-week trial, the Senate voted down both articles of impeachment, 55–45 on perjury and 50–50 on obstruction of justice—both votes well short of the necessary two-thirds vote needed to convict.

(See 62 What is the procedure for impeaching the president? 376 Who brought the Monica Lewinsky scandal to light?)

Q 66. Have any vice presidents committed impeachable offenses?

A Three vice presidents committed offenses serious enough to raise the question of impeachment, but Congress did not begin formal proceedings against any of them. In the first case, Vice President Aaron Burr killed his political rival Alexander Hamilton in a duel on July 11, 1804. Both New York and New Jersey indicted him on murder charges, but Burr fled back to Washington. Despite a considerable public outcry, Congress refused to begin impeachment proceedings, in part because Burr had less than a year left to serve and the impeachment process would have been long and controversial.

Vice President Schuyler Colfax also was near the end of his term when in December 1872 news broke that he had been indirectly involved in the Crédit Mobilier scandal during his years as a member of Congress. This time the House investigated the charges, but decided Colfax could only be impeached for offenses committed while he occupied the vice presidency.

Congress also refused to impeach Spiro T. Agnew, President Richard M. Nixon's vice president, after the Justice Department revealed plans to indict him for allegedly taking bribes when he served in the Maryland state government. At the time Congress was more concerned about possibly impeaching President Nixon, and Agnew's resignation removed him as a possible successor to Nixon.

(See 369 What was the Crédit Mobilier scandal about?)

67. Can the vice president really preside over his own impeachment trial?

A Technically, yes. The Constitution gives vice presidents the job of presiding over the Senate, allowing them to vote only to break a tie vote. In only one situation are they required to step aside as presiding officer—during a Senate trial for the impeachment of the president, when the chief justice of the United States presides. In an apparent oversight, however, the Constitution makes no mention of vice presidents stepping aside during their own impeachment trial. The Senate has the power to make a rule requiring the vice president to do so, but because no vice president has been impeached, no such rule is on the books.

FOR FURTHER INFORMATION

More information on the questions in this chapter can be found in the books listed below. Two encyclopedias on the presidency stand out: Congressional Quarterly's two-volume *Guide to the Presidency* and Leonard Levy and Louis Fisher's multivolume *Encyclopedia of the American Presidency.* Both cover facets of the presidency by topic, present the information in a very readable fashion, and provide more than enough depth to satisfy general reference needs. One or the other should be available at most libraries, although the second edition of the *Guide to the Presidency* is more current. For readers who want to explore the areas covered in this chapter further, the following books will prove especially useful:

Boller, Paul F. *Presidential Anecdotes.* New York: Oxford University Press, 1996.

Bowen, Catherine Drinker. *Miracle at Philadelphia: The Story of the Constitutional Convention, May to September 1787.* Boston: Little, Brown, 1966.

Connolly, Thomas, and Michael Senegal. *Almanac of the American Presidents.* New York: Facts on File, 1991.

Couch, Ernie. *Presidential Trivia.* New York: Routledge, 1996.

Dallek, Robert. *Hail to the Chief: The Making and Unmaking of American Presidents.* Westport, Conn.: Hyperion, 1996.

DeGregorio, William A. *The Complete Book of U.S. Presidents.* New York: Barricade Books, 1997.

Epstein, Lee, and Thomas G. Walker. *Constitutional Law for a Changing America: A Short Course.* 2d ed. Washington, D.C.: CQ Press, 2000.

Every Four Years: The American Presidency. Rev. ed. Ed. Robert C. Post. Washington, D.C.: Smithsonian Exposition Press; dist by W. W. Norton, 1984.

Garrison, Webb. *A Treasury of White House Tales.* Nashville: Rutledge Hill Press, 1996.

Graf, Henry F. *The Presidents: A Reference History.* New York: Macmillan, 1996.

Historic Documents on the Presidency, 1776–1989. Ed. Michael Nelson. Washington, D.C.: Congressional Quarterly, 1989.

Inaugural Addresses of the Presidents of the United States: From George Washington 1789 to George Bush 1989. Washington, D.C.: Government Printing Office, 1989.

Kane, Joseph Nathan. *Presidential Fact Book.* New York: Random House, 1998.

Levy, Leonard W., and Louis Fisher. *Encyclopedia of the American Presidency.* New York: Simon and Schuster, 1993.

Lott, Davis Newton. *The Presidents Speak: The Inaugural Addresses of the American Presidents, from Washington to Clinton.* New York: Henry Holt, 1994.

Martin, Fenton S., and Robert U. Goehlert. *How to Research the Presidency.* Washington, D.C.: Congressional Quarterly, 1996.

Milkis, Sidney M., and Michael Nelson. *The American Presidency: Origins and Development, 1776–1998.* Washington, D.C.: CQ Press, 1999.

Nelson, Michael, ed. *Congressional Quarterly's Guide to the Presidency.* 2d ed. 2 vols. Washington, D.C.: Congressional Quarterly, 1996.

————, ed. *The Evolving Presidency: Addresses, Cases, Essays, Letters, Reports, Resolutions, Transcripts, and Other Landmark Documents, 1787–1998.* Washington, D.C.: CQ Press, 1999.

Powers of the Presidency. 2d ed. Washington, D.C.: Congressional Quarterly, 1997.

The Presidency A to Z. 2d ed. Michael Nelson, advisory editor. Washington, D.C.: Congressional Quarterly, 1998.

Ragsdale, Lyn. *Vital Statistics on the Presidency: Washington to Clinton.* Rev. ed. Washington, D.C.: Congressional Quarterly, 1998.

Rejai, Mostafa, and Kay Phillips. *Demythologizing an Elite: American Presidents in Empirical, Comparative, and Historical Perspective.* Westport, Conn.: Greenwood Press, 1993.

Ryan, Halford R. *The Inaugural Addresses of Twentieth Century American Presidents.* Westport, Conn.: Greenwood Press, 1993.

Van Tassel, Emily Field, and Paul Finkelman. *Impeachable Offenses: A Documentary History from 1787 to the Present.* Washington, D.C.: Congressional Quarterly, 1999.

Wetterau, Bruce. *Congressional Quarterly's Desk Reference on American Government.* 2d ed. Washington, D.C.: CQ Press, 2000.

———. *Congressional Quarterly's Desk Reference on the Federal Budget.* Washington, D.C.: CQ Press, 1998.

II

THE PRESIDENTS, PERSONALLY SPEAKING

GROWING UP TO BE PRESIDENT

Q 68. Were any presidents actually born in log cabins?

A During the mid-1800s, being born in a log cabin became a big plus for presidential candidates because it symbolized their ties to the common citizen and the pioneering life. But not all presidents whose campaigns made that claim were born in log cabins. Of the first twenty presidents, only six actually were—Andrew Jackson, Franklin Pierce, James Buchanan, Abraham Lincoln, Andrew Johnson, and James A. Garfield.

William Henry Harrison, a member of the Whig Party whose campaign championed the "log cabin and hard cider" image in 1840, was not one of them. He had been born in a three-story brick mansion on his father's Virginia plantation. Harrison the candidate did not live in a log cabin either. The original section of Harrison's home on what was called his "tiny farm" was in fact a log cabin. But voters who helped put him in the White House never discovered that the much-enlarged house was worth $20,000 (a huge sum in those days), nor did they find out that Harrison's tiny farm encompassed two thousand acres.

(See 420 Why was the Log Cabin campaign of 1840 a success?)

Q 69. Did George Washington really chop down a cherry tree?

A No. This popular story about Washington was in fact invented by Mason Weems, an itinerant bookseller and author of the biography *Life and Memorable Actions of George Washington*. Weems published his highly romanticized, semifictional biography in 1800, soon after Washington's death, and it proved tremendously popular. The story, in which the young Washington chopped down a cherry tree and then admitted to his angry father, "I cannot tell a lie," was added to the fifth edition of Weems's book in 1806. The adult Washington's stature as an American patriot, and his hard-earned reputation as an honest and dedicated public official, lent credence to Weems's fabrication.

Q 70. How did a sickly Theodore Roosevelt transform himself into a rugged outdoorsman?

A From the time he was a very young child, Theodore Roosevelt suffered from severe attacks of asthma and debilitating bouts of diarrhea. He was a bright, intelligent boy, but his health problems left him a weak and puny adolescent. Two incidents in the boy's life changed all that, however. The first was advice from his father, who installed a small gym in their home and told his son, "You have brains but you have a sickly body. In order to make your brains bring you what they ought, you must build up your body—it depends on you." The young Roosevelt took those words to heart and not only began exercising, but also became obsessed with sports that required the stamina and strength he lacked. Then at age fourteen he tried to fight two boys who were making sport of him, only to find he was still too weak to inflict any harm whatsoever.

Roosevelt threw himself into boxing and other sports, building up his body and unexpectedly lessening the frequency of his asthma attacks. By the time he completed college, Roosevelt was pursuing physical activities with the vigor and enthusiasm he showed for the rest of his life. After college the once sickly Roosevelt could, and did, scale Switzerland's Matterhorn, one of its more difficult and dangerous mountain climbs.

(See 1 Which president gave us the expression "bully pulpit"? 109 What military service did the future presidents perform?)

Q 71. What advice did President Grover Cleveland give a young Franklin D. Roosevelt?

A Roosevelt, who grew up in a wealthy, well-connected family, had opportunities that many other youngsters his age could only dream of. On one such occasion the young Roosevelt met President Grover Cleveland, but it was not so uplifting an event as one might want. The president greeted the young boy, patted him on the head, and solemnly advised him to never become president of the United States. Roosevelt, however, chose to ignore the warning.

Q 72. Was Dwight D. Eisenhower always so mild mannered?

A Eisenhower began life as a scrappy, energetic youth who had one serious flaw: he had a terrible temper. When he was just ten, his parents refused to let him go trick-or-treating with his brothers, and, on being rebuffed, the boy completely lost his temper. He ran outside crying and began pounding an apple tree with his bare fists, not feeling the cuts and bruises being inflicted on his hands. After his father sent him inside, his mother bandaged the wounds and had a talk with him about his temper. She repeated a biblical proverb, "He that conquereth his own soul is greater than he who taketh a city." Then she told him about the self-destructiveness of anger and how much he had to do to conquer his temper. Eisenhower never forgot that conversation, and, although it took him some time, he eventually got far better control of his temper than most.

Q 73. Who was the first president born an American citizen?

A The eighth president, Martin Van Buren, was the first born after America declared its independence from Britain. All earlier presidents had been born under British colonial rule. William Henry Harrison, the ninth president, was the last born in pre-revolutionary times.

Abraham Lincoln was the first president born outside the original thirteen colonies (in Kentucky). Almost seventy years would pass, however, before a president born west of the Mississippi took office—Herbert Hoover. He was born in Iowa.

Q 74. Which states produced the most presidents?

A Virginia leads with eight native sons who became president, all but one of whom served during the 1800s. They were George Washington, Thomas Jefferson, James Madison, James Monroe, William Henry Harrison, John Tyler, and Zachary Taylor. Only Virginia native Woodrow Wilson served in the 1900s.

Ohio produced the next largest crop of presidential native sons. The seven were Ulysses S. Grant, Rutherford B. Hayes, James A. Garfield, Benjamin Harrison, William McKinley, William Howard Taft, and Warren G. Harding. Massachusetts and New York sent four presidents each to the White House. John Adams, John Quincy Adams, John F. Kennedy, and George Bush were all Massachusetts born. Martin Van Buren, Millard Fillmore, Theodore Roosevelt, and Franklin D. Roosevelt were New Yorkers.

In all, only nineteen states have been represented in the White House, and only six of those states have been west of the Mississippi (Arkansas, California, Iowa, Missouri, Nebraska, and Texas).

(See 137 In what state have the most vice presidents been born?)

Q 75. Which president's mother fell overboard while immigrating to America?

A President Woodrow Wilson's mother, Jessie Wilson, suffered that misfortune, but she lived to tell about it. She was a girl when her mother and father emigrated from Scotland to America in the 1830s. Crossing the Atlantic by sailing ship was a long and dangerous voyage, especially in winter. One day, while standing on the ship's deck in rough weather, Jessie was swept overboard and might easily have been lost at sea, but she saved herself by grabbing hold of a rope. Jessie never completely forgot that experience and grew up fearing storms and the water. Perhaps as a result, Woodrow never learned to swim.

Q 76. Which future president nearly fell overboard?

A Gerald R. Ford, who gained something of a reputation for clumsiness while president, nearly fell overboard and drowned while serving in the navy during World War II. Stationed aboard the carrier U.S.S. *Monterey* in 1944, Ford smelled smoke and went out on the flight deck during a typhoon to investigate. Waves were tossing the ship about, and Ford fell as the deck under him heaved. He rolled helplessly off the edge of the deck and just managed to arch his body so that he landed on a catwalk. Had he missed, he almost surely would have been lost in the stormy seas.

Q 77. Which presidents were born into wealthy families?

A Some but not most presidents hailed from the wealthy families that made up the American aristocracy. George Washington's family owned several plantations, and Washington later inherited his stepbrother Lawrence's estate, Mount Vernon. Thomas Jefferson also was born into a wealthy family and at age fourteen inherited his father's thousand-acre estate in Virginia. James Madison likewise grew up on his family's estate in Virginia and eventually came to own it. Other presidents who were born into wealthy families and who had the advantages of wealth and family connections were: John Quincy Adams, John Tyler, William Henry Harrison, Benjamin Harrison, the Roosevelts, William Howard Taft, John F. Kennedy, and George Bush.

Some presidents found their way to the nation's highest office even though their families were poor. These self-made men included Andrew Jackson, Abraham Lincoln, Andrew Johnson, James A. Garfield, Richard M. Nixon, and Bill Clinton. Jackson, the son of Irish immigrant farmers, lost both of his parents as a youth and was raised by his mother's relatives. Lincoln, born in a log cabin, also made his way despite the hardships of life in a poor farming family. Andrew Johnson's parents, neither of whom could read or write, apprenticed him to a tailor as a young teenager. Garfield, his two brothers, and two sisters were raised by his widowed mother, who, with the children's help, lived by farming a thirty-acre plot. Richard Nixon's parents managed a general store and gas station. Bill Clinton's father died three months before he was born, and his stepfather reportedly was an abusive alcoholic. Nevertheless, both Nixon and Clinton went on to college and excelled in their studies.

Q 78. Have any presidents been related?

A Eight presidents were related to other presidents. John Adams and his son John Quincy Adams are to date the only father and son presidents. (However, George Bush's son George W. Bush was the Republican presidential nominee in 2000.)

Franklin D. Roosevelt's family ties were not as close. He was a fifth cousin of Theodore Roosevelt and claimed eleven other presidents as distant relatives (five through his parents and six through marriage). Roosevelt's wife, Eleanor, was Theodore Roosevelt's niece.

Four other presidents also were related. President William Henry Harrison was the grandfather of Benjamin Harrison. Zachary Taylor was a second cousin of James Madison.

Q 79. Who had the most brothers and sisters?

A Benjamin Harrison, the twenty-third president, had the most—seven brothers and five sisters, though five died in infancy. Other presidents also came from large families, especially those who grew up during the country's first century or so. There were eleven in James Buchanan's family and ten in George Washington's, Thomas Jefferson's, James Madison's, James K. Polk's, and William Howard Taft's.

Just three presidents—Franklin D. Roosevelt, Gerald R. Ford, and Bill Clinton—were only children by their parents' marriage. But all three presidents grew up with half brothers or sisters by their parents' second marriages. Roosevelt's half brother was by his father's previous marriage; Ford's three half brothers were by his mother's second marriage; and Clinton's half brother was by his mother's second marriage.

Q 80. When are the presidents' birthdays?

A October has been a good month for presidents—more have been born in that month than any other. John Adams, Chester A. Arthur, Rutherford B. Hayes, Theodore Roosevelt, Dwight D. Eisenhower, and Jimmy Carter all took their first breaths in October. As for the rest of the year, three or four presidents share most months, but only one president's birthday falls in June (George Bush) and September (William Howard Taft).

President	Date of Birth	Birthplace
George Washington	February 22, 1732	Westmoreland County, Va.
John Adams	October 30, 1735	Braintree, Mass.
Thomas Jefferson	April 13, 1743	Shadwell, Va.
James Madison	March 16, 1751	Port Conway, Va.
James Monroe	April 28, 1758	Westmoreland County, Va.
John Quincy Adams	July 11, 1767	Braintree, Mass.
Andrew Jackson	March 15, 1767	Waxhaw, S.C.
Martin Van Buren	December 5, 1782	Kinderhook, N.Y.
William Henry Harrison	February 9, 1773	Berkeley, Va.
John Tyler	March 29, 1790	Greenway, Va.
James K. Polk	November 2, 1795	Mecklenburg County, N.C.
Zachary Taylor	November 24, 1784	Orange County, Va.
Millard Fillmore	January 7, 1800	Cayuga County, N.Y.
Franklin Pierce	November 23, 1804	Hillsboro, N.H.
James Buchanan	April 23, 1791	Cove Gap, Pa.
Abraham Lincoln	February 12, 1809	Hardin County, Ky.
Andrew Johnson	December 29, 1808	Raleigh, N.C.
Ulysses S. Grant	April 27, 1822	Point Pleasant, Ohio
Rutherford B. Hayes	October 4, 1822	Delaware, Ohio
James A. Garfield	November 19, 1831	Orange, Ohio
Chester A. Arthur	October 5, 1829	Fairfield, Vt.
Grover Cleveland	March 18, 1837	Caldwell, N.J.
Benjamin Harrison	August 20, 1833	North Bend, Ohio
William McKinley	January 29, 1843	Niles, Ohio
Theodore Roosevelt	October 27, 1858	New York, N.Y.
William Howard Taft	September 15, 1857	Cincinnati, Ohio
Woodrow Wilson	December 29, 1856	Staunton, Va.
Warren G. Harding	November 2, 1865	Corsica, Ohio

President	Date of Birth	Birthplace
Calvin Coolidge	July 4, 1872	Plymouth, Vt.
Herbert Hoover	August 10, 1874	West Branch, Iowa
Franklin D. Roosevelt	January 30, 1882	Hyde Park, N.Y.
Harry S. Truman	May 8, 1884	Lamar, Mo.
Dwight D. Eisenhower	October 14, 1890	Denison, Texas
John F. Kennedy	May 29, 1917	Brookline, Mass.
Lyndon B. Johnson	August 27, 1908	Near Stonewall, Texas
Richard M. Nixon	January 9, 1913	Yorba Linda, Calif.
Gerald R. Ford	July 14, 1913	Omaha, Neb.
Jimmy Carter	October 1, 1924	Plains, Ga.
Ronald Reagan	February 6, 1911	Tampico, Ill.
George Bush	June 12, 1924	Milton, Mass.
Bill Clinton	August 19, 1946	Hope, Ark.

(See 119 When did the presidents marry? 137 In what state have the most vice presidents been born? 173 When did the presidents and vice presidents die? 348 When did the presidents and vice presidents serve?)

Q 81. Which presidents lost their mothers or fathers while growing up?

A Seventeen presidents suffered the death of one or both parents before reaching the age of twenty-one. Three lost both parents (Andrew Jackson, William Henry Harrison, and Herbert Hoover), and three were born after their fathers had died (Andrew Jackson, Rutherford B. Hayes, and Bill Clinton). John F. Kennedy was the only president survived by both of his parents; Warren G. Harding was survived by his father; and James K. Polk and James A. Garfield were survived by their mothers.

Seven presidents lost their mothers during their youth. They were: Andrew Jackson, William Henry Harrison, John Tyler, Abraham Lincoln, Benjamin Harrison, Calvin Coolidge, and Herbert Hoover.

The thirteen presidents who lost their fathers before reaching age twenty-one were: George Washington, Thomas Jefferson, James Monroe, Andrew Jackson, William Henry Harrison, Andrew Johnson, Rutherford B. Hayes, James A. Garfield, Grover Cleveland, Theodore Roosevelt, Herbert Hoover, Franklin D. Roosevelt, and Bill Clinton.

Q 82. Which president's parents divorced?

A Although seventeen presidents lost a father or mother before growing up, only one came from a family with divorced parents—Gerald R. Ford. His birth parents, Dorothy and Leslie King, divorced in 1911, when he was just two years old. Dorothy moved to Grand Rapids, Michigan, with her son, then named Leslie Lynch King Jr., and some years later married Gerald R. Ford. Gerald senior adopted young Leslie, and the boy took his stepfather's name, becoming Gerald R. Ford Jr. Mrs. Ford later gave birth to three other sons.

Q 83. Did any presidents grow up as the oldest child?

A Twelve presidents were the oldest children in their families; seven others, the youngest. Abraham Lincoln and Herbert Hoover were middle children raised in families of three. Presidents are grouped below by order of birth, which includes brothers and sisters who died in infancy and children from a parent's previous marriage:

First Child
John Adams, James Madison, James Monroe, James K. Polk, Ulysses S. Grant, Warren G. Harding, Calvin Coolidge, Harry S. Truman, Lyndon B. Johnson, Gerald R. Ford, Jimmy Carter, Bill Clinton

Second Child
John Quincy Adams, Millard Fillmore, James Buchanan, Abraham Lincoln, Andrew Johnson (youngest of two), Theodore Roosevelt, Herbert Hoover, Franklin D. Roosevelt (youngest of two), John F. Kennedy, Richard M. Nixon, Ronald Reagan (youngest of two), George Bush

Third Child
Thomas Jefferson, Andrew Jackson (youngest of three), Martin Van Buren, Zachary Taylor, Woodrow Wilson, Dwight D. Eisenhower

Fourth Child
Benjamin Harrison

Fifth Child
George Washington, Rutherford B. Hayes (youngest of four), James A. Garfield (youngest of five), Chester A. Arthur, and Grover Cleveland

Sixth Child
John Tyler

Seventh Child
William Henry Harrison (youngest of seven), Franklin Pierce, and William McKinley

Youngest Child
Andrew Jackson, William Henry Harrison, Andrew Johnson, Rutherford B. Hayes, James A. Garfield, Franklin D. Roosevelt, and Ronald Reagan

▶ *Which president came from the biggest family? See 79 Who had the most brothers and sisters?*

Q 84. Have all the presidents been married?

A All but one president was married at some point during his lifetime; James Buchanan was the only lifelong bachelor. Grover Cleveland also entered the White House as a bachelor, but he married the daughter of a former law partner in 1886, during his first term. Four other presidents were widowers when they took office—Thomas Jefferson, Andrew Jackson, Martin Van Buren, and Chester A. Arthur—and none remarried.

(See 116 Which first lady got married the youngest? Which president? 117 Who was married the longest? 118 Which first ladies were widows when they married the president? Divorcees? 119 When did the presidents marry? 350 When was the first White House wedding?)

Q 85. Which presidents fathered illegitimate children?

A Grover Cleveland, campaigning for president as a reform candidate in 1884, was forced to admit, after a newspaper broke the story, that he had fathered an illegitimate child (and was providing support for it). Embarrassed by the revelations, he nevertheless ordered his campaign staff to "tell the truth" and managed to weather that political storm. Cleveland also came under fire for having avoided service during the Civil War, but his Republican opponent, James G. Blaine, had done so as well. In the end Cleveland won the election by just 60,000 votes (219–182 electoral votes).

Warren G. Harding, who had no children by his wife, fathered a child out of wedlock in 1919. He carried on a long affair with newspaperwoman Nan Britton, but news of the child did not become public until Britton revealed the birth three years after Harding's death in 1923.

Thomas Jefferson has long been rumored to have fathered children by a mulatto named Sally Hemings, who was his slave and also the half sister of his wife, Martha. (Martha's father had a long-standing relationship with Sally's mother, a slave in his household.) Sally gave birth to her first child in 1789 or 1790, and eventually bore seven children, all of whom she claimed were Jefferson's. Jefferson never commented on the matter, but recent DNA tests indicate that either Thomas or his younger brother Randolph had likely fathered Sally's children.

Q 86. Who was the first divorced president?

A Ronald Reagan became the first when he took office in 1981, and to date he remains the only divorced president. His first marriage, to actress Jane Wyman, ended in divorce in 1948, after eight years. He married another actress, Nancy Davis, four years later in 1952. President Reagan and his second wife had been married for almost twenty-nine years when he took office in 1981.

(See 82 Which president's parents divorced? 118 Which first ladies were widows when they married the president? Divorcees?)

Q 87. When was the first time George Washington led troops in battle?

A As a young lieutenant colonel in Virginia's colonial militia, Washington gained his first combat experience in 1754, while leading 160 recruits to reinforce a British outpost on the Ohio and Monongahela Rivers. But the outcome was not a happy one. Along the way his nervous troops ambushed a group of thirty French soldiers and killed ten, thus firing the first shots of the French and Indian War. Worse yet, one of the dead Frenchmen was on a diplomatic mission to meet with the British.

A few weeks later Washington was surrounded and defeated by the French at Fort Necessity. Before being released, he was forced to sign a statement in which he admitted to being an "assassin" for having led the troops that killed the diplomat. Washington said he had not understood the text because it was written in French, but he was nevertheless heavily criticized on his return.

Q 88. Who was the most inventive president?

A Certainly among the most talented of all presidents, Thomas Jefferson was accomplished in the fields of architecture, science, agriculture, politics, law, foreign languages, and music. He also was noted for his inventions. Among the devices he created and built were a pantograph for duplicating letters, a pedometer, and a walking stick chair. Preferring that his inventions be used by anyone who wanted, Jefferson never bothered to patent any of them. That distinction fell to Abraham Lincoln, who did patent a device for lessening the draft of steamboats operating in shallow waters. Lincoln never built the device though.

Q 89. Why did Andrew Jackson's wife die prematurely?

A Social propriety and personal pride were important virtues in Andrew Jackson's day. When Jackson met his future wife, Rachel Donelson Robards, she had been divorced from her first husband, or so she thought (her husband had sued for the divorce). After Jackson married Rachel in 1794, however, questions arose about the status of her divorce. The Jacksons remarried just to be sure, but the gossip and slanderous comments about Rachel's divorce from Robards *after* her marriage to Jackson haunted her for the rest of her life. Jackson even fought several duels (and was wounded in one) defending her honor.

Over thirty years later, in 1828, Jackson's victory in the presidential campaign stirred the gossip anew. In talking about the impending move to the White House, Rachel privately admitted she would rather be "a doorkeeper in the house of God than to live in that palace in Washington." She talked of staying home at the Jackson estate, the Hermitage, outside Nashville, but later reluctantly agreed to accompany her husband to Washington. She never did, however. On a trip into Nashville to buy clothes for her debut in Washington society, something snapped. By some accounts, an insulting comment made within earshot finally broke her. Whatever the cause, friends found her hysterical and crouching in a corner. She deteriorated quickly after that and died a few days later. She repeated her comment about preferring to be a "doorkeeper in the house of God" just twenty minutes before her death. Jackson never remarried.

(See 123 What was the Eaton affair about?)

Q 90. Why did Abraham Lincoln grow a beard?

A Various people had suggested that Lincoln grow a beard, saying it would give him a more dignified appearance and soften his rugged-looking face. But a young girl is often credited with having convinced the president to actually do so. Eleven-year-old Grace Bedell wrote Lincoln a letter in 1860, advising him that he would "look a great deal better" with a beard because his face was so thin. Lincoln, then in the midst of his presidential campaign, wrote her back. Then, as legend has it, he met the girl during a campaign stop near her hometown, told the crowd the story, and then gave the girl a kiss. While no proof of the meeting exists, Lincoln did write her the letter and began growing the beard soon after his election. He was the first president to wear a beard.

Q 91. How did Ulysses S. Grant get his name?

A Born Hiram Ulysses Grant, Grant decided to change his name to Ulysses Hiram Grant when he entered the U.S. Military Academy at West Point. But officials there mistakenly recorded his name as Ulysses S. Grant, adding an unexpected twist to the new name. Though he never bothered with the legal formalities of changing his name, Grant went through the rest of his life as Ulysses S. Grant. The initial *S.*, he maintained, did not stand for anything.

Seven other presidents also changed their names in one way or another:

Stephen Grover Cleveland became Grover Cleveland

John Calvin Coolidge became Calvin Coolidge

Thomas Woodrow Wilson became Woodrow Wilson

David Dwight Eisenhower became Dwight David Eisenhower

Leslie Lynch King Jr. became Gerald R. Ford Jr. (after his mother's remarriage)

James Earl Carter Jr. became Jimmy Carter

William Jefferson Blythe became William Jefferson Clinton (after his mother's remarriage)

Q 92. How many presidents were left-handed?

A Only five presidents grew up left-handed, and all but one served in the modern era, after the stigma of being left-handed had been erased. The first left-handed president was James A. Garfield (who could also use his right hand), followed decades later by Harry S. Truman (also ambidextrous), Gerald R. Ford, George Bush, and Bill Clinton. President Ronald Reagan apparently used both hands—he waved with his left but signed bills with his right, and in some movies during his film career he seemed to be left-handed.

Q 93. Which presidents were the most prolific writers?

A Theodore Roosevelt pursued writing the way he lived his life—vigorously—and published over three dozen books in his lifetime. His works ranged from adventure stories such as *Ranch Life and the Hunting Trail* (1888) and *The Rough Riders* (1899) to the four-volume *The Winning of the West* (1889–1896). Woodrow Wilson produced a half dozen or so scholarly works, including *Congressional Government: A Study in American Politics* (1885) and the five-volume *A History of the American People* (1902). Herbert Hoover also wrote substantially, including his three-volume *Memoirs* (1951–1952) and *The Ordeal of Woodrow Wilson* (1958). Among recent presidents, both Richard Nixon and Jimmy Carter have eleven books to their credit. Among them are Nixon's *Six Crises* (1962) and Carter's *Why Not the Best?* (1975). John F. Kennedy's *Profiles in Courage* (1956) won a Pulitzer Prize for biography (1959).

Q 94. Which future president passed up the opportunity to play football professionally?

A Gerald R. Ford, who played center on two championship teams at the University of Michigan in the 1930s, turned down the chance to play professional football. Instead he took a job at Yale University, where he served as an assistant coach and eventually earned his law degree (1941). Dwight D. Eisenhower also played football while at the U.S. Military Academy at West Point; Woodrow Wilson coached football at Wesleyan University.

Q 95. Was Bill Clinton the only musically talented president?

A Bill Clinton was the first president to play the saxophone, but six other presidents played instruments as well. Both Harry S. Truman and Richard M. Nixon were proficient on the piano, Calvin Coolidge played the harmonica, and Warren G. Harding played the alto horn and cornet. Early presidents Thomas Jefferson and John Tyler were violinists.

Q 96. Which president's hobbies included riding a mechanical horse?

A Calvin Coolidge listed riding the mechanical horse among his hobbies. He also liked to pitch hay. The two poker-playing presidents were Warren G. Harding and Harry S. Truman. George Bush liked to pitch horseshoes, while an earlier president, Herbert Hoover, went in for heavier objects—he preferred throwing a medicine ball. Franklin D. Roosevelt was an avid stamp collector.

Q **97. What are the presidents' favorite sports?**

A Although golf, fishing, and swimming have been favored by many presidents, horseback riding has been the sport of choice for the most, twelve in all. Theodore Roosevelt probably is the president best known for his hunting exploits, but Benjamin Harrison, Dwight D. Eisenhower, Lyndon B. Johnson, and George Bush all enjoyed hunting as well. The most popular sports of the presidents are as follows:

Horseback riding: George Washington, Thomas Jefferson, Andrew Jackson, Martin Van Buren, Zachary Taylor, William McKinley, Theodore Roosevelt, William Howard Taft, Woodrow Wilson, Warren G. Harding, Lyndon B. Johnson, and Ronald Reagan

Golf: William Howard Taft, Woodrow Wilson (he even had special black golf balls made so he could play in the snow), Warren G. Harding, Calvin Coolidge, Dwight D. Eisenhower (probably the most famous golfer among the presidents), Richard M. Nixon, Gerald R. Ford, George Bush, and Bill Clinton

Fishing: George Washington, Thomas Jefferson, Chester A. Arthur, Grover Cleveland, Calvin Coolidge, Herbert Hoover, Dwight D. Eisenhower, Lyndon B. Johnson, Jimmy Carter, and George Bush

Swimming: John Quincy Adams, Ulysses S. Grant, William McKinley, Franklin D. Roosevelt, Harry S. Truman, John F. Kennedy, Gerald R. Ford, Jimmy Carter, and Ronald Reagan

BACKGROUND OF THE PRESIDENTS

Q **98. Which president is known as the father of the Constitution?**

A Many people helped to write and ratify the Constitution, but James Madison's numerous key contributions earned him the distinction of being called the "father of the Constitution." Early in the 1780s, as a member of Continental Congress, Madison realized the need for a strong central government, and by 1787 he had became a leader in the movement to replace the weak government formed under the Articles of Confederation. At the Constitutional Convention, Madison largely wrote the Virginia Plan, which proposed establishing a bicameral Congress as the heart of the government. (Article II, creating the presidency, was largely the work of other delegates.)

Once the Constitution was drafted, Madison joined Alexander Hamilton and John Jay in writing the *Federalist Papers,* essays arguing for ratification of the Constitution by the states. Later, as a member of the newly created U.S. House of Representatives, Madison proposed nine amendments to the Constitution that formed the basis of the Bill of Rights.

(See 4 Which presidents are counted among the Founding Fathers?)

Q 99. What three characteristics have all presidents shared?

A All presidents to date have been white males; all have traced their ancestry to the nations of northern Europe; and all have had substantial experience as a public servant or military officer. All but two presidents also have been married and belonged to a Protestant church. Only James Buchanan never married, and only John F. Kennedy was a Catholic.

(See 84 Have all the presidents been married? 101 Has anyone ever become president without winning any previous elective office? 107 To what religious denominations did the presidents belong? 108 How many presidents once served as generals?)

Q 100. What profession produced the most presidents?

A Twenty-five were lawyers, the most common occupation of presidents. Two other presidents, Theodore Roosevelt and Warren G. Harding, studied law but did not become lawyers. Among the recent presidents, only Gerald R. Ford, Richard M. Nixon, and Bill Clinton actually practiced law.

(See 105 What careers did presidents pursue before reaching the White House? 108 How many presidents once served as generals?)

Q 101. Has anyone ever become president without winning any previous elective office?

A Zachary Taylor, Ulysses S. Grant, Herbert Hoover, and Dwight D. Eisenhower all became president without having held any other elective office. Three were war heroes—Taylor was a hero of the Mexican War; Grant helped bring about the Union victory during the Civil War; and Eisenhower became famous for his part in the Allied victory during World War II. Hoover, an engineer, gained his reputation as the head of war relief organizations during World War I and for his work in appointive government posts.

Q 102. Which president entered politics at the earliest age?

A George Washington holds that distinction, having been appointed to his first political office—official surveyor for Culpeper County—at age seventeen. Andrew Johnson was just three years older when he won his first political post, city alderman in Greeneville, Tennessee. Andrew Jackson was twenty-one when he entered politics as a prosecuting attorney, as was John Tyler when he was elected to the state legislature.

Ronald Reagan got the latest start in politics. He was fifty-five when he became governor of California (and was the oldest president to take office as well). Woodrow Wilson came in second by only a year, though, leaving the academic world for the New Jersey governorship at age fifty-four.

The first political offices held by the presidents are as follows:

President	First Political Office	Age
George Washington	County surveyor	17
John Adams	Highway surveyor	39
Thomas Jefferson	State legislator	26
James Madison	State legislator	25
James Monroe	State legislator	24
John Quincy Adams	Minister to the Netherlands	27
Andrew Jackson	Prosecuting attorney	21
Martin Van Buren	County surrogate	30
William Henry Harrison	Territorial delegate to Congress	26
John Tyler	State legislator	21
James K. Polk	State legislator	28
Zachary Taylor	None	—
Millard Fillmore	State legislator	28
Franklin Pierce	State legislator	25
James Buchanan	County prosecutor	22
Abraham Lincoln	State legislator	25
Andrew Johnson	City alderman	20
Ulysses S. Grant	None	—
Rutherford B. Hayes	City solicitor	36
James A. Garfield	State legislator	28
Chester A. Arthur	State engineer	31
Grover Cleveland	District attorney	26
Benjamin Harrison	City attorney	24

President	First Political Office	Age
William McKinley	Prosecuting attorney	26
Theodore Roosevelt	State legislator	24
William Howard Taft	Prosecuting attorney	24
Woodrow Wilson	Governor	54
Warren G. Harding	State legislator	35
Calvin Coolidge	City councilman	26
Herbert Hoover	Relief administrator	43
Franklin D. Roosevelt	State legislator	28
Harry S. Truman	County judge	38
Dwight D. Eisenhower	None	—
John F. Kennedy	U.S. House Representative	29
Lyndon B. Johnson	U.S. House Representative	28
Richard M. Nixon	U.S. House Representative	34
Gerald R. Ford	U.S. House Representative	36
Jimmy Carter	Member, county board of education	38
Ronald Reagan	Governor	55
George Bush	U.S. House Representative	42
Bill Clinton	State attorney general	30

Q 103. How many presidents have served as governors?

A Sixteen presidents served as state governor before entering the nation's highest office. The first was Thomas Jefferson, former governor of Virginia, and the most recent was Bill Clinton, former governor of Arkansas. (As of early 2000, another state governor, George W. Bush of Texas, was the Republican presidential nominee). State governors who went on to become president were:

Governor	State	Term
Thomas Jefferson	Virginia	1779–1781
James Monroe	Virginia	1799–1802, 1811
Martin Van Buren	New York	1829
John Tyler	Virginia	1825–1827
James K. Polk	Tennessee	1839–1841
Rutherford B. Hayes	Ohio	1868–1872, 1876–1877
Andrew Johnson	Tennessee	1853–1857, 1862–1865
Grover Cleveland	New York	1883–1885

Governor	State	Term
William McKinley	Ohio	1892–1896
Theodore Roosevelt	New York	1899–1901
Woodrow Wilson	New Jersey	1911–1913
Calvin Coolidge	Massachusetts	1919–1921
Franklin D. Roosevelt	New York	1929–1933
Jimmy Carter	Georgia	1971–1975
Ronald Reagan	California	1967–1975
Bill Clinton	Arkansas	1979–1981, 1983–1992

(See 142 Have any political offices served as stepping-stones to the vice presidency?)

▶ *Which presidents served as cabinet members? See 467 Which presidents once served as cabinet members?*

Q 104. Has serving in Congress proved to be an effective springboard to the presidency?

A Although twenty-four of the nation's forty-two presidents served in either the House or Senate (or both) before entering the White House, just seven of the twenty-four took office after 1900—Warren G. Harding, Harry S. Truman, John F. Kennedy, Lyndon B. Johnson, Richard M. Nixon, Gerald R. Ford, and George Bush.

James A. Garfield was the first (and only) sitting member of the House to be elected to the presidency, and Warren G. Harding and John F. Kennedy went directly from the Senate to the White House. The only House Speaker elected president was James K. Polk. Gerald R. Ford went from House minority leader to the vice presidency (by being appointed), and from there to the presidency by succession after President Richard M. Nixon resigned.

The 2000 Democratic presidential nominee—Vice President Al Gore—once served in the U.S. Senate. Presidents who were members of Congress are (D–Democrat; DR–Democratic-Republican; R–Republican; W–Whig):

President	Representing Party-State	House Term	Senate Term
James Madison	DR-Va.	1789–1797	
James Monroe	DR-Va.		1790–1794

President	Representing Party-State	House Term	Senate Term
John Quincy Adams	DR-Mass.	1831–1848	1803–1808
Andrew Jackson	D(DR)-Tenn.	1796–1797	1797–1798 1823–1825
Martin Van Buren	D(DR)-N.Y.		1821–1828
William Henry Harrison	W-Ohio	1799–1800 1816–1819	1825–1828
John Tyler	W-Va.	1817–1821	1827–1836
James K. Polk	D-Tenn.	1825–1839	
Millard Fillmore	W-N.Y.	1833–1835 1837–1843	
Franklin Pierce	D-N.H.	1833–1837	1837–1842
James Buchanan	D-Pa.	1821–1831	1834–1845
Abraham Lincoln	R-Ill.	1847–1849	
Andrew Johnson	D-Tenn.	1843–1853	1857–1862 1875
Rutherford B. Hayes	R-Ohio	1865–1867	
James A. Garfield	R-Ohio	1863–1880	
Benjamin Harrison	R-Ind.		1881–1887
William McKinley	R-Ohio	1877–1884 1885–1891	
Warren G. Harding	R-Ohio	1915–1921	
Harry S. Truman	D-Mo.		1935–1945
John F. Kennedy	D-Mass.	1947–1953	1953–1960
Lyndon B. Johnson	D-Texas	1937–1949	1949–1961
Richard M. Nixon	R-Calif.	1947–1950	1950–1953
Gerald R. Ford	R-Mich.	1949–1973	
George Bush	R-Texas	1967–1971	

(See 142 Have any political offices served as stepping-stones to the vice presidency?)

Q 105. What careers did presidents pursue before reaching the White House?

A Presidents have come from all walks of life. Storekeepers, farmers, businessmen, generals, teachers, and even a former tailor and a former movie actor have served in the nation's highest office. By far, however, the biggest group of future presidents spent at least some of their years before the White House working in the field of law. And most future presidents served in political office before reaching the White House.

The careers of the presidents are listed below. Some presidents are listed twice because they established themselves in more than one career before entering politics.

Lawyer: John Adams, Thomas Jefferson, James Monroe, John Quincy Adams, Andrew Jackson, Martin Van Buren, John Tyler, James K. Polk, Millard Fillmore, Franklin Pierce, James Buchanan, Abraham Lincoln, Rutherford B. Hayes, James A. Garfield, Chester A. Arthur, Grover Cleveland, Benjamin Harrison, William McKinley, Theodore Roosevelt, William Howard Taft, Calvin Coolidge, Franklin D. Roosevelt, Richard M. Nixon, Gerald R. Ford, Bill Clinton

Farmer/rancher: George Washington, John Adams, Thomas Jefferson, James Madison, James Monroe, Lyndon B. Johnson, Jimmy Carter

Military: William Henry Harrison, Zachary Taylor, Ulysses S. Grant, Dwight D. Eisenhower

Educator: James A. Garfield, Woodrow Wilson, Lyndon B. Johnson

Other: George Washington (surveyor), Andrew Johnson (tailor), Theodore Roosevelt (author), Warren G. Harding (newspaper editor), Herbert Hoover (mining engineer), Harry S. Truman (clerk, store owner), Jimmy Carter (businessman), Ronald Reagan (entertainer), George Bush (businessman)

Q 106. Did most presidents attend college?

A Thirty-two presidents did, and twenty-eight earned a bachelor's degree or better. Every president in the twentieth century spent at least some time in college studies, except for Harry S. Truman. Woodrow Wilson is the only president who earned a Ph.D., for his studies in politics and government. He managed to get his advanced degree despite the fact that he was dyslexic.

Among the other presidents, all but one—Andrew Johnson—had at least some formal education while growing up. Johnson learned to read and write while working as a tailor.

President	College or University	Years Attended	Degree
John Adams	Harvard	1751–1755	B.A.
Thomas Jefferson	William and Mary	1760–1762	—
James Madison	Princeton	1768–1771	B.A.
James Monroe	William and Mary	1774–1776	—
John Quincy Adams	Harvard	1786–1787	B.A.
William Henry Harrison	Hampden-Sydney	1781–1790	—
John Tyler	William and Mary	1802–1807	B.A.
James K. Polk	North Carolina	?–1818	B.A.
Franklin Pierce	Bowdoin	1820–1824	B.A.
James Buchanan	Dickinson	1807–1809	B.A.
Ulysses S. Grant	U.S. Military Academy	1839–1843	B.S.
Rutherford B. Hayes	Kenyon	?–1842	B.A.
James A. Garfield	Williams	1854–1856	B.A.
Chester A. Arthur	Union	1845–1848	B.A.
Benjamin Harrison	Miami (Ohio)	1850–1852	B.A.
William McKinley	Allegheny	1859–1860	—
Theodore Roosevelt	Harvard	1876–1880	B.A.
William Howard Taft	Yale	1874–1878	B.A.
Woodrow Wilson	Princeton	1875–1879	B.A.
	Johns Hopkins	1883–1886	Ph.D.
Warren G. Harding	Ohio Central	1879–1882	—
Calvin Coolidge	Amherst	1891–1895	B.A.
Herbert Hoover	Stanford	1891–1895	B.A.
Franklin D. Roosevelt	Harvard	1900–1903	B.A.

President	College or University	Years Attended	Degree
Dwight D. Eisenhower	U.S. Military Academy	1911–1915	B.S.
John F. Kennedy	Harvard	1936–1940	B.S.
Lyndon B. Johnson	Southwest Texas State Teacher's College	1927–1930	B.S.
Richard M. Nixon	Whittier	1930–1934	B.A.
Gerald R. Ford	Michigan	1931–1935	B.A.
Jimmy Carter	U.S. Naval Academy	1943–1946	B.S.
Ronald Reagan	Eureka	1928–1932	B.A.
George Bush	Yale	1945–1948	B.A.
Bill Clinton	Georgetown	1964–1968	B.S.

(See 124 Who was the first wife of a president to have a college degree?)

Q **107. To what religious denominations did the presidents belong?**

A Three presidents—Thomas Jefferson, Abraham Lincoln, and Andrew Johnson—expressed no preference for a religious denomination, although they did profess a belief in God. All other presidents belonged to one or another of the Christian denominations. The majority of them were Episcopalian, Presbyterian, Unitarian, Baptist, or Methodist. James A. Garfield and Lyndon B. Johnson were Disciples of Christ; Martin Van Buren and Theodore Roosevelt belonged to the Dutch Reformed Church; Herbert Hoover and Richard M. Nixon were Quakers; Calvin Coolidge was a Congregationalist; and John F. Kennedy was a Catholic. Following are the denominations to which three or more presidents belonged:

Episcopalian
George Washington, James Madison, James Monroe, William Henry Harrison, John Tyler, Zachary Taylor, Franklin Pierce, Chester A. Arthur, Franklin D. Roosevelt, Gerald R. Ford, Ronald Reagan, George Bush

Presbyterian
Andrew Jackson, James K. Polk, James Buchanan, Grover Cleveland, Benjamin Harrison, Woodrow Wilson, Dwight D. Eisenhower

Unitarian

John Adams, John Quincy Adams, Millard Fillmore, William Howard Taft

Baptist

Warren G. Harding, Harry S. Truman, Jimmy Carter, Bill Clinton

Methodist

Ulysses S. Grant, Rutherford B. Hayes, William McKinley

(See 99 What three characteristics have all presidents shared?)

Q 108. How many presidents once served as generals?

A Twelve presidents were war heroes who won promotions to the rank of general, although just three of them were true career soldiers—Zachary Taylor, Ulysses S. Grant, and Dwight D. Eisenhower. Grant and Eisenhower graduated from the U.S. Military Academy at West Point, and both reached the highest rank of their time—four-star general and five-star general, respectively.

George Washington, who served whenever there was a national emergency, retired as a three-star general, the highest rank at that time. Two-star generals were Andrew Jackson, William Henry Harrison, Zachary Taylor, Andrew Johnson, Rutherford B. Hayes, and James A. Garfield. One-star generals were Franklin Pierce, Chester A. Arthur, and Benjamin Harrison.

Q 109. What military service did the future presidents perform?

A Twenty-eight presidents served in the armed forces, all but three of them during wartime. Not all presidents who were in the military during wars saw combat, however. Among those who did, George Washington was the first and most famous, having served as commanding general of the Continental Army during the American Revolution. Gen. Ulysses S. Grant played a pivotal role in the Civil War, Gen. Dwight Eisenhower commanded the allied invasion of Europe during World War II, and Theodore Roosevelt won fame as the leader of the rough riders. The presidents and the wars in which they served were:

President	*War Experience*
George Washington	Revolutionary War
James Madison	Revolutionary War

President	War Experience
James Monroe	Revolutionary War
Andrew Jackson	Revolutionary War, Creek War, War of 1812, Seminole War
William Henry Harrison	Northwest Territory Wars, Shawnee Confederation, War of 1812
John Tyler	War of 1812
Zachary Taylor	War of 1812, Seminole, Black Hawk, Mexican Wars
Millard Fillmore	Mexican War
Franklin Pierce	Mexican War
James Buchanan	War of 1812
Abraham Lincoln	Black Hawk War
Andrew Johnson	Civil War
Ulysses S. Grant	Mexican War, Civil War
Rutherford B. Hayes	Civil War
James A. Garfield	Civil War
Chester A. Arthur	Civil War
Benjamin Harrison	Civil War
William McKinley	Civil War
Theodore Roosevelt	Spanish-American War
Harry S. Truman	World War I
Dwight D. Eisenhower	World War I, World War II
John F. Kennedy	World War II
Lyndon B. Johnson	World War II
Richard M. Nixon	World War II
Gerald R. Ford	World War II
Jimmy Carter	Korean War
Ronald Reagan	World War II
George Bush	World War II

Q 110. How many presidents once taught school?

A Seven presidents spent part of their careers teaching—John Adams, James A. Garfield, Chester A. Arthur, William McKinley, Woodrow Wilson, Lyndon B. Johnson, and Bill Clinton. Adams, Arthur, McKinley, and Johnson all taught briefly early on in their careers. Wilson's first career, however, was as an educator. He taught at colleges from 1885 to 1902 and Princeton in 1890. He then served as president of Princeton from 1902 to 1910, when he resigned to run for the New Jersey governorship. Clinton taught law at the University of Arkansas for several years in the 1970s before entering politics.

(See 105 What careers did presidents pursue before reaching the White House?)

Q 111. Which presidents served as ambassadors to foreign countries?

A Eight future presidents were ministers to foreign countries. John Adams served in various diplomatic capacities in Europe from 1778 to 1779 and from 1780 to 1788, including minister to Great Britain (in 1783 he signed the armistice ending the war between the United States and Britain). Thomas Jefferson was minister to France from 1784 to 1789. James Monroe, while minister to France (1803–1807), concluded the Louisiana Purchase (for $15 million). John Quincy Adams became minister to Russia in 1809, and from there went in 1814 to Belgium to lead the delegation negotiating the Treaty of Ghent, which ended the War of 1812. He then served as minister to Great Britain from 1814 to 1817.

President Andrew Jackson appointed three future presidents to diplomatic posts. William Henry Harrison served just eight months as minister to Colombia in 1828. Martin Van Buren's appointment as ambassador to Great Britain 1831 (and his trip there) proved pointless, because the Senate refused to confirm him. James Buchanan negotiated a commercial treaty while minister to Russia (1831–1833). Later, while minister to Great Britain (1853–1856) under President Franklin Pierce, Buchanan helped to write the Ostend Manifesto, a controversial document that called for the United States to take Cuba from Spain by force if Spain refused to sell it.

Over a century passed before the eighth future president accepted a diplomatic posting. George Bush first served as ambassador to the United Nations (1970–1972) under President Richard M. Nixon and then briefly as chief of the U.S. Liaison Office in communist China (1974–1975) under President Gerald R. Ford.

(See 105 What careers did presidents pursue before reaching the White House?)

Q **112. What are the most famous homes of the presidents?**

A *Mount Vernon,* George Washington's plantation, in Mount Vernon, Virginia, on the banks of the Potomac River. He first lived there as a child for several years beginning in 1735. After inheriting the estate from his half brother Lawrence, he made it his home from 1759 on. He died and was buried there in 1799.

Monticello, Thomas Jefferson's plantation outside Charlottesville, Virginia. Jefferson designed and built the dome-shaped mansion that is the centerpiece of the property. Jefferson is buried in the family cemetery there.

Montpelier, James Madison's plantation at Montpelier, Virginia. The mansion house was built by Madison's father. Madison remodeled and added to the house while serving as president.

Ash Lawn, James Monroe's plantation outside Charlottesville, Virginia (not far from Monticello). According to some experts, the existing house at Ash Lawn is not the original one Monroe built.

The Hermitage, Andrew Jackson's estate outside Nashville, Tennessee. In 1819 he built (and probably designed) the two-story brick house on the estate.

Lindenwald, Martin Van Buren's home at Kinderhook, New York. Bought by Van Buren in 1840, the original estate included a brick mansion and two hundred acres in the town where he had been born.

Sherwood Forest, John Tyler's home in Charles County, Virginia. Tyler greatly enlarged the original house soon after he bought the estate in 1842 (while he was still president).

Wheatland, James Buchanan's estate at Wheatland, Pennsylvania. Buchanan bought the two-and-a-half-story mansion in 1848.

Spiegel Grove, Rutherford B. Hayes's estate at Fremont, Ohio. Hayes inherited it from an uncle and expanded the brick house considerably.

Sagamore Hill, Theodore Roosevelt's home at Oyster Bay, New York. He died while at his home in 1919.

The Beeches, Calvin Coolidge's home at Northampton, Massachusetts.

Springwood, Franklin D. Roosevelt's estate at Hyde Park, New York. Roosevelt is buried on the estate.

LBJ Ranch, Lyndon B. Johnson's ranch near Johnson City, Texas.

PRESIDENTIAL FAMILIES

Q **113. Who was the first president's wife to be called the first lady?**

A Julia Grant became the first in 1870, but the term *first lady* was not widely used until Lucy Hayes's tenure at the White House (1877–1881). A play about Dolley Madison, *First Lady in the Land*, produced in New York in 1911, further helped to popularize the title. Before first lady, president's wives had been variously called Mrs. President, presidentress, and Lady ——.

▶ *Were any first ladies related to former presidents? See 78 Have any presidents been related?*

Q **114. Which first lady was a descendant of Pocahontas?**

A Edith Bolling Galt, President Woodrow Wilson's second wife, was a descendant of the famous Indian woman Pocahontas and her husband, the early Virginia colonist John Rolfe. Rolfe married the Indian princess in 1619.

Raised in a well-to-do Virginia family, Edith first married a Washington jeweler named Norman Galt. Galt died in 1908, however, and in 1915 Edith met President Wilson, who had lost his first wife the previous year. Woodrow was immediately taken with Edith and soon proposed marriage. They married in December 1915.

Q **115. Who were the most popular first ladies? The highest rated?**

A Among the early first ladies, Dolley Madison stands out as the country's first popular White House hostess and successful entertainer. Julia Grant also was a lavish entertainer. Her flamboyance caught the public's fancy, and for the first time the first lady became a national celebrity. Grover Cleveland's beautiful young wife, Frances Folsom, proved an even bigger celebrity. She was so popular that women across the country began imitating the way she dressed and wore her hair. Jacqueline Kennedy ranks as the most glamorous first lady of the twentieth century. Hugely popular with both the media and the public, she too sparked national fads, and her public appearances always drew large crowds.

Not all first ladies were social successes, however. Abigail Adams, unlike the women of her day, was known for expressing her views on political and social matters. The first true political activist among the first ladies, Eleanor Roosevelt, has been ranked first among all presidents' wives by one poll of history professors. Other highly rated first ladies are Edith Wilson, Lady Bird Johnson, Rosalynn Carter, and Hillary Rodham Clinton. Clinton became the first first lady to run for political office when she announced her candidacy for a U.S. Senate seat in 2000 (representing New York).

(See 122 Which first lady became famous for her skills as White House hostess?)

▶ *Who was the only first lady to be married in the White House? See 350 When was the first White House wedding?*

Q 116. Which first lady got married the youngest? Which president?

A The youngest first lady to wed was Eliza Johnson, Andrew Johnson's wife. She was only sixteen years, seven months, at the time. Elizabeth Monroe was seventeen going on eighteen. Rosalynn Carter was nearly nineteen when she wed, and four other first ladies married when they were nineteen—Abigail Adams, Alice Roosevelt, Mamie Eisenhower, and Barbara Bush.

The youngest president to marry was Andrew Johnson; he was almost eighteen and a half. George Bush was twenty and a half, and Jimmy Carter was twenty-one.

The oldest president to marry was Benjamin Harrison—he was sixty-two when he married his second wife—though Millard Fillmore and Woodrow Wilson were not much younger. Both were fifty-eight when they married their second wives. James Madison was forty-three when he married.

Caroline Fillmore, Millard's second wife, was the oldest president's wife to wed. She was forty-four when she married Fillmore, five years after he left office. Edith Wilson, Woodrow's second wife, was just a year younger when she wed, making her the oldest of those who actually served as first lady.

Four presidents married older women: Warren G. Harding (Florence was five years senior), Millard Fillmore (Abigail was a year and ten months senior), Herbert Hoover (Lou was just over four months older), and Richard M. Nixon (Pat was less than a year older).

Q 117. Who was married longest?

A Abigail and John Adams had the longest marriage—just over fifty-four years. Four other presidents and their wives also were married for fifty or more years: Louisa and John Quincy Adams (almost fifty-one years), Bess and Harry Truman (over fifty-three years), Mamie and Dwight Eisenhower (nearly fifty-three years), and Pat and Richard Nixon (fifty-three years).

Q 118. Which first ladies were widows when they married the president? Divorcees?

A Four future first ladies were widows when they married. Martha Washington had been widowed at age twenty-five, Martha Jefferson at nineteen, and Dolley Madison at twenty-five. They all remarried within a few years of their husbands' deaths. The other widow, First Lady Edith Wilson, married a president who was a widower. Caroline Fillmore and Mary Harrison also were widows, but they married presidents who had already left the White House.

Three presidents' wives were divorcees—Andrew Jackson's wife, Rachel; Warren G. Harding's wife, Florence; and Gerald R. Ford's wife, Betty.

(See 84 Have all the presidents been married? 86 Who was the first divorced president? 119 When did the presidents marry?)

Q 119. When did the presidents marry?

A All the presidents except James Buchanan eventually did marry, and some married twice—two names are given in the list below. The previous married names of widows or divorcees who married presidents are given in brackets.

President	Wife's Maiden Name	Date Married
George Washington	Martha Dandridge [Custis]	January 6, 1759
John Adams	Abigail Smith	October 25, 1764
Thomas Jefferson	Martha Wayles [Skelton]	January 1, 1772
James Madison	Dorothea (Dolley) Payne [Todd]	September 15, 1794
James Monroe	Elizabeth Kortright	February 16, 1786
John Quincy Adams	Louisa Catherine Johnson	July 26, 1797

President	Wife's Maiden Name	Date Married
Andrew Jackson	Rachel Donelson [Robards]	January 17, 1794
Martin Van Buren	Hannah Hoes	February 21, 1807
William Henry Harrison	Anna Symmes	November 25, 1795
John Tyler	Letitia Christian	March 29, 1813
	Julia Gardiner	June 26, 1844
James K. Polk	Sarah Childress	January 1, 1824
Zachary Taylor	Margaret Mackall Smith	June 21, 1810
Millard Fillmore	Abigail Powers	February 5, 1826
	Caroline Carmichael [McIntosh]	February 10, 1858
Franklin Pierce	Jane Means Appleton	November 19, 1834
James Buchanan	Not married	
Abraham Lincoln	Mary Todd	November 4, 1842
Andrew Johnson	Eliza McCardle	May 17, 1827
Ulysses S. Grant	Julia Boggs Dent	August 22, 1848
Rutherford B. Hayes	Lucy Ware Webb	December 30, 1852
James A. Garfield	Lucretia Rudolph	November 11, 1858
Chester A. Arthur	Ellen Lewis Herndon	October 25, 1859
Grover Cleveland	Frances Folsom	June 2, 1886
Benjamin Harrison	Caroline Lavinia Scott	October 20, 1853
	Mary Scott Lord [Dimmick]	April 6, 1896
William McKinley	Ida Saxton	January 25, 1871
Theodore Roosevelt	Alice Hathaway Lee	October 27, 1880
	Edith Kermit Carow	December 2, 1886
William Howard Taft	Helen Herron	June 19, 1886
Woodrow Wilson	Ellen Louise Axson	June 24, 1885
	Edith Bolling [Galt]	December 18, 1915
Warren G. Harding	Florence Kling [DeWolfe]	July 8, 1891

President	Wife's Maiden Name	Date Married
Calvin Coolidge	Grace Anna Goodhue	October 4, 1905
Herbert Hoover	Lou Henry	February 10, 1899
Franklin D. Roosevelt	Anna Eleanor Roosevelt	March 17, 1905
Harry S. Truman	Elizabeth Virginia (Bess) Wallace	June 28, 1919
Dwight D. Eisenhower	Marie (Mamie) Geneva Doud	July 1, 1916
John F. Kennedy	Jacqueline Lee Bouvier	September 12, 1953
Lyndon B. Johnson	Claudia Alta (Lady Bird) Taylor	November 17, 1934
Richard M. Nixon	Thelma Catherine (Pat) Ryan	June 21, 1940
Gerald R. Ford	Elizabeth (Betty) Bloomer [Warren]	October 15, 1948
Jimmy Carter	Rosalynn Smith	July 7, 1946
Ronald Reagan	Sarah June Fulks [Futterman] (Jane Wyman) Ann Frances Robbins (Nancy Davis)	January 24, 1940 March 4, 1952
George Bush	Barbara Pierce	January 6, 1945
Bill Clinton	Hillary Rodham	October 11, 1975

(See 116 Which first lady got married the youngest? Which president? 350 When was the first White House wedding?)

Q 120. What did Martha Washington do during the Revolutionary War?

A Rather than stay at home surrounded by the comforts of Mount Vernon, Martha was determined to remain at her husband's side and so traveled from one battlefront headquarters to another throughout the war. She faced the privations of life in camp without complaint, keeping house for General Washington, helping to tend the sick, and even knitting socks for the soldiers. She later said she had heard "the opening and closing shot of almost every important campaign in the war." But she also paid a tremendous price—her last living child, John Custis (by her first marriage), died of camp fever in 1781.

Q **121. What were Abigail Adams's opinions about slavery and the status of women?**

A Of the early first ladies, Abigail Adams was the most politically active and outspoken in her beliefs. Because women in her day were expected to be ladylike and keep their distance from the unwholesomeness of politics, her influence as a political adviser to President John Adams aroused considerable criticism. Nevertheless, she was highly regarded for her intelligence and sharp wit, not the least by Adams himself. Perhaps most remarkable among Abigail's strongly held beliefs were her staunch opposition to slavery and strong support for better treatment of women, including more education. On both issues she was well ahead of her time.

(See 126 How did Eleanor Roosevelt reshape the role of first lady?)

Q **122. Which first lady became famous for her skills as White House hostess?**

A Using her charm, finely honed social skills, and great beauty, Dolley Madison earned her reputation as "the nation's hostess." Dolley's first turn as White House hostess came in 1801, when Thomas Jefferson, a widower, became president. Jefferson needed a hostess, and Dolley, wife of Secretary of State James Madison, quickly proved her ability to organize lavish social events that became the talk of Washington. Certainly her social skills, considerable energy, and intelligence contributed to her success, but Dolley also was genuinely interested in people. She acted as White House hostess on many occasions through Jefferson's two terms (1801–1809), as did Jefferson's daughter, Martha Jefferson Randolph. Dolley then returned for her husband's two terms (1809–1817).

(See 115 Who were the most popular first ladies? The highest rated?)

▶ *How did the British upset Dolley Madison's dinner plans during the War of 1812? See 305 Why did the British burn the White House in 1814?*

Q **123. What was the Eaton affair about?**

A John Eaton, a longtime friend of Andrew Jackson, lived at a Washington, D.C., inn in the years leading up to Jackson's election to the presidency in 1828. Eaton became friends with the innkeeper's daughter, Peggy Timberlake, who was married to a navy purser and who also lived at the inn. Soon after Peggy's husband committed suicide while on a sea voyage in 1828, Eaton proposed marriage, and in January 1829 the two married.

Because marriage and keeping up proper appearances were so important in the 1800s, Peggy's friendship with Eaton became the subject of considerable gossip before the marriage. Then, President-elect Jackson's appointment of John Eaton as his secretary of war thrust the Eatons, and the gossip, into the center of Washington's social scene. Despite Jackson's demand that Peggy be treated courteously, the wives of government officials—including most of the wives of Jackson's cabinet secretaries—treated her as a social outcast. Jackson became so angry with his cabinet secretaries that he formed an informal cabinet of advisers—his Kitchen Cabinet—in order to avoid dealing with them. The affair continued until John Eaton resigned in 1831, and Jackson reshuffled his cabinet. Eaton went on to become governor of Florida and later minister to Spain.

(See 89 Why did Andrew Jackson's wife die prematurely? 189 Who advises the president on policy matters?)

Q **124. Who was the first wife of a president to have a college degree?**

A Lucy Hayes, President Rutherford B. Hayes' wife, was the first, having graduated from Ohio Wesleyan Woman's College in 1850. Many first ladies, both before and after Lucy Hayes, had at least some formal education. But because of the attitudes of the times, only a few continued to the college level and graduated. First ladies who received their college degrees were:

First Lady	College or University	Degree	Date
Lucy Hayes	Wesleyan	B.A.	1850
Frances Cleveland	Wellesley College	B.A.	1885
Grace Coolidge	Vermont	B.A.	1902
Lou Hoover	Stanford	B.A.	1898
Jacqueline Kennedy	George Washington	B.A.	1951
Lady Bird Johnson	Texas	B.A.	1933
Pat Nixon	Southern California	B.A.	1937
Nancy Reagan	Smith	B.A.	1943
Hillary Rodham Clinton	Wellesley College	B.A.	1969
	Yale Law School	L.L.B.	1973

(See 106 Did most presidents attend college?)

Q **125. What did Edith Wilson do when her husband became seriously ill?**

A From the very beginning of her marriage to President Woodrow Wilson in 1915, Edith helped her husband on a daily basis with the business of running the government. She read papers and discussed matters at his direction, and even learned secret codes so she could code and decode his messages.

When President Wilson collapsed with a stroke in 1919 that left him partially paralyzed, she already had a firm idea of what government matters were most important to the president. So, to allow him the rest doctors insisted meant life or death, Edith placed herself between the president and the outside world, screening out all but the most important business and shutting off all but essential access to the president.

For several months, until he regained his strength, Edith essentially ran the government insofar as the outside world was concerned. Afterward, however, she maintained that her role had been limited to deciding what matters needed the president's attention. She read the necessary papers to him or summarized them, and, according to Edith, the president made the final decision from his sickbed.

(See 114 Which first lady was a descendant of Pocahontas? 157 What medical condition left President Wilson incapacitated for several months?)

Q **126. How did Eleanor Roosevelt reshape the role of first lady?**

A Both admired and criticized, Eleanor Roosevelt was the first politically active first lady. She made numerous public appearances, gave speeches, held news conferences, wrote articles, and traveled widely—both to promote her husband's presidency and in behalf of her own causes. Her ability to sway (at times even badger) the president on issues she supported gave her considerable political clout. On many of her travels—she was the first first lady to fly by airplane—she served as the president's eyes and ears, and during World War II she visited the troops as a representative of her husband.

Among the many causes Eleanor supported were women's rights, ending racial discrimination, and the humanitarian programs put in place by the New Deal, such as those aimed at child welfare and helping the poor. After President Roosevelt's death, she was named U.S. delegate to the infant United Nations where, as chairwoman of the UN Commission on Human Rights (1946–1951), she helped to write the UN's Universal Declaration of Human Rights.

(See 78 Have any presidents been related? 115 Who were the most popular first ladies? The highest rated? 180 What does the first lady do?)

Q **127. What careers have the first ladies pursued?**

A Wives of almost all the recent presidents had careers of their own at some point in their lives. A few of the earlier first ladies also held jobs, despite the social pressures against women working outside the home. First ladies and their occupations were:

First Lady	Occupation
Abigail Fillmore	Teacher
Ellen Wilson	Painter
Florence Harding	Circulation manager, Marion, Ohio, newspaper
Grace Coolidge	Teacher (for deaf children)
Lou Hoover	Girl Scout official (served as president of Girl Scouts of America)
Eleanor Roosevelt	Spokeswoman and emissary, Roosevelt administration; newspaper columnist; UN delegate and head of UN Commission on Human Rights
Bess Truman	Secretary to Senator Truman
Jacqueline Kennedy	Newspaper columnist, book editor
Lady Bird Johnson	Owner, broadcasting network
Pat Nixon	Movie extra, teacher, government worker
Betty Ford	Model, dancer, dance teacher
Rosalynn Carter	Bookkeeper (at the Carter family peanut warehouse)
Nancy Reagan	Actress (Broadway and movies)
Hillary Rodham Clinton	Attorney

(See 105 What careers did presidents pursue before reaching the White House?)

(See 105 What careers did presidents pursue before reaching the White House?)

Q **128. What social causes have recent first ladies advocated?**

A Although first ladies today have a much higher public profile and more freedom to speak out than they once did, some early first ladies did not hesitate to stand up for causes they believed in. For example, Abigail Adams spoke out against slavery and for women's equality. Lucy Hayes banned alcohol from the White House during the Hayes administration, earning her the nickname "Lemonade Lucy." More recent first ladies and the social causes they became identified with were:

First Lady	Cause
Edith Wilson	Red Cross
Eleanor Roosevelt	Human rights, rights of minorities and underprivileged
Jacqueline Kennedy	The arts
Lady Bird Johnson	Beautification of highways and urban areas
Betty Ford	Equal Rights Amendment, aid for handicapped children, treatment of alcohol and drug addiction
Rosalynn Carter	Mental health
Nancy Reagan	Fight against drug abuse
Barbara Bush	Literacy, voluntarism
Hillary Rodham Clinton	Children's rights

Q 129. Who is the only first lady to give birth in the White House?

A Frances Folsom Cleveland, President Grover Cleveland's wife, gave birth to the first and only president's child born in the White House. The baby girl, Esther, was born in 1893 during Cleveland's second term. She was Frances's second child.

The first child born in the White House was a slave's baby (1803). Three years later Thomas Jefferson's grandson became the first child related to a president to be born in the White House.

Q 130. Which presidential family had the most children? The fewest?

A John Tyler had fifteen children, more than any other president, but they were the product of two marriages. Tyler's first wife, Letitia, bore eight children, and his second, Julia, had seven. William Henry Harrison had ten children, and Rutherford B. Hayes, had eight. Six presidents, including George Washington, had no children, and both Harry S. Truman and Bill Clinton had only one child (both daughters). Andrew

Jackson adopted his wife's nephew, Andrew Jackson Jr. Neither adopted children nor the few illegitimate children of presidents are included in the list below.

President	Boys	Girls
George Washington	0	0
John Adams	3	2
Thomas Jefferson	1	5
James Madison	0	0
James Monroe	1	2
John Quincy Adams	3	1
Andrew Jackson	0	0
Martin Van Buren	4	0
William Henry Harrison	6	4
John Tyler	8	7
James K. Polk	0	0
Zachary Taylor	1	5
Millard Fillmore	1	1
Franklin Pierce	3	0
James Buchanan	0	0
Abraham Lincoln	4	0
Andrew Johnson	3	2
Ulysses S. Grant	3	1
Rutherford B. Hayes	7	1
James A. Garfield	5	2
Chester A. Arthur	2	1
Grover Cleveland	2	3
Benjamin Harrison	1	2
William McKinley	0	2
Theodore Roosevelt	4	2
William Howard Taft	2	1
Woodrow Wilson	0	3
Warren G. Harding	0	0
Calvin Coolidge	2	0
Herbert Hoover	2	0
Franklin D. Roosevelt	5	1
Harry S. Truman	0	1
Dwight D. Eisenhower	2	0

President	Boys	Girls
John F. Kennedy	2	1
Lyndon B. Johnson	0	2
Richard M. Nixon	0	2
Gerald R. Ford	3	1
Jimmy Carter	3	1
Ronald Reagan	2	2
George Bush	4	2
Bill Clinton	0	1

(See 85 Which presidents fathered illegitimate children?)

Q **131. Which presidents' sons sought the presidency?**

A Four presidents' sons tried to follow in their fathers' footsteps. President John Adams's son John Quincy was the first president's offspring to run for the White House, and in 1825 he succeeded in becoming the nation's chief executive. Two other presidents' sons did not fare as well—Robert Todd Lincoln lost out in the race for the Republican nomination in 1884 and 1888, and Robert A. Taft failed to get the Republican nod in 1940, 1948, and 1952.

Two other presidents' sons were offered party nominations but refused them. John Scott Harrison, son of William Henry Harrison, declined nomination as a Whig candidate in 1856, but his son Benjamin did become president in 1888. John Van Buren turned down a nomination by Free Soil Democrats in 1848 so that his father could run (Martin lost the election).

Most recently, President George Bush's son George W. was the candidate for the Republican presidential nomination in 2000.

▶ *Which presidents' children were married in the White House? See 350 When was the first White House wedding?*

▶ *Who is the only man to be both the son and father of a president? See 78 Have any presidents been related?*

Q **132. Which presidents' wives died prematurely?**

A Five wives died before their husbands reached the White House: Martha Jefferson, Rachel Jackson, Hannah Van Buren, Ellen Arthur, and Alice Lee Roosevelt. Alice Roosevelt was the youngest, twenty-two, when she died in 1884. Martha Jefferson was thirty-three when she died in 1782; Hannah Van Buren was also young, thirty-five at her death in 1819. Rachel Jackson was sixty-one when she died in 1828, just before her husband's inauguration in 1829. Ellen Arthur died in 1880, having reached age forty-two. Of the five widowers, only Theodore Roosevelt remarried.

Three other presidents' wives died while their husbands were in the White House. Fifty-one-year-old Letitia Tyler died in 1842, the second year of John Tyler's term. Sixty-year-old Caroline Harrison passed away in 1892, just two weeks before Benjamin Harrison lost his bid for a second term. Ellen Wilson, fifty-four, died in 1914, a year into Woodrow's first term.

(See 135 Where are the presidents' wives buried? 295 Which presidents and first ladies died in the White House?)

Q **133. Which presidents' children died while their fathers were in office?**

A Five presidents' children died while their fathers were still in office. The first was John Adams's son Charles, who died in 1800 at age thirty. Four years later in 1804, Thomas Jefferson's daughter Mary died at age twenty-five (her mother had died in 1782). President Abraham Lincoln's son William died of pneumonia in 1862, the only president's child to die in the White House.

The two other children died during the twentieth century. Calvin Coolidge Jr. died of blood poisoning when his toe became infected in 1924. He was just sixteen. In 1963 President John F. Kennedy's son Patrick died just two days after his birth.

Q **134. Which former first ladies outlived their husbands?**

A Twenty-four first ladies lived on after their husbands' deaths, beginning with Martha Washington, who survived George by almost two and a half years. Andrew Johnson's wife, Eliza, died the soonest after her husband, just six months, and Benjamin Harrison's second wife, Mary, survived the longest—she lived for another forty-six years. James K. Polk's wife, Sarah, survived him by forty-two years (Polk died at age fifty-three). Grover Cleveland's wife, Frances, who was twenty-eight years younger than Grover when they married, survived him by forty years. Jacqueline Kennedy lived for another thirty years after her husband's assassination.

Q **135. Where are the presidents' wives buried?**

A Eight presidents' wives are buried in Virginia and seven in New York, which are also the two states where the most presidents are buried. Jacqueline Kennedy Onassis is buried at Arlington National Cemetery with her first husband, John F. Kennedy.

President's Wife	Date of Death	Age	Burial Place
Martha Washington	May 22, 1802	70	Mount Vernon, Va.
Abigail Adams	October 28, 1818	73	Quincy, Mass.
Martha Jefferson	September 6, 1782	33	Monticello, Va.
Dolley Madison	July 12, 1849	81	Montpelier, Va.
Elizabeth Monroe	September 23, 1830	62	Richmond, Va.
Louisa Adams	May 14, 1852	77	Quincy, Mass.
Rachel Jackson	December 22, 1828	61	Nashville, Tenn.
Hannah Van Buren	February 5, 1819	35	Kinderhook, N.Y.
Anna Harrison	February 25, 1864	88	North Bend, Ohio
Letitia Tyler	September 10, 1842	51	Cedar Grove, Va.
Julia Tyler	July 10, 1889	69	Richmond, Va.
Sarah Polk	August 14, 1891	87	Nashville, Tenn.
Margaret Taylor	August 18, 1852	63	Louisville, Ky.
Abigail Fillmore	March 30, 1853	55	Buffalo, N.Y.
Caroline Fillmore	August 11, 1881	67	Buffalo, N.Y.
Jane Pierce	December 2, 1863	57	Concord, N.H.
Mary Lincoln	July 16, 1882	63	Springfield, Ill.
Eliza Johnson	January 15, 1876	65	Greeneville, Tenn.
Julia Grant	December 14, 1902	76	New York, N.Y.
Lucy Hayes	June 25, 1889	57	Fremont, Ohio
Lucretia Garfield	March 14, 1918	85	Cleveland, Ohio
Ellen Arthur	January 12, 1880	42	Albany, N.Y.
Frances Cleveland	October 29, 1947	83	Princeton, N.J.

President's Wife	Date of Death	Age	Burial Place
Caroline Harrison	October 25, 1892	60	Indianapolis, Ind.
Mary Harrison	January 5, 1948	88	Indianapolis, Ind.
Ida McKinley	May 26, 1907	59	Canton, Ohio
Alice Roosevelt	February 14, 1884	22	Cambridge, Mass.
Edith Roosevelt	September 30, 1948	87	Oyster Bay, N.Y.
Helen Taft	May 22, 1943	82	Arlington, Va.
Ellen Wilson	August 6, 1914	54	Rome, Ga.
Edith Wilson	December 28, 1961	89	Washington, D.C.
Florence Harding	November 21, 1924	64	Marion, Ohio
Grace Coolidge	July 8, 1957	78	Plymouth Notch, Vt.
Lou Hoover	January 7, 1944	69	Palo Alto, Calif. (reinterred West Branch, Iowa)
Eleanor Roosevelt	November 7, 1962	78	Hyde Park, N.Y.
Bess Truman	October 18, 1982	97	Independence, Mo.
Mamie Eisenhower	November 1, 1979	82	Abilene, Kan.
Jacqueline Kennedy	May 19, 1994	64	Arlington National Cemetery, Va.
Pat Nixon	June 22, 1993	81	Yorba Linda, Calif.

(See 173 When did the presidents and vice presidents die?)

THE VICE PRESIDENTS

Q **136. Where did the term *Veep* originate?**

A Although the vice president's formal title is "Mr. Vice President," Alben W. Barkley's young grandson found it too cumbersome to say. The boy shortened his grandfather's title to "veep," and in 1949 the *New York Times* published a story telling the world about his unconventional adaptation. The informal title veep caught on and has since become a common alternative term for vice president.

Q 137. In what state have the most vice presidents been born?

A New York was the birthplace of eight vice presidents, twice the number of the next closest state, Kentucky. The eight New York–born vice presidents were George Clinton, Daniel D. Tompkins, Martin Van Buren, Millard Fillmore, Schuyler Colfax, William A. Wheeler, Theodore Roosevelt, and James S. Sherman.

Q 138. Did any vice presidents come from wealthy families?

A The parents of ten vice presidents were wealthy, and those of six others were considered well-to-do. Vice President Nelson A. Rockefeller came from one of the country's wealthiest families. Among the other vice presidents with monied backgrounds were Thomas Jefferson, John C. Calhoun, George M. Dallas, Theodore Roosevelt, George Bush, and Dan Quayle.

Eleven vice presidents came from poor families, including Millard Fillmore, Andrew Johnson, Charles W. Fairbanks, Harry S. Truman, and Alben W. Barkley.

(See 77 Which presidents were born into wealthy families?)

Q 139. Who was the first vice president married while in office?

A Harry S. Truman's vice president, Alben W. Barkley, became the first in 1949 when he married a widow, Elizabeth Jane Rucker Hadley. The couple was wed in a St. Louis, Missouri, ceremony.

(See 84 Have all the presidents been married?)

Q 140. Which vice president had the most children?

A John Tyler, who was vice president for only a few weeks before President William Henry Harrison died, had the most children—fifteen by his first and second wives. Tyler holds the same record among the presidents as well. Vice President Elbridge Gerry had the second largest family, with ten children, and John C. Calhoun fathered nine. Among the recent vice presidents, Nelson A. Rockefeller had seven and George Bush, had six.

Charles G. Dawes and his wife adopted two children and had two others. Richard M. Johnson fathered two illegitimate daughters by his mistress, a mulatto who was his slave.

(See 85 Which presidents fathered illegitimate children?)

Q 141. Has a Native American descendant ever served as vice president?

A Charles Curtis, vice president under Herbert Hoover, was a descendant of the Kaw Indian tribe on his mother's side of the family. His maternal grandmother was a Kaw Indian and the granddaughter of an Osage Indian chief. Curtis served during Hoover's one term, from 1929 to 1933.

▶ *Who was the first African American contender for the vice-presidential nomination of a major party? See 400 Has an African American ever been nominated for president or vice president by a major party?*

Q 142. Have any political offices served as stepping-stones to the vice presidency?

A If a steppingstone to the vice presidency exists, serving in Congress is surely it. Of the forty-five vice presidents, thirty-five served either in the Continental Congress or in its successor, the U.S. Congress, before becoming vice president. John Adams, Thomas Jefferson, George Clinton, and Elbridge Gerry all served in the Continental Congress (but not the U.S. Congress). Daniel D. Tompkins was elected to the House of Representatives but resigned his seat before beginning his term. Fourteen vice presidents served as a state governor before taking office. The following vice presidents served in the U.S. Congress (D–Democratic; DR–Democratic-Republican; R–Republican; W–Whig):

Vice President	Representing Party-State	House Term	Senate Term
Aaron Burr	DR-N.Y.		1791–1797
Elbridge Gerry	DR-Mass.	1789–1793	
John C. Calhoun	DR-S.C.	1811–1817	1832–1843 1845–1850
Martin Van Buren	D-N.Y.		1821–1828
Richard M. Johnson	R-Ky.	1807–1819 1899–1837	1819–1829
John Tyler	R-W.Va.	1817–1821	1827–1836
George M. Dallas	D-Pa.		1831–1833

Vice President	Representing Party-State	House Term	Senate Term
Millard Fillmore	W-N.Y.	1833–1835 1837–1843	
William R. King	Ala.*	1811–1816	1819–1844 1848–1852
John C. Breckinridge	D-Ky.	1851–1855	1861 (expelled)
Hannibal Hamlin	Maine*	1843–1847	1848–1857 1857–1861 1869–1881
Andrew Johnson	D-Tenn.	1843–1853	1857–1862 1875
Schuyler Colfax	R-Ind.	1855–1869	
Henry Wilson	R-Mass.		1855–1873
William A. Wheeler	R-N.Y.	1861–1863 1869–1877	
Thomas A. Hendricks	D-Ind.	1851–1855	1863–1869
Levi P. Morton	R-N.Y.	1879–1881	
Adlai E. Stevenson	D-Ill.	1875–1877 1879–1881	
Charles W. Fairbanks	R-Ind.		1897–1905
James S. Sherman	R-N.Y.	1887–1891 1893–1909	
Charles Curtis	R-Kan.	1893–1907	1907–1913 1915–1929
John N. Garner	D-Texas	1903–1933	
Harry S. Truman	D-Mo.		1935–1945
Alben W. Barkley	D-Ky.	1913–1927	1927–1949 1955–1956
Richard M. Nixon	R-Calif.	1947–1950	1950–1953
Lyndon B. Johnson	D-Texas	1937–1949	1949–1961

Vice President	Representing Party-State	House Term	Senate Term
Hubert H. Humphrey	D-Minn.		1949–1964 1971–1978
Gerald R. Ford	R-Mich.	1949–1973	
Walter F. Mondale	D-Minn.		1964–1976
George Bush	R-Texas	1967–1971	
Dan Quayle	R-Ind.	1977–1981	1981–1989
Al Gore	D-Tenn.	1977–1985	1985–1993

*Switched parties

(See 104 Has serving in Congress proved to be an effective springboard to the presidency?)

Q 143. Which former vice president was tried for treason?

A Vice President Aaron Burr earned that dubious distinction in 1807, when he was arrested for trying to incite a rebellion in the Louisiana Territory. After killing Alexander Hamilton in a duel (1804), Burr realized his political future in the federal government was at an end. He was both ambitious and a schemer, however, and in 1805—while still vice president—he began to seek backing for the revolt, which was to have created an independent republic under his leadership.

The British government turned him down, but an Irish millionaire gave him financial backing and Gen. James Wilkinson, governor of the Louisiana Territory, joined in the plot. In 1806, with Burr out of office and the plot moving forward, Wilkinson had second thoughts and revealed Burr's treasonous plan to President Thomas Jefferson. Arrested as he headed down the Mississippi with some sixty soldiers of fortune, Burr was tried for treason, with Chief Justice John Marshall presiding. Despite the evidence, Burr was acquitted of the charges.

Q 144. Why was Vice President Charles G. Dawes awarded the Nobel Peace Prize?

A Dawes, the only vice president to receive a Nobel Prize, was honored for his work in helping end the economic crisis in Germany after World War I. The director of the newly formed Bureau of the Budget in the Harding administration, Dawes was appointed chairman of the Allied Reparations Commission in 1923. In that post he oversaw the development of the Dawes Plan, which in 1924 restructured the war reparations payments Germany had been forced to make after losing World War I. The high payments had thrown the German economy into a tailspin. Dawes's plan reduced the payments and included a foreign loan to help revive Germany's economy.

Dawes received the Nobel Peace Prize in 1925. That same year he became vice president in the Coolidge administration.

(See 147 Which two presidents won Nobel Prizes?)

▶ *How old were the vice presidents? See 145 Who were the oldest and youngest presidents? Vice presidents? 172 Which president and vice president lived the longest?*

▶ *Has the country ever been without a vice president? See 60 Has the office of vice president ever been vacant?*

▶ *Under which presidents did the vice presidents serve? See 348 When did the presidents and vice presidents serve?*

FOR THE RECORD

Q 145. Who were the oldest and youngest presidents? Vice presidents?

A President Ronald Reagan was inaugurated just weeks before his seventieth birthday, making him the oldest president. He was nearly seventy-eight when he completed his second term. William Henry Harrison ranks as the second oldest—at just over sixty-eight—but he died after serving less than a month.

The youngest president was Theodore Roosevelt; he succeeded to the presidency at forty-two. The next youngest, John F. Kennedy, was forty-three years and seven months old at his inauguration.

Harry S. Truman's vice president, Alben W. Barkley, holds the record for being the oldest veep—seventy-one at his inauguration. Sixty-nine-year-old George Clinton, James Madison's first vice president, became the second oldest at his inauguration. The youngest was thirty-six-year-old John C. Breckinridge, James Buchanan's vice president.

(See 173 When did the presidents and vice presidents die? 348 When did the presidents and vice presidents serve?)

146. Who were the tallest, shortest, and heaviest presidents?

A At six feet, four inches, Abraham Lincoln was the tallest, but not by much—Lyndon B. Johnson was six feet, three inches. Thomas Jefferson was six feet, two and a half inches, and five others were six feet, two inches (George Washington, Chester A. Arthur, Franklin D. Roosevelt, George Bush, and Bill Clinton).

James Madison was the shortest—he stood just five feet, four inches—and weighed the least, only about a hundred pounds. Both Martin Van Buren and Benjamin Harrison were only two inches taller, however.

The heaviest president was William Howard Taft, who was six feet tall and weighed in at between 300 and 332 pounds. At 260 pounds, Grover Cleveland was also overweight for his five-foot-eleven frame.

Q **147. Which two presidents won Nobel Prizes?**

A Theodore Roosevelt and Woodrow Wilson, who were both instrumental in increasing U.S. involvement in foreign affairs, are the only two presidents to win the Nobel Peace Prize. Roosevelt won his in 1906 for mediating a peace agreement between Russia and Japan to end the Russo-Japanese War in 1905. Wilson was honored in 1919 for his work in establishing the League of Nations, the forerunner of the United Nations.

(See 144 Why was Vice President Charles G. Dawes awarded the Nobel Peace Prize?)

Q **148. Who was the first president to be photographed?**

A John Quincy Adams became the first in 1848, shortly before his death. The photograph was a daguerrotype, itself one of the earliest types of photographs, and it shows the eighty-year-old Adams seated in a chair, hands folded and staring intently at the camera. He had been out of office for nineteen years when the picture was taken.

By the twentieth century posing for photographs had become a regular part of a president's routine. Two presidents were more than ready to take on the task—both Gerald R. Ford and Ronald Reagan had worked for a time as professional models. Ford helped to pay for law school at Yale by modeling men's clothing. Reagan took advantage of his celebrity status as a movie actor to do ads for cigarettes and other consumer products.

Q 149. Who were the first presidents heard on radio and seen on television?

A The first president to have his speech broadcast on radio was Warren G. Harding. The occasion was his dedication of the Francis Scott Key Memorial in Baltimore on June 14, 1922. Franklin D. Roosevelt had the distinction of being the first president seen on television. NBC aired his speech marking the opening of the New York World's Fair on April 30, 1939. Herbert Hoover had appeared in an early experimental television picture twelve years earlier, in 1927, but at that time he was secretary of commerce in the Coolidge administration.

President Calvin Coolidge, who was running for reelection in 1924, became the first presidential candidate filmed for movie newsreels on August 11. His opponents that year also appeared in the newsreel.

(See 280 Who was the first president to hold televised news conferences?)

Q 150. Which president has been the subject of the most films?

A Abraham Lincoln has been the subject of more films than any other president, including George Washington. Lincoln, portrayed as "Honest Abe" and the Union's savior, was especially popular in the early years of the motion picture industry, and by 1930 studios had produced nine motion pictures based on his life. Eleven other films included Lincoln as a historical character. By contrast, by 1930 studios had released only four motion pictures depicting Washington's life.

Ronald Reagan appeared in some fifty-five movies, but as an actor, not the subject of the films.

Q 151. Who is the only former president to sit on the Supreme Court?

A Once a judge on the U.S. Sixth Circuit Court, William Howard Taft went on to become president and then returned to the bench years later as chief justice of the United States. Taft became president of the American Bar Association after failing to win a second term as president in 1912. Then in 1921 Taft's friend Warren G. Harding took office as president. When Chief Justice Edward White died later in 1921, Harding named Taft to succeed him on the Supreme Court.

A moderate conservative, Taft served on the Court from 1921 until 1930, when heart problems forced his resignation. He was instrumental in passage of the Judiciary Act of 1925, which reduced the Supreme Court's backlog of cases by allowing it almost unlimited discretion in deciding which cases to review.

Q 152. Did George Washington really have false teeth?

A Washington suffered from bad teeth as an adult—he may have had periodontal problems. By the time he reached middle age, he had lost all his teeth and was forced to depend on a strange array of custom-made dentures. His first set of false teeth had a steel spring in back and tended to push his lips outward. Later he tried dentures made of seahorse ivory, hippopotamus teeth, pig's teeth, and cow's teeth.

Q 153. From what condition did President Lincoln suffer?

A While it cannot be said with certainty, Abraham Lincoln exhibited the symptoms of a congenital disorder called Marfan's disease, which affects the skeleton, circulatory system, and eyes. The most obvious outward signs, which Lincoln exhibited, are abnormally long, thin arms, legs, and fingers. Its victims also tend to be unusually tall—like Lincoln. People with untreated Marfan's disease usually die in their forties or fifties, but Lincoln was well into his fifties when he was assassinated.

Q 154. Did President Garfield's doctors contribute to his death from an assassin's bullet?

A Certainly the lack of medical knowledge in the 1880s contributed to James A. Garfield's death from a gunshot wound, which was not serious by today's standards. In 1881 doctors had no anesthetics and no knowledge of germs and sterilization. Nor did they have any way of determining where the bullet was lodged, except by probing the wound in his back with their unsterilized fingers and instruments (the bullet nicked Garfield's backbone and lodged below his pancreas). Although doctors at first thought the president would soon die of his wound, Garfield seemed to stabilize the day after the assassin's bullet struck him.

Over the next weeks doctors again probed Garfield's wound in an effort to locate the bullet, but otherwise they could do nothing beyond draining the wound and trying to make him comfortable in the sweltering summer heat. By the end of August the infection from his wound was spreading, and the president was showing signs of weakening. He died in September, eleven weeks after being shot.

Q 155. Why did Grover Cleveland conceal his cancer surgery from the public?

A Early in President Cleveland's second term, doctors discovered a cancerous growth on the roof of his mouth. They saw no alternative but surgery to remove it. Cleveland had other problems to worry about though—the country was in the midst of the financial panic of 1893, and news of his illness might well have made matters even worse. When his doctors insisted on operating, Cleveland finally agreed, but only on the condition that it be done in complete secrecy.

To that end, Cleveland and his doctors met aboard a private yacht in New York harbor on June 30, 1893. The next day they anesthetized the president and then removed the cancerous tissue and the most of his upper jawbone. A few days later the president recovered enough to travel to his summer home, and two months after that he was able to resume his duties. The operation remained a secret until 1917, which was well after Cleveland's death from heart disease.

Q 156. Which president suffered from dyslexia as a child?

A Woodrow Wilson, the only president to earn a Ph.D. and who also served as president of Princeton University, probably was dyslexic. During his early years, Wilson had been too sickly to attend school and was taught at home by his father. He was unquestionably intelligent, but his reading problem kept him from learning to read until age eleven.

(See 106 Did most presidents attend college? 110 How many presidents once taught school?)

Q 157. What medical condition left President Wilson incapacitated for several months?

A In mid-August 1919, Woodrow Wilson began a cross-country campaign to win public support for ratification of the Treaty of Versailles, which ended World War I and called for creation of the League of Nations. Ratification had become a personal crusade for Wilson, but he was already exhausted and ill from overwork during the treaty negotiations. On his cross-country tour, he made it as far as Pueblo, Colorado, before suffering a stroke on September 23, 1919, that abruptly ended his crusade.

Rushed back to the White House, he suffered another debilitating stroke that left him paralyzed on the left side. For the next several months Wilson's doctors and First Lady Edith Wilson kept secret the extent of the president's illness. Even presidential aides were not allowed to visit him. Wilson recovered slowly and with Edith's help began taking an active part in running the government again. After several months, he was able to walk with help, and he eventually completed his second term. He never fully recovered from the stroke, however, and died in 1924—of yet another one.

(See 125 What did Edith Wilson do when her husband became seriously ill?)

Q 158. What was the cause of Warren G. Harding's death?

A Various rumors surrounded President Harding's death in 1923, in part because of the Teapot Dome scandal that broke soon afterward. Some chalked his death up to food poisoning; others suspected poisoning by his unhappy wife; and still others voiced suspicions that the impending scandal had somehow killed him. But some months before his death he had begun losing strength and looking sickly. At least one doctor who met him in late 1922 predicted the president would be dead from coronary disease in a matter of months.

In the spring of 1923, when Harding began a trip to Alaska, he was losing strength rapidly. Partway through the excursion he suffered a collapse of sorts—after receiving a coded message from Washington. Things only got worse from there. In Vancouver he barely managed to get through a speech and that night complained of chest pains. The president's physician blamed acute indigestion from a crabmeat snack, but Harding was rushed to San Francisco, where heart specialists diagnosed a cardiac collapse and bronchial pneumonia. Treated with digitalis and caffeine, Harding seemed to improve over the next two days, only to die suddenly after a brief convulsion, probably as a result of coronary artery disease. Mrs. Harding refused to permit an autopsy.

(See 372 What happened in the Teapot Dome scandal?)

Q 159. When did Franklin D. Roosevelt contract polio?

A Roosevelt contracted polio while on vacation with his family during the summer of 1921, some months after losing his bid to become vice president of the United States. The disease began after a severe chill and progressed rapidly. His lower limbs were paralyzed after just three days. Roosevelt refused to let the paralysis hinder his political ambitions, however. His handicap was no secret, but by various means he managed to keep it out of the public eye, or at least to minimize the impression that he was disabled.

Roosevelt served three full presidential terms and part of a fourth before the hard work and ill health finally brought on his death. It was not the polio, however, that ended his life; it was severe hardening of the arteries of the brain. Roosevelt died at age sixty-three of a cerebral hemorrhage.

(See 285 Which presidents served the longest and shortest periods of time?)

Q 160. How many heart attacks did Dwight D. Eisenhower have while in office?

A President Eisenhower suffered his first heart attack (September 27, 1955) and a stroke (November 25, 1957) while still in office. (In 1956 he also was operated on for ileitis, a disease of the intestine.) The stroke left him with a slight speech defect, but he otherwise recovered and finished out his term. In the years after leaving office, however, his heart condition worsened. He suffered heart attacks in November 1965 and in April 1968, and from that time on remained hospitalized (and suffered three more heart attacks) until his death in March 1969.

Q 161. What medical condition left John F. Kennedy near death before he became president?

A Although his supporters publicly denied it, evidence exists that Kennedy suffered from Addison's disease, a loss of function in the adrenal glands. Apparently, it had developed in the years after World War II. A serious condition, the disease leads to weight loss, fatigue, indigestion, diarrhea, poor resistance to infection, and, if left untreated, failure of the adrenal glands and death.

According to reports, symptoms of the disease began appearing—along with persistent back problems—soon after a Japanese destroyer rammed and sank the U.S. Navy patrol boat, *PT 109*, that Kennedy commanded during World War II. After the war, Kennedy became thin and ill and suffered from indigestion. While on a trip to Europe in 1947 he was finally diagnosed with Addison's disease. During the voyage back to the United States in October of that year, he became so sick that he was given last rites. This was the first of three occasions on which he nearly died (1947, 1951, and 1954). The first two attacks appeared to have been caused directly by the Addison's disease; the third—when he was again given last rites—resulted from the severe infection that followed surgery for his back pain.

Q 162. How seriously was Ronald Reagan wounded during the 1981 assassination attempt?

A While the fact that President Reagan walked into the hospital after being shot led many people to believe his wound was not serious, only quick medical treatment and good fortune saved his life. For one thing, just one of the bullets fired by John W. Hinckley Jr. struck the president, missing his heart by a mere inch before lodging in a lung. That wound could have been far worse, however. The bullet was the kind that explodes after penetration, but fortunately for Reagan it did not. Still, he was bleeding internally, and by the time he got to the hospital he had lost at least 30 percent of his blood, a potentially life-threatening amount. In addition, doctors kept him on the operating table for three hours trying to find the bullet, much longer than they had anticipated.

AFTER THE PRESIDENCY

Q 163. Why was President Washington's Farewell Address important?

A George Washington's final message to the nation is perhaps the first truly significant address by a president. Written with the help of Alexander Hamilton, John Jay, and James Madison, the address circulated widely in print form from 1796 onward, but Washington never delivered it in person before an audience. He did, however, set the precedent for presidents delivering farewell addresses at the end of their terms, and he voiced several important concerns about the future of America that remain relevant today. Washington emphasized the need for national unity and warned against the dangers of political parties and special interests. He also spoke out against accumulating a large national debt and against becoming entangled in foreign politics.

Historians also regard a few other presidents' farewell addresses as especially important. Dwight D. Eisenhower's address, with its warning against the immense power of what he called the military-industrial complex, is a good example.

Q 164. Did any presidents run for political office after leaving the presidency?

A Although former presidents differed on what they believed ex-presidents should or should not do after leaving office, two did eventually serve in elective offices. John Quincy Adams followed up his term as president by running for the U.S. House of Representatives and spent eighteen years as a representative from Massachusetts (1831–1848). In late 1861 during the Civil War, former president John Tyler, a native Virginian, ran for a seat in the Confederate Congress. He won but died before beginning his term. Ex-president Andrew Johnson was elected to the U.S. Senate by the Tennessee legislature in 1874, but he died after serving only a few months.

(See 385 Which incumbent presidents lost their reelection bids?)

Q **165. When were the most former presidents alive?**

A Twice in the nation's history five ex-presidents have been alive at the same time. The first group of five endured for less than a year, from March 1861 to January 1862, and was made up of Martin Van Buren, John Tyler, Franklin Pierce, Millard Fillmore, and James Buchanan. Tyler's death in January 1862 ended the first period. Some 130 years later the country again had a bumper crop of five living ex-presidents—Richard M. Nixon, Gerald R. Ford, Jimmy Carter, Ronald Reagan, and George Bush. This group of five living ex-presidents lasted for just over a year, from January 20, 1993, to April 22, 1994, when Nixon died.

Q **166. Do all of the presidents have presidential libraries?**

A Former presidents since Herbert Hoover have all established libraries to house their presidential papers, films, photographs, and other materials of historical interest from their years in the White House. The first such library was privately organized in 1916 for the papers of Rutherford B. Hayes. Franklin D. Roosevelt used Hayes's as a model for setting up his presidential library, which was the first official one. Except for the Hayes and Richard M. Nixon libraries (both privately funded), presidential libraries are run by the National Archives. The libraries are:

Rutherford B. Hayes Memorial Museum and Library, 1337 Hayes Ave., Fremont, OH 43420

Herbert Hoover Presidential Library, Parkside Drive, West Branch, IA 52358 (www.hoover.nara.gov)

Franklin D. Roosevelt Library, Albany Post Road, Hyde Park, NY 12538 (academic.marist.edu/fdr/)

Harry S. Truman Library, U.S. Highway 24 and Delaware St., Independence, MO 64050
(www.trumanlibrary.org)

Dwight D. Eisenhower Library, Southeast Fourth Street, Abilene, KS 67410 (www.eisenhower.utexas.edu)

John F. Kennedy Library, Morrissey Boulevard, Boston, MA 02125 (www.cs.umb.edu/jfklibrary/)

Lyndon B. Johnson Library, 2313 Red River Street, Austin, TX 78705 (www.lbjlib.utexas.edu)

Richard M. Nixon Library and Birthplace, 18001 Yorba Linda Blvd., Yorba Linda, CA 92686
(www.nara.gov/nixon/)

Gerald R. Ford Library, 1000 Beal Avenue, Ann Arbor, MI 48109
(www.ford.utexas.edu)

Jimmy Carter Library, One Copenhill Avenue, Atlanta, GA 30307
(www.carterlibrary.galileo.peachnet.edu)

Ronald Reagan Presidential Library, 40 Presidential Drive, Simi Valley, CA 93065
(www.reagan.utexas.edu)

George Bush Presidential Library, Texas A&M University, College Station, TX 77843
(http://bushlibrary.tamu.edu)

Q 167. What retirement benefits do presidents get?

A Until former President Harry S. Truman complained to Congress about having to spend $30,000 a year just to answer mail, presidents received no pension whatsoever. Truman, who was not wealthy, refused a number of business offers after leaving the White House because he did not want to trade on his reputation as a former president. But the cost of being an ex-president was proving too much, and in 1958 Congress passed the Former Presidents Act.

Under the act, Truman received a pension plus $50,000 annually for office expenses. Since then, Congress has fattened the retirement package considerably. On leaving office, presidents get a $1.5 million transition payment, an annual pension equal to a cabinet member's salary (about $150,000), $96,000 a year for staff (more during the first thirty months), lifetime Secret Service protection (for their spouses and for children sixteen and under as well), and generous funding for a presidential library.

(See 183 What is the president's salary?)

Q 168. Did any of the presidents die in poverty?

A Thomas Jefferson, who owned a Virginia plantation, was the first. His inability to live within his salary as president and the lavish hospitality he extended an endless stream of guests at his home left him $100,000 in debt by the time he died. Jefferson's plantation, Monticello, was sold at auction after his death to settle his debts. James Monroe's years of public service also put him heavily in debt, and even a $30,000 payment voted by Congress did not solve his problems. Unable to sell his Virginia estate, Monroe lost it and died penniless. Andrew Jackson's debts were much smaller—he owed $26,000—but he also died in debt. Ulysses S. Grant's final years were marked by the failure of his brokerage firm, which cost him most of his property, and the onset of cancer. He hoped that by writing and selling his memoirs, he could provide his wife with financial security. Despite the cancer, he finished the book four days before his death, and it became a bestseller, earning his wife $500,000. The last president to die in debt was Warren G. Harding. Stock market trading (through a blind account) ruined him, and he died owing a broker $200,000.

Q 169. How many presidents died on the Fourth of July?

A Three presidents died on July 4, the day commemorating U.S. independence. In a remarkable coincidence, Thomas Jefferson and John Adams both died on July 4, 1826, the fiftieth anniversary of the Declaration of Independence. The third president, James Monroe, died five years later, on July 4, 1831, six years after completing his two terms in office.

One president was born on July 4—Calvin Coolidge (in 1872).

Q 170. What ceremonies are observed when a president dies while in office?

A The deceased president first lies in state in the East Room of the White House. Then, by means of an elaborate funeral procession, the casket is transported to the Capitol Building, where it is placed in the Rotunda so the public can pay its last respects before the burial.

James A. Garfield is the only sitting president whose body was taken directly to the Capitol Building without first lying in state in the White House. Garfield had died in New Jersey and his body was transported back to Washington for funeral services.

(See 154 Did President Garfield's doctors contribute to his death from an assassin's bullet? 296 Which presidents were assassinated?)

Q 171. Who is the only president buried in Washington, D.C.?

A Woodrow Wilson is the only one. Most presidents are buried in their home states, but Wilson's body was interred in the National Cathedral in the District of Columbia. Wilson might have had some company in the District had the planners of the Capitol Building had their way. When the Capitol was constructed, provisions were made for a crypt in which to place George Washington's body. But when the former first president died, his family had him buried on the grounds of his beloved home at Mount Vernon, Virginia, and the Capitol crypt remained empty.

Arlington National Cemetery in Virginia is the burial place for two presidents, William William Howard Taft and John F. Kennedy. First Ladies Helen Taft and Jacqueline Kennedy Onassis also are buried there.

Q 172. Which president and vice president lived the longest?

A President John Adams died just a few months shy of ninety-one, making him the longest-living president. Herbert Hoover lived until ninety, and Harry S. Truman was almost eighty-nine when he died. In all, seven now-deceased presidents lived to be eighty or older, and ten more reached their seventies.

Two of the assassinated presidents had the shortest life spans. John F. Kennedy died at forty-six, and James A. Garfield died two months before his fiftieth birthday.

Some vice presidents enjoyed extraordinary longevity. Franklin D. Roosevelt's first vice president, John Nance Garner, lived until just two weeks shy of his ninety-ninth birthday. Levi P. Morton, Benjamin Harrison's vice president, did nearly as well; he died at ninety-six. The vice president with the shortest life span was Daniel D. Tompkins, James Monroe's vice president. Tompkins died just before his fifty-first birthday.

Q 173. When did the presidents and vice presidents die?

A Seven presidents died in July, more than any other month, and six others passed away in June. May was the only month in which no president has died, perhaps because of the month's pleasant spring weather.

Seven presidents are buried in Virginia, the most of any state. New York is the final resting place for six presidents, and Ohio, five. Here is the complete list of presidents and vice presidents:

President	Date of Death	Age	Burial Site
George Washington	December 14, 1799	67	Mount Vernon, Va.
John Adams	July 4, 1826	90	Quincy, Mass.
Thomas Jefferson	July 4, 1826	83	Charlottesville, Va.
James Madison	June 28, 1836	85	Montpelier, Va.
James Monroe	July 4, 1831	73	Richmond, Va.
John Quincy Adams	February 23, 1848	80	Quincy, Mass.

President	Date of Death	Age	Burial Site
Andrew Jackson	June 8, 1845	78	Nashville, Tenn.
Martin Van Buren	July 24, 1862	79	Kinderhook, N.Y.
William Henry Harrison	April 4, 1841	68	North Bend, Ohio
John Tyler	January 18, 1862	71	Richmond, Va.
James K. Polk	June 15, 1849	53	Nashville, Tenn.
Zachary Taylor	July 9, 1850	65	Louisville, Ky.
Millard Fillmore	March 8, 1874	74	Buffalo, N.Y.
Franklin Pierce	October 8, 1869	64	Concord, N.H.
James Buchanan	June 1, 1868	77	Lancaster, Pa.
Abraham Lincoln	April 15, 1865	56	Springfield, Ill.
Andrew Johnson	July 31, 1875	66	Greeneville, Tenn.
Ulysses S. Grant	July 23, 1885	63	New York, N.Y.
Rutherford B. Hayes	January 17, 1893	70	Fremont, Ohio
James A. Garfield	September 19, 1881	49	Cleveland, Ohio
Chester A. Arthur	November 18, 1886	56	Albany, N.Y.
Grover Cleveland	June 24, 1908	71	Princeton, N.J.
Benjamin Harrison	March 13, 1901	67	Indianapolis, Ind.
William McKinley	September 14, 1901	58	Canton, Ohio
Theodore Roosevelt	January 6, 1919	60	Oyster Bay, N.Y.
William Howard Taft	March 8, 1930	72	Arlington, Va.
Woodrow Wilson	February 3, 1924	67	Washington, D.C.
Warren G. Harding	August 2, 1923	57	Marion, Ohio
Calvin Coolidge	January 5, 1933	60	Plymouth Notch, Vt.
Herbert Hoover	October 20, 1964	90	West Branch, Iowa
Franklin D. Roosevelt	April 12, 1945	63	Hyde Park, N.Y.
Harry S. Truman	December 26, 1972	88	Independence, Mo.
Dwight D. Eisenhower	March 28, 1969	78	Abilene, Kan.
John F. Kennedy	November 22, 1963	46	Arlington, Va.
Lyndon B. Johnson	January 22, 1973	64	Johnson City, Texas
Richard M. Nixon	April 22, 1994	81	Yorba Linda, Calif.

Vice President	Date of Death	Age	Burial Site
John Adams	July 4, 1826	90	Quincy, Mass.
Thomas Jefferson	July 4, 1826	83	Charlottesville, Va.
Aaron Burr	September 14, 1836	80	Princeton, N.J.
George Clinton	April 20, 1812	73	Kingston, N.Y.

Vice President	Date of Death	Age	Burial Site
Elbridge Gerry	November 23, 1814	70	Washington, D.C.
Daniel D. Thompkins	June 11, 1825	51	New York, N.Y.
John C. Calhoun	March 31, 1850	68	Charleston, S.C.
Martin Van Buren	July 24, 1862	79	Kinderhook, N.Y.
Richard M. Johnson	November 19, 1850	70	Frankfort, Ky.
John Tyler	January 18, 1862	71	Richmond, Va.
George M. Dallas	December 31, 1864	72	Philadelphia, Pa.
Millard Fillmore	March 8, 1874	74	Buffalo, N.Y.
William R. King	April 18, 1853	67	Selma, Ala.
John C. Breckinridge	May 17, 1875	54	Lexington, Ky.
Hannibal Hamlin	July 4, 1891	81	Bangor, Maine
Andrew Johnson	July 31, 1875	66	Greeneville, Tenn.
Schuyler Colfax	January 13, 1885	61	South Bend, Ind.
Henry Wilson	November 22, 1875	63	Natick, Mass.
William A. Wheeler	June 4, 1887	67	Malone, N.Y.
Chester A. Arthur	November 18, 1886	56	Albany, N.Y.
Thomas A. Hendricks	November 25, 1885	66	Indianapolis, Ind.
Levi P. Morton	May 16, 1920	96	Rhinebeck, N.Y.
Adlai E. Stevenson	June 14, 1914	78	Bloomington, Ill.
Garret A. Hobart	November 21, 1899	55	Paterson, N.J.
Theodore Roosevelt	January 6, 1919	60	Oyster Bay, N.Y.
Charles W. Fairbanks	June 4, 1918	66	Indianapolis, Ind.
James S. Sherman	October 30, 1912	57	Utica, N.Y.
Thomas R. Marshall	June 1, 1925	71	Indianapolis, Ind.
Calvin Coolidge	January 5, 1933	60	Plymouth Notch, Vt.
Charles G. Dawes	April 23, 1951	85	Chicago, Ill.
Charles Curtis	February 8, 1936	76	Topeka, Kan.
John Nance Garner	November 7, 1967	98	Uvalde, Texas
Henry A. Wallace	November 18, 1965	77	Des Moines, Iowa
Harry S. Truman	December 26, 1972	88	Independence, Mo.
Alben W. Barkley	April 30, 1956	78	Paducah, Ky.
Richard M. Nixon	April 22, 1994	81	Yorba Linda, Calif.
Lyndon B. Johnson	January 22, 1973	64	Johnson City, Texas
Hubert H. Humphrey	January 13, 1978	66	Minneapolis, Minn.
Spiro T. Agnew	September 17, 1996	77	Timonium, Md.
Nelson A. Rockefeller	January 26, 1979	70	North Tarrytown, N.Y.

Q **174. Why did Congress wait so long before authorizing construction of the Washington Monument?**

A Washington himself discouraged plans to erect an equestrian statue in his honor while he was still alive, and after his death in 1799 his family refused to allow his body to be interred in the crypt constructed for that purpose in the U.S. Capitol. But Washington was too great a hero for the American people to forget completely, and in 1832 a private group won approval from Congress to build the Washington Monument. Construction of the 555-foot-high obelisk did not begin until 1848, though, and was further delayed by lack of funds and the Civil War. The monument was finally dedicated in 1885.

Other presidents also have been honored with memorials in Washington, D.C. The two best known, the Lincoln Memorial and the Jefferson Memorial, were constructed on the Mall in Washington in the first half of the twentieth century. The Lincoln Memorial was dedicated in 1922 and the Jefferson Memorial on April 13, 1943, the two hundredth anniversary of Jefferson's birth. The Franklin D. Roosevelt Memorial is the newest presidential memorial; it opened to the public in 1997. An island in the Potomac is maintained in honor of Theodore Roosevelt, and the Lyndon B. Johnson Grove on the Potomac honors his memory.

Q **175. Which four presidents are represented on Mount Rushmore?**

A The faces of George Washington, Thomas Jefferson, Abraham Lincoln, and Theodore Roosevelt are carved into the granite face of Mount Rushmore, in South Dakota. Sculptor Gutzon Borglum began carving the 60-foot-high likenesses in 1927 and worked until his death in 1941. That year his son Lincoln added the finishing touches to the massive job, which involved cutting away some 450,000 tons of rock (a task largely paid for by the federal government). The four presidents had been selected to represent the nation's founding (Washington), political philosophy (Jefferson), national unity (Lincoln), and expansion and conservation (Roosevelt).

Likenesses of Confederate president Jefferson Davis and two other heroes of the Confederacy, Robert E. Lee and Stonewall Jackson, were carved out of the rock at Stone Mountain, Georgia, between 1963 and 1972.

(See 14 Which president's image appears on the $100,000 bill? 15 On how many postage stamps has President George Washington appeared? 16 How many state capitals are named after presidents?)

FOR FURTHER INFORMATION

Most libraries have a number of basic reference sources for biographical and factual information about the presidents and their families. For quick reference information, Joseph Nathan Kane's *Presidential Fact Book* provides a wide range of list-type information and is available at most libraries. The *Almanac of the American Presidents* organizes its coverage around broad topics, which are broken up into fact-filled text entries. Biographical references, such as *The Presidents, First Ladies, and Vice Presidents: White House Biographies,* by Daniel C. Diller and Stephen L. Robertson, give an overview of the individual's life in narrative form. But for the fullest coverage of a president's life, readers should consult biographies of individual presidents. The White House also operates a web site that has biographical sketches of past presidents, among other things (www.whitehouse.gov/ WH/glimpse/ presidents/html).

American Presidential Families. New York: Macmillan, 1994.

Boller, Paul F. *Presidential Anecdotes.* New York: Oxford University Press, 1996.

Bungarner, John R. *The Health of the Presidents: The Forty-one U.S. Presidents through 1993 from a Physician's Point of View.* Jefferson, N.C.: McFarland, 1993.

Carpenter, Glenn J. *From George to George: A Book of Anecdotes, Facts, and Other Trivia about Our Forty-one Presidents.* Fargo, N.D.: Prairie House, 1992.

Clark, James C. *Faded Glory: Presidents Out of Power.* Westport, Conn.: Praeger, 1985.

Connolly, Thomas, and Michael Senegal. *Almanac of the American Presidents.* New York: Facts on File, 1991.

Couch, Ernie. *Presidential Trivia.* New York: Routledge, 1996.

Cunningham, Homer F. *The Presidents' Last Years: George Washington to Lyndon B. Johnson.* Jefferson, N.C.: McFarland, 1989.

DeGregorio, William A. *The Complete Book of U.S. Presidents.* New York: Barricade Books, 1997.

Diller, Daniel C., and Stephen L. Robertson. *The Presidents, First Ladies, and Vice Presidents: White House Biographies.* Washington, D.C.: Congressional Quarterly, 1996.

Garrison, Webb. *A Treasury of White House Tales.* Nashville: Rutledge Hill Press, 1996.

Graf, Henry F. *The Presidents: A Reference History.* New York: Macmillan, 1996.

Hyland, Pat. *Presidential Libraries and Museums: An Illustrated Guide.* Washington, D.C.: Congressional Quarterly, 1995.

Kane, Joseph Nathan. *Presidential Fact Book.* New York: Random House, 1998.

Kochmann, Rachel. *Presidents: A Pictorial Guide to Presidents' Birthplaces, Homes, and Burial Sites.* Osage, Minn.: Osage Publications, 1997.

Laird, Archibald. *The Near Great: Chronicle of the Vice Presidents.* North Quincy, Mass.: Christopher Publishing House, 1980.

Levy, Leonard W., and Louis Fisher. *Encyclopedia of the American Presidency.* New York: Simon and Shuster, 1993.

MacMahon, Edward B., and Leonard Cory. *Medical Coverups in the White House.* Washington, D.C.: Farragut, 1987.

Messick, William L. *America's Fighting Presidents: Chief Executives Who Served Their Country Long Before They Entered the White House.* Santa Barbara: Harbor House West, 1992.

Nelson, Michael, ed. *Congressional Quarterly's Guide to the Presidency.* 2d ed. 2 vols. Washington, D.C.: Congressional Quarterly, 1996.

The Presidency A to Z. 2d ed. Michael Nelson, advisory editor. Washington, D.C.: Congressional Quarterly, 1998.

Purcell, Edward L., ed. *The Vice Presidents: A Biographical Dictionary.* New York: Facts on File, 1998.

Smith, Richard, and Timothy Walch. *Farewell to the Chief: Former Presidents in American Life.* Glendo, Wyo.: High Plains Press, 1990.

Steiner, Franklin. *The Religious Beliefs of Our Presidents: From Washington to FDR.* Buffalo: Prometheus Books, 1995.

Sullivan, Michael J. *Presidential Passions: The Love Affairs of American Presidents.* New York: Sure Seller, 1992.

Whitney, David C., and Robin V. Whitney. *The American Presidents: Biographies of the Chief Executives from Washington through Clinton.* New York: Doubleday, 1996.

III

THE PRESIDENT'S
POWERS AND DUTIES

IN GENERAL

Q **176. What does the president do?**

A As the top official of the executive branch the president wears many hats. First and foremost, the occupant of the Oval Office is the country's chief executive, who oversees the vast federal government bureaucracy and is responsible for seeing that the laws Congress passes are carried out. As chief executive, the president keeps the day-to-day operations of the government running as smoothly as possible and in times of emergency provides the leadership needed to guide the nation through the crisis. The president appoints the top officials in the executive branch, proposes an annual federal budget, submits proposed new legislation to Congress, and oversees both the government's law enforcement bureaucracy and its foreign policy apparatus.

As the commander in chief of the armed forces, the president takes responsibility in times of war and emergency for deploying troops and committing them to battle. Presidents act as the nation's chief of state as well, performing many ceremonial functions, such as receiving ambassadors and foreign dignitaries.

(See 191 How much control over federal departments and agencies does the president actually have? 204 How does the president enforce the laws of the land? 207 What does the president do as commander in chief? 212 Which president made the greatest use of emergency powers? 226 Who has the power to make laws, Congress or the president? 252 Do presidents have the constitutional authority to recognize foreign governments?)

Q **177. How long do presidents serve?**

A The president's term of office is four years, beginning and ending at noon on inauguration day, January 20. The number of full terms the president can serve is limited to two by the Twenty-second Amendment, which allows one exception. Any president who succeeds to office and serves two years or less of an unexpired term can run for two additional full terms. That way, the most any president can serve is ten years.

(See 26 Which amendments to the Constitution deal with the presidency? 52 When was January 20 set as inauguration day? 285 Which presidents served the longest and shortest periods of time?)

Q 178. Why was the two-term limit imposed on the presidency?

A Originally, the Constitution set no limits on the number of terms a president could serve if reelected. President George Washington began the tradition of presidents refusing to run for more than two terms, but he made it clear he simply wanted to retire and did not intend to set a precedent. Thomas Jefferson did consider it a matter of principle, however, and became the first president to propose a constitutionally mandated two-term limit when he declined to run for a third term in 1807.

The custom of presidents serving just two terms became accepted in the years after Jefferson served, and during the 1800s few presidents proved popular enough (or lived long enough) to serve two terms, much less three. Theodore Roosevelt, who succeeded to the presidency after William McKinley's assassination in 1901, provided the first real test for the tradition. He had served nearly all of McKinley's term and a full term of his own when, in 1908, he refused "a third cup of coffee." Serving only two terms, he said, was a "wise custom." (Four years later, however, he changed his mind and tried unsuccessfully for another term.)

Franklin D. Roosevelt, a Democrat, was the first president to actually break the 143-year-old tradition. Tremendously popular as the president who led the country through the Great Depression, Roosevelt had said in the late 1930s he would not run for a third term. But when World War II broke out in 1939, he changed his mind and in 1940 won election to an unprecedented third term (and then a fourth in 1944).

Roosevelt's long tenure in office fueled a Republican drive to limit presidents to two terms. When they gained control of Congress in 1946, they pushed through the Twenty-second Amendment (1951) imposing the limit.

(See 26 Which amendments to the Constitution deal with the presidency?)

Q 179. What is a lame duck president?

A A president who has been defeated for reelection or who is nearing the end of a second term (and so cannot run again) or who has decided not to run for a second term is called a lame duck president. Because the lame duck president has so little time left in power and because a new president will soon be in control, Congress can easily ignore or delay action on any legislation or appointments the outgoing president wants approved. With this lack of political clout, a president finds it very difficult to undertake any new initiatives in the last year or so in office.

The problem of a president's lame duck status was addressed in the Twentieth Amendment, ratified in 1933. Before then, presidents had remained in office for four months after the November elections (until March 4). The amendment moved inauguration day to January 20, putting the new president in office a month and a half sooner.

Lame duck originated as a British term for a bankrupt businessman, but in the 1830s Americans began applying the term to politicians who were nearing the end of their terms and so were running out of political capital.

Q 180. What does the first lady do?

A The president's wife has no official role in the government but is nevertheless an important public figure who can help shape the administration's image. Early first ladies oversaw the domestic operations of the White House, answered mail, and were expected to be successful hostesses for White House functions. In modern times, though, first ladies have tended to be more active, making appearances to support administration policies and in behalf of causes they have chosen to support. They can and do affect the president's decisions on matters, have their own administrative and public relations staffers, and may take on duties as the president requests. President Franklin D. Roosevelt, for example, sent First Lady Eleanor Roosevelt on many goodwill and fact-finding missions.

(See 115 Who were the most popular first ladies? The highest rated? 126 How did Eleanor Roosevelt reshape the role of first lady? 283 Which first lady was first to head a presidential commission?)

Q 181. Is the president's power to appoint important?

A Although the civil service merit system is used to fill most positions in the government today, presidents still exercise considerable control over the executive branch because they appoint its top officials, including cabinet officials, agency heads, ambassadors, Supreme Court justices, and other federal judges. The Senate must approve the appointments, but the president chooses the nominees in the first place, and they owe their jobs to the president.

By carefully selecting top officials who have the necessary experience, willingness to implement administration policies, and loyalty, the president can exert strong influence over the direction the executive branch departments and agencies take. President Ronald Reagan, for example, had more control over the government than any recent president because he placed special emphasis on recruiting appointees whose political philosophy matched his own.

The process of appointing officials was haphazard in earlier times. Before the advent of civil service reforms in the late 1800s, all government posts were filled on the basis of patronage. And political party bosses, not the president, usually chose the appointees. As the civil service expanded during the 1900s, the number of political appointees declined steadily and presidents began to exercise greater control over appointments. President Harry S. Truman appointed the first full-time staffer to oversee personnel matters, and since the Kennedy-Johnson era, personnel staffers have been a part of every administration's White House Office.

(See 190 Can the president fire any government official? 202 How do presidents turn patronage and pork-barrel projects to their advantage? 205 How does the president control law enforcement policy? 247 Which presidents have had the greatest success in using appointments to influence the direction of Supreme Court rulings? 248 Which president appointed the most Supreme Court justices? The fewest? 253 Why is the president's power to appoint ambassadors important?)

Q 182. About how many executive posts does the president fill by appointment?

A The president appoints about 5,000 top government officials whose jobs are outside the control of the civil service's merit-based hiring system. Although the number varies from one administration to the next, the appointees include about 200 White House staffers, the 14 heads of cabinet departments, 400–500 subordinate officials in the departments, and 150 ambassadors.

(See 190 Can the president fire any government official? 191 How much control over federal departments and agencies does the president actually have? 498 What have presidents said about the bureaucracy? 499 What does the civil service system do?)

Q 183. What is the president's salary?

A Thanks to a 1999 pay raise authorized by Congress and to take effect in 2001, the president receives an annual salary of $400,000, double what it once was. While that is an impressive figure by most people's standards, it is still far less than what the heads of major corporations earn. The president enjoys many extra perks, however, not the least of which is a place in history as the head of one of the world's most powerful countries. The first family lives rent-free in the White House—a place few people get to visit, much less live in—and the government picks up the $8 million tab for official state functions, domestic staff, maintenance, security, and the like. Free use of the presidential retreat at Camp David also is part of the bargain. The president's expense accounts cover the out-of-pocket costs associated with the job— $50,000 for general expenses, $100,000 for travel, and $19,000 for entertainment. Other presidential perks include a presidential plane, *Air Force One*, helicopters, and a bullet-proof limousine.

(See 185 Why is the president's plane called Air Force One? *216 How much is the vice president's salary?)*

Q 184. Can presidents accept gifts?

A The president, first lady, and their dependent children may receive gifts from the public, but the president must report any gift worth $250 or more on his annual financial disclosure statement. Gifts from foreign governments, foreign groups, and the officials representing them are regulated much more closely. The Constitution requires congressional approval of any gifts from foreigners, and today only gifts worth less than a few hundred dollars are permitted. The president is allowed to accept a gift of greater value if refusing it would offend the foreign dignitary offering the gift or somehow damage relations with that dignitary's country, but the gift must be turned over to the government.

Q 185. Why is the president's plane called *Air Force One*?

A *Air Force One* was first used as a call sign for the president's aircraft in September 1961, during the Kennedy administration. But the first plane popularly identified as *Air Force One* was a Boeing 707 jet built for President John F. Kennedy's use in 1962. It had special markings and a luxurious interior that First Lady Jacqueline Kennedy helped to design.

Kennedy's successors continued using the 707 until the early 1970s, when another 707 replaced it (Kennedy's plane became a backup). By the late 1980s, though, the 707 model had become outmoded, and in 1990 President George Bush became the first president to fly in the new *Air Force One*, a Boeing 747-200B. The 747s (two were made for the president) can fly at 640 miles an hour, and they have a range of over

7,000 miles and can carry over 100 passengers and crew. They cost $400 million each. These presidential aircraft are a far cry from the first presidential aircraft, a Douglas DC-4 used by Franklin D. Roosevelt in 1945. It was unofficially named *Sacred Cow.*

(See 351 Who was the first president to fly in an airplane?)

Q 186. What is the Presidential Medal of Freedom?

A This medal, which only the president can award, is the nation's highest civilian honor. It recognizes outstanding contributions to culture, world peace, and national security. President John F. Kennedy created the medal in 1963 in order to help promote idealism and pride in America's achievements. JFK selected the first recipients, but he was assassinated in Dallas, Texas, before the presentation ceremony in December 1963. Thus it fell to his successor, Lyndon B. Johnson, to present the first medals, and since then every president has presented the medal to at least a few persons. In all, about three hundred medals have been awarded since 1963. The recipients represent a wide range of backgrounds and include a few foreign dignitaries as well. Scientists, writers, movie stars, sports figures, artists, and government officials have been among the honorees.

Q 187. Is the president immune from criminal prosecution?

A The president's immunity from criminal prosecution is far from clear. Some scholars believe a sitting president can be prosecuted for criminal actions only through the impeachment process. In 1974 President Richard M. Nixon's involvement in the Watergate affair might have provided a legal test, but the special prosecutor avoided that outcome by deliberately naming Nixon an unindicted co-conspirator. More recently, President Bill Clinton claimed immunity from civil suits for actions taken before he took office—his lawyers argued that a trial on the Paula Jones lawsuit for sexual harassment could not begin until after Clinton left office. In early 1996 a federal appeals court ruled the trial could in fact begin.

Presidents do enjoy absolute immunity against civil suits arising from their official acts. The U.S. Supreme Court provided a clear ruling on that in *Nixon* v. *Fitzgerald* (1982), but presidents can still be called on to testify in criminal trials and investigations of others. Videotaped testimony is usually permitted.

(See 203 What is executive privilege?)

THE CHIEF EXECUTIVE

Q **188. Does the president create the agencies and departments of the government?**

A The Constitution gives Congress the power to create, fund, and abolish all the departments, agencies, and programs that make up the executive branch. As chief executive the president is responsible for administering the executive branch, including ensuring that policies and programs legislated by Congress are carried out. Within those broad guidelines, however, the president has considerable control over agencies through the power to appoint top officials for all agencies and programs (subject to Senate approval), which influences how they are run. The president also can ask Congress to change the way existing departments and agencies are set up and can influence Congress when plans for new ones are being drawn up. In addition, the laws Congress writes for setting up programs often are written in very broad language, leaving the job of filling in the details to the executive branch. This the president does by issuing executive orders, which do not require congressional approval.

(See 176 What does the president do? 194 What is an executive order?)

Q **189. Who advises the president on policy matters?**

A Top staff members in the White House Office form the inner circle of the president's most trusted policy advisers. Heads of other offices and councils in the Executive Office of the President also play a key role in advising the president, including top officials in the Office of Management and Budget, the Council of Economic Advisers, the National Security Council, and the Office of Policy Development (for domestic policy issues).

Cabinet secretaries originally were intended to serve as an advisory body to the president, but the competing interests of the departments and the practice of using cabinet posts to reward political allies have forced all presidents to downplay the importance of cabinet meetings. Presidents do consult individually with cabinet members on policy matters concerning their departments, however.

In the past, presidents have relied on trusted friends and informal groups of advisers for policy advice. Andrew Jackson depended on his "kitchen cabinet" for much of his first term. Among them were longtime associates, such as John Eaton and Andrew Donelson, politicians Martin Van Buren and Roger B. Taney, and newspaperman Amos Kendall. President Woodrow Wilson relied on his confidant Col. Edward House. Early in his first administration, Franklin D. Roosevelt sought advice from his "brain trust," a group of academics that included Rexford Tugwell and Raymond Moley. Roosevelt also relied heavily on two longtime associates, Harry Hopkins and a journalist named Louis Howe. President John F. Kennedy's brother Robert F. Kennedy was his closest adviser.

(See 455 How is the White House staff organized? 460 What does the Executive Office of the President do? 464 What does the president's cabinet do?)

Q 190. Can the president fire any government official?

A The Constitution explicitly grants the president the power to appoint executive branch officials (with Senate approval), but it is silent on the subject of the president's power to remove them. Certainly one powerful way the president can control appointees is to threaten to remove them from office.

During Andrew Johnson's administration (1865–1869), Radical Republicans in Congress passed the Tenure of Office Act (1867) requiring Senate approval before the president fired appointed officials. Johnson tried to force the issue into the courts by firing Secretary of War Edwin M. Stanton, a staunch supporter of the Radical Republicans. But the Republicans impeached him instead (Johnson was acquitted), and the law remained on the books until Congress repealed it during the Cleveland administration.

The Supreme Court finally ruled on the president's removal power in 1926. In *Myers v. United States* the justices held that the president needed the power to fire officials for political and other reasons in order to run the executive branch effectively. In 1935, however, the Court limited that broad power in *Humphrey's Executor v. United States*, when it overturned President Franklin D. Roosevelt's firing of a Federal Trade Commission official for political reasons. The Court ruled that any president removing appointed officials from independent regulatory agencies did need approval from Congress.

(See 64 Why was President Andrew Johnson impeached?)

Q 191. How much control over federal departments and agencies does the president actually have?

A The sheer number of tasks performed by the hundreds of departments and agencies within the federal government make tight control of the federal bureaucracy all but impossible for the president. Even with the help of the some 1,700 people who work in the Executive Office of the President, presidents often find it difficult just to keep track of what the government bureaucracy is doing.

In fact, in trying to make a change in a single agency can be a daunting task. First, the president and the president's advisers must know in great detail what the agency does and how it goes about its job—information that usually must be obtained from bureaucrats within the agency itself. The president also must assess how the bureaucrats will react to changes, the political implications of the new policy, and what pressures the agency's client groups exert on it (such as the elderly on the Social Security Administration). Even the president's own appointees at the agency may prove a negative factor. Once they become attuned to the needs of the agency and the client groups it serves, they may work against the president's policy goals.

Q 192. How long can it take to get an agency to act on a presidential directive?

A President Richard M. Nixon's chief assistant for bureaucratic reorganization, Frank Carlucci, claimed that it took agencies six to eight months to translate a presidential directive into agency guidelines and then put them into action. Sometimes, he claimed, action by the agency could be delayed as long as two or three years.

(See 498 What have presidents said about the bureaucracy?)

Q 193. Are there any agencies the president cannot control?

A Yes, independent regulatory agencies like the Federal Reserve Board and the Federal Communications Commission lie outside the president's direct control, and the White House is powerless to remove members of such agencies if they institute policies contrary to the president's liking. For that matter, neither can Congress. The board members of independent regulatory agencies are appointed by the president and approved by the Senate, but once in office they serve fixed terms that generally run four to seven years. They do not have to report to the president or Congress, and they can only be removed for misconduct, inefficiency, or neglect of duty. The president's control is effectively limited to appointing commissioners who are likely to have the same political philosophy.

(See 190 Can the president fire any government official? 502 What is an independent agency?)

Q 194. What is an executive order?

A Executive orders are directives issued by the president that apply to agencies or individuals within the executive branch. They have the force of law even though Congress does not approve them, and presidents use them for a variety of purposes, from giving agencies basic operational orders to imposing sweeping policy changes within the executive branch of the federal government. For example, President Franklin D. Roosevelt centralized budget authority in the Executive Office of the President by executive order. Among the more sweeping policy changes accomplished by executive order were President Harry S. Truman's order to racially integrate the armed services, John F. Kennedy's order to racially integrate federally subsidized housing, and Lyndon B. Johnson's requirement that federal contractors have minority hiring programs. Executive orders even created the government's entire system for classifying documents as secret.

Although Congress has challenged certain executive orders, the Supreme Court has generally upheld the president's power to issue them. In fact, executive orders are frequently used to provide detailed instructions to agencies, because Congress is unwilling or unable to include such details in legislation creating programs and policies.

(See 259 Why have executive agreements become so important?)

Q 195. Which modern president issued the fewest executive orders?

A Among presidents serving since the beginning of the twentieth century, George Bush resorted to the fewest executive orders per year while in office—just over 41, for a total of 165 over his four years in office. President Gerald R. Ford issued only 152 orders, but because he served just part of Richard M. Nixon's unexpired term, his yearly average (about 63) was well above Bush's.

President Franklin D. Roosevelt issued the most executive orders, 3,522, and had the highest yearly average as well, almost 286. His predecessor, President Herbert Hoover, had the next highest yearly average, 242; he issued a total of 968 executive orders during his four years in office.

President George Washington issued the first eight executive orders, but presidents for the most part used them sparingly until the second half of the nineteenth century. Since World War II, the number of executive orders issued by presidents has declined.

Q 196. Is the president's role as chief of state important?

A Although largely ceremonial, the president's duties as chief of state provide opportunities to act publicly as the nation's leader and to build public support. The Constitution specifies only three ceremonial duties that the president is obliged to perform as chief of state: take the oath of office, deliver an annual report on the state of the Union, and receive ambassadors and other foreign dignitaries. Certainly, the State of the Union address reinforces the president's image as the nation's leader. The fact that foreign dignitaries deal directly with the president as head of state (and not Congress) projects that image abroad as well.

As the nation's ceremonial spokesperson, the president participates in many other functions the Constitution does not mention. The speeches the president gives at such functions highlight special occasions or accomplishments, promote domestic or foreign policy objectives, or simply widen his public support.

Broadly speaking, these ceremonies fall into four categories: *celebrations,* including building dedications, important national events, patriotic speeches, proclamations, and eulogies; *honorific ceremonies,* including university commencement speeches, award ceremonies, and testimonials; *initiating ceremonies,* such as bill signings, the president's inaugural address, and the swearing in of public officials; and *greeting and departure ceremonies,* for distinguished White House visitors and during presidential trips.

(See 176 What does the president do? 256 What advantages does the president have over Congress in conducting foreign affairs? 334 What have presidents done in the battle for the public's favor? 349 Which president proclaimed the first national holiday?)

Q **197. How did presidents come to be regarded as the "Managers of Prosperity"?**

A Americans today expect the president to avoid recessions and keep the economy growing; in effect, they want a "manager of prosperity." As chief executive, the president is directly involved in economic matters, even though the Constitution does not grant any specific economic powers. That involvement includes implementing all of Congress's taxing and spending decisions, vetoing legislation affecting the economy, proposing economic policies in the State of the Union address, and concluding commercial treaties with foreign nations that can affect the economy.

The modern president's influence over the economy, however, has grown well beyond even those considerable powers. As the U.S. economy, and the federal budget, became increasingly complex during the twentieth century, Congress delegated greater economic powers to the president such as preparing a proposed federal budget each year. At the same time, presidents used the growing prestige and visibility of their office to promote their own formulas for producing economic prosperity.

Not surprisingly, as presidents began to claim the ability to produce good economic times, voters came to expect them to deliver—to be the managers of prosperity. Thus voters today can and do hold them accountable for such economic problems as inflation, high unemployment, sluggish economic growth, and outright recessions, just as they would for a failure to enforce the laws or defend national security.

(See 37 Has the president always been responsible for preparing a proposed federal budget? 199 What limits the president's ability to manage the economy? 379 Is the economy a factor in presidential elections? 511 In what ways does the government influence the economy?)

Q 198. When did presidents begin to try controlling the economy through taxing and spending decisions?

A Although President Franklin D. Roosevelt dramatically increased federal spending in the early 1930s, he did so not to stimulate the economy but to help ease the suffering of millions of Americans hurt by the Great Depression. The connection between increasing federal spending and economic stimulation did not become clear to Roosevelt until later in the 1930s. Responding to a recession in 1937, Roosevelt at first cut spending to make up for lost revenue and so kept the budget deficit from getting too large. But when the cuts only made unemployment—and the recession—worse, Roosevelt became convinced that more federal spending could provide the stimulus needed to finally end the Great Depression. From 1938 onward, he worked to increase government spending, but the depression did not end until the early 1940s, when Congress approved truly massive spending increases to prepare the country for World War II.

(See 511 In what ways does the government influence the economy?)

Q 199. What limits the president's ability to manage the economy?

A While presidents probably have more power over the economy than any other government official, neither they nor anyone else can completely control it. In the first place, presidents share what control they do have with Congress, the Federal Reserve Board, and other executive branch organizations. Congress, for example, can block a president's economic policy because it has the final authority on raising or lowering taxes and spending.

The art of handling the economy and countering its ups and downs is also imprecise at best. As a result, presidents often find it difficult to know what steps to take and when. Providing too much of an economic stimulus, for example, or stimulating the economy at the wrong time can dangerously overheat it.

Finally, the government is not the only factor in the economy—large corporations, worker productivity, prices of raw materials such as oil, consumer confidence, state and local government spending, and even economic crises in other countries can affect the performance of the U.S. economy.

(See 511 In what ways does the government influence the economy?)

Q 200. Does Congress have to accept the president's budget?

A No, the president's annual budget proposal is just that, a proposal that Congress can accept, reject, or modify as it pleases. However, the power and prestige of the presidency are such that even in the most contentious battles, Congress usually gives presidents at least some of what they want in the way of new programs or added spending for favored programs. Furthermore, the president's budget proposal includes many basic costs that cannot be ignored, such as funding for entitlement programs, payments on the national debt, and salaries for federal employees. Congress must either fund such items at the required level or take the politically difficult step of cutting them back.

(See 37 Has the president always been responsible for preparing a proposed federal budget?)

Q 201. Do presidents control the Federal Reserve System?

A The Federal Reserve System (also known as the Fed) is an independent regulatory agency that sets federal monetary policy and so has a powerful influence over the nation's economy. Members of the Fed's board of governors are appointed to fixed fourteen-year terms by the president, with Senate approval. One member is designated by the president to serve as chair for a four-year term and can be reappointed. Because it is an independent agency, the Fed operates outside of the president's direct control and can institute monetary policies that conflict with the president's economic goals. In practice, though, the president influences the Fed by informal means, and the Fed usually does try to accommodate the president's economic policies.

(See 508 How does the Federal Reserve affect the economy?)

Q 202. How do presidents turn patronage and pork-barrel projects to their advantage?

A The president's power to fill thousands of government jobs by appointment represents an important reserve of political capital called patronage. Beyond the top White House and cabinet posts, the president also appoints federal judges, attorneys, ambassadors, marshals, customs collectors, and the like. These jobs can be used to reward campaign workers, campaign donors, and political allies, or even to win the favor of members of Congress who want their constituents in the job.

The president's personal patronage is another valuable political commodity. Inviting members of Congress and others to the White House, campaigning for congressional candidates, and providing tickets to special events all can help win political allies or soften opposition to a specific policy.

Although Congress actually provides the funding for programs and public works projects that benefit a region or locality (some of which are branded by critics as pork-barrel projects), the president can reward political allies by supporting public works that benefit a congressional district or interest group, or punish political opponents in Congress by threatening to veto projects designed to appeal to voters in their districts.

(See 306 Which president introduced the "spoils system"?)

Q 203. What is executive privilege?

A The president's right to withhold sensitive information from Congress and the courts is called executive privilege. The act of withholding the information has been around much longer than the term, however. President George Washington refused to give Congress information about negotiations for the Jay Treaty with Britain, and similar confrontations between the president and Congress, which sometimes has insisted on its right to know, have arisen in almost every administration since then. During one such confrontation, President Dwight D. Eisenhower coined the term *executive privilege* to refer to the president's power to hold back information, especially when negotiations and other sensitive business involving national security are involved.

Usually there is some basis for compromise in these conflicts, but during the Watergate affair President Richard M. Nixon's insistence on withholding tape recordings of his Oval Office conversations with staffers took the question of executive privilege all the way to the Supreme Court. In *United States v. Nixon* (1974) the Court ruled for the first time that the president did have a constitutional right to executive privilege. But the Court also said it was not an absolute right and ordered him to turn over the tapes. The tapes proved Nixon's involvement in the Watergate cover-up and forced him to resign.

(See 373 What happened in the Watergate scandal?)

Q **204. How does the president enforce the laws of the land?**

A As the country's chief law enforcement officer, the president has a huge law enforcement bureaucracy at his disposal, including the Justice Department and a host of regulatory agencies, that can investigate and prosecute virtually all types of illegal activities. In the unlikely event of a riot or full-scale rebellion, however, the president also can mobilize National Guard units or the regular military to restore order.

The Justice Department forms the core of the president's law enforcement apparatus. The attorney general and the department's many U.S. attorneys prosecute cases for the federal government, and the department's main enforcement arm, the Federal Bureau of Investigation, investigates federal crimes and apprehends criminals. If a criminal is convicted, the sentence is served in a jail operated by the Justice Department's Bureau of Prisons. Other law enforcement agencies within the Justice Department are the Immigration and Naturalization Service, Drug Enforcement Administration, and U.S. Marshals Service.

Law enforcement and regulatory agencies reside in other cabinet departments as well. Treasury oversees the U.S. Secret Service, Bureau of Alcohol, Tobacco, and Firearms, Internal Revenue Service, and U.S. Customs Service. The Food and Drug Administration in the Department of Health and Human Services regulates food and drug quality, Transportation's Federal Aviation Administration ensures compliance with aviation safety regulations, and the Labor Department's Occupational Safety and Health Administration monitors workplace safety.

(See 24 What is the source of the president's law enforcement powers? 507 Which president established the forerunner of the FBI?)

Q **205. How does the president control law enforcement policy?**

A Presidents use their appointment power as their chief means of controlling law enforcement policy. They do so by selecting top officials who agree with their policy aims, political philosophy, or both. Although the attorney general and other top presidential appointees at the Justice Department must be confirmed by the Senate, the president can fire them for any reason and so has considerable control over how they do their jobs. That is not the case, however, with other high-ranking law enforcement officials. For example, the director of the Federal Bureau of Investigation cannot be fired before the end of his ten-year term without just cause. The president's power to fire top officials at independent regulatory agencies such as the Federal Trade Commission also is limited.

(See 181 Is the president's power to appoint important? 190 Can the president fire any government official? 247 Which presidents have had the greatest success in using appointments to influence the direction of Supreme Court rulings? 249 Do presidents become involved in judicial nominations to lower federal courts?)

Q 206. Can the president pardon criminals?

A The Constitution gives the president the power to grant pardons and reprieves for any federal crime except in cases of impeachment of government officials. Pardons eliminate all guilt and punishment for a criminal act, even one not yet been proved, and restore the person pardoned to the legal status enjoyed before the alleged crime was committed. A reprieve only reduces a criminal's sentence; it does not remove the conviction itself from the record.

George Washington became the first president to issue a pardon. Seeking to quell the 1792 Whiskey Rebellion, he used his power to pardon farmers who had revolted against the government's excise tax on whiskey. Presidents Abraham Lincoln and Andrew Johnson both issued pardons to Confederates after the Civil War to help reunite the nation. Just over a hundred years later, Presidents Gerald R. Ford and Jimmy Carter used much the same thinking when they issued amnesties for Vietnam War era draft evaders and those who left the country to avoid military service.

President Ford's full pardon of former President Richard M. Nixon for any crimes relating to the Watergate scandal ranks among the most controversial pardons of recent years. President Nixon had resigned before impeachment proceedings could begin in the House of Representatives, so the pardon was within Ford's right to grant. President Ford said he issued the pardon to avoid the unhappy spectacle of a former president standing trial.

President George Bush also aroused criticism when in 1992 he pardoned six former Reagan administration members charged with withholding information or lying to Congress. More recently, President Bill Clinton was heavily criticized for offering pardons to sixteen Puerto Rican nationalists serving prison sentences for their involvement in terrorist activities.

Q 207. What does the president do as commander in chief?

A As leader of all U.S. military forces, the president oversees military preparedness during peacetime, commits troops to battle in times of hostility or outright war, and approves plans for military operations. The president could even take direct command of troops on the battlefield, but only one president has ever done so (in actual combat). During the War of 1812, President James Madison, who was personally overseeing the unsuccessful attempt to stop the 1814 British invasion of Washington, D.C., briefly assumed personal command of an artillery unit.

Since the advent of the cold war in the late 1940s, the president's peacetime responsibility for defense preparedness has grown considerably. The president and the Pentagon take the lead in running the armed forces, even though Congress has legislative and budgetary authority over the military. They develop military policy on such matters as force levels, overseas deployment, weapons procurement, and recruitment, as well as prepare basic strategies and estimates of defense needs.

Before the nuclear age, presidents generally kept close watch on the overall strategy and plans for war campaigns, while leaving battlefield strategies and command of troops to their generals and admirals. With the advent of atomic weapons, however, presidents had to become more directly involved in planning and executing military operations. Indeed, especially during the cold war a small conflict could have easily escalated into global nuclear war. And even today, in politically tense regions such as the Middle East a local commander who oversteps his bounds or a bomber pilot who mistakenly bombs the wrong target could ignite a political firestorm.

(See 33 How has American military power grown over the years? 41 Which cabinet department occupies the world's largest office building? 176 What does the president do? 301 What happened during the Whiskey Rebellion?)

Q 208. How quickly can the president give an order to strike with conventional military forces?

A Surprisingly quickly, if military forces are already in position in a military theater. The case of a U.S. navy pilot in 1988 provides a good example of how fast an attack order can be transmitted, even halfway around the world. While on patrol over the Persian Gulf, the navy fighter pilot spotted Iranian gunboats attacking oil rigs, but he did not have the authority to fire on them. So he radioed his ship, and the request was relayed up the navy's chain of command via satellite to the Pentagon. The secretary of defense then called President Ronald Reagan, who gave permission to attack, and the order was relayed back down the chain of command to the pilot. Just three minutes after his request, the pilot received the order and launched an attack on the gunboats.

Q 209. Are there limits on the president's power to order a nuclear attack?

A Because of the speed and devastating power of nuclear weapons, the president has full authority to order their use should the United States, its military forces, or a close ally be attacked. A surprise nuclear attack allows so little time to launch a counterattack—a matter of minutes—that there is simply no time to consult Congress or to go through the formalities of a declaration of war.

Ordering a preemptive, first-strike attack with nuclear weapons is another matter, however, because the president would in effect be starting a war, not defending against an attack. Unless Congress had actually declared war in the first place, or the president had consulted with Congress before the crisis developed, the president would not have the legal authority to launch such a strike.

One final check on the president's power does exist, however. While the president could conceivably order a surprise nuclear attack even though no crisis existed, others actually fire the missiles. Military officers and White House advisers involved in the launch probably would resist the order to push the button.

(See 478 How would the military respond to a nuclear attack?)

Q 210. Who declares war, the president or Congress?

A Here the Constitution provides what appears to be a clear separation between Congress and the president. Congress has the power to declare war; the president is empowered to send the military into battle once war has been declared. But as with many rules, exceptions abound. If the United States is attacked, for example, the president has the authority to order a military response. A formal declaration of war by Congress would surely follow.

Over the years, presidents have deployed U.S. troops overseas hundreds of times in order to quell revolts against pro-American governments, to advance U.S. interests, or to take part in peacekeeping operations. None of these actions was ever sanctioned by a congressional declaration of war though. In fact, Congress has formally declared war only five times—for the War of 1812, Mexican War (1846), Spanish-American War (1898), World War I (1917), and World War II (1941).

Authority for ending a war is also divided. The president has the power to stop the fighting, to pull out the troops, and to negotiate an armistice. But if Congress has formally declared war, it must vote to formally end the state of war.

Q 211. Has Congress supported the expansion of the president's war powers?

A Until recently, Congress routinely approved expansion of the president's wartime powers. Whenever war threatened, Congress willingly passed legislation giving presidents emergency powers to deal with the crisis. For example, President Abraham Lincoln claimed, and Congress approved, wide-ranging powers after the Civil War broke out. During the two world wars in the twentieth century, Congress handed presidents Woodrow Wilson and Franklin D. Roosevelt sweeping powers to help ensure victory.

Most of these war powers were intended only for the duration of the crisis. But after World War II, presidents faced an almost constant state of emergency—the ongoing cold war, the threat of communist expansion into the free world, and the possibility of nuclear war. Congress accepted the president's authority to commit troops to fight communists without a congressional declaration of war—notably in Korea (1950–1953) and Vietnam (1960s and early 1970s)—and to send them to other hot spots around the world as needed to further U.S. interests.

But American losses during the Vietnam War, and the war's growing unpopularity, prodded Congress into trying to restrict the president's wide powers over the military. The War Powers Act of 1973 essentially set a sixty-day limit on any deployment of American troops that Congress had not specifically approved. The act also gave Congress the power to order a troop withdrawal at any time in an undeclared war and urged the president to consult with Congress before committing troops. Critics have questioned the act's constitutionality, and presidents have largely ignored it since 1973. Only twice has there been any prospect of the act being invoked: during deployments of U.S. Marines in Lebanon (1982–1983) and U.S. troops in Somalia (1993).

Q 212. Which president made the greatest use of emergency powers?

A President Abraham Lincoln claimed such wide-ranging emergency powers during the Civil War (1861–1865) that some critics accused him of becoming a constitutional dictator. The Constitution does not explicitly grant presidents emergency powers. Instead, the powers derive from the Constitution's mandate that the president "preserve, protect, and defend" the Constitution.

Faced with a civil war and the imminent breakup of the Union at a time when Congress was not in session, Lincoln relied on these implied emergency powers to begin enlarging the army and navy, spend federal funds on war preparations without congressional authorization, mobilize the militia, and blockade southern ports. Because of the severity of the national emergency, Congress eventually gave him authority retroactively, and for the most part the courts refused to rule on the president's actions during the emergency.

In 1861 a lower court did rule against Lincoln's suspension of writs of habeas corpus (*Ex parte Merryman*), but Lincoln ignored the court, and Congress later gave him its approval. As for other war actions taken by President Lincoln, the Supreme Court ruled in Lincoln's favor in the 1863 *Prize Cases*, and against him in a decision after the war had ended (*Ex parte Milligan*, 1866).

(See 241 Did the Supreme Court rule against expansion of presidential powers in the last century?)

Q 213. What emergency powers does the president have today?

A War, civil unrest, and other times of crisis call for extraordinary measures by the president, and in the past Congress has been willing to ratify most any emergency powers the president has deemed necessary. Wartime has justified the most extreme emergency powers—including censorship, limitations on personal freedoms, and regulation of prices, distribution of goods, and production. But presidents also can use emergency powers in times of economic crisis, domestic disorders, and natural disasters. For example, Franklin D. Roosevelt declared a national emergency and ordered banks to close in 1933 to prevent the collapse of the banking system, and years later, Lyndon B. Johnson used 55,000 soldiers to quell the race riots that broke out after the 1968 assassination of Martin Luther King Jr.

During the 1970s, Congress passed legislation giving it greater oversight of the president's emergency powers and imposed some limits on the president's emergency powers outside of wartime. The presidents' wartime powers as they now stand include the power to:

— declare martial law
— keep sensitive information from the public and Congress
— censor communications with foreign countries
— deploy troops overseas
— suspend writs of habeas corpus
— confine persons believed to be a threat to national security
— restrict movement of citizens in the United States and abroad

— order registration of foreign representatives

— fire federal employees considered a security risk

— fix wages and prices

— control industrial production

— order stockpiling of strategic materials

— control distribution of raw materials needed for defense production

— restrict exports of critical products and materials.

(See 322 What reason did Truman give for seizing the steel mills?)

Q 214. Has the president ever declared martial law?

A Because martial law substitutes military rule for civilian law and can sharply curb citizens' rights, it is considered a drastic measure reserved only for emergency situations. No president has ever declared martial law nationwide, although during the Civil War President Abraham Lincoln did order it for certain areas of the country. Since Lincoln, no president has directly declared martial law, although some have supported emergency use of martial law in certain areas by military officers and other government officials. After the Japanese attacked Pearl Harbor in 1941, for example, President Franklin D. Roosevelt supported the territorial governor's declaration of martial law on the Hawaiian Islands.

THE VICE PRESIDENT

Q 215. What does the vice president do?

A The vice presidency was created primarily to provide a successor should the president die or otherwise become unable to fulfill his duties. At one time, vice presidents were held in rather low regard because they had little purpose other than to mark time until either their term or the president expired. Even their constitutionally mandated duty to serve as president of the Senate was largely ceremonial. From time to time, a vice president would cast the tie-breaking vote in that body, but the vote was expected to be in support of the president.

Modern vice presidents have far more duties than they once did. Because they must be ready to take over the complex job of president at any time, they attend meetings of the National Security Council and the cabinet, receive full national security briefings, and have regular private meetings with the president. At the president's direction, vice presidents also chair presidential commissions, go overseas on diplomatic and goodwill missions, help lobby members of Congress for the president's legislative proposals, and otherwise actively support the president's policies.

(See 25 How did the vice presidency come about? 222 How many vice presidents have succeeded to the presidency?)

Q 216. How much is the vice president's salary?

A Congress voted the president a hefty pay raise in 1999, but the vice president was not so fortunate. Apart from incremental cost of living increases, the vice president's salary has remained stable in recent years. As of 1997 it was $171,500 a year, a considerable improvement over what the first vice president earned in 1789—$5,000—but not stellar by today's corporate standards. The vice president does get a few other perks, however, including $10,000 a year for expenses, an official residence, three offices (including one in the West Wing of the White House), limousines, and an airplane (*Air Force Two*).

(See 183 What is the president's salary? 346 When did the vice president get an official residence?)

Q 217. What did Daniel Webster say when offered the chance to run for the vice presidency?

A The venerable Daniel Webster, a Massachusetts senator and longtime aspirant to the presidency, flatly refused the Whig Party's offer to nominate him for vice president in 1848 by saying, "I do not proposed to be buried before I am dead." Webster was not alone in his low opinion of the office. President Woodrow Wilson's vice president, Thomas R. Marshall put his feelings about the office in fable form: "Once there were two brothers. One ran away to sea, the other was elected vice president, and nothing was ever heard of either of them again." Franklin D. Roosevelt's vice president, John Nance Garner once told Lyndon B. Johnson that the vice presidency "wasn't worth a bucket of warm spit." In spite of his advice, Johnson accepted the vice-presidential nomination in 1960. Historian Arthur Schlesinger Jr. echoed Nance's dismal assessment: "It is a doomed office. The Vice President has only one serious thing to do: that is to wait around for the president to die."

Q **218. Why was the vice presidency held in such low regard during the nineteenth century?**

A Ratification of the Twelfth Amendment in 1804, which called for separate electoral votes for the president and vice president, eliminated an important element of the vice president's prestige—that of being the second highest vote-getter in the presidential election. Moreover, in the early 1800s party leaders began the practice of selecting the vice-presidential running mate. The leaders did not pick candidates because they were competent or personally compatible with the presidential candidate. Rather, they selected those who would balance the ticket, placate a party faction, or deliver a swing state needed for the election. As a result, the best potential candidates, such as Sen. Daniel Webster of Massachusetts, wanted nothing to do with the post, and often those who did run were old, in bad health, or prone to corruption and scandal. In fact, six nineteenth-century vice presidents died in office. After the early 1800s, no vice president was nominated to a second term by his party until the 1900s, and after Martin Van Buren in 1836, no vice president was nominated for president until the 1900s.

(See 59 Have any vice presidents resigned from office? 60 Has the office of the vice president ever been vacant? 143 Which former vice president was tried for treason?)

Q **219. Do modern vice presidents have more responsibility?**

A Vice presidents began to see an improvement in their political prestige almost immediately in the twentieth century. In 1900, vice-presidential candidate Theodore Roosevelt became the first to gain a national reputation by campaigning actively nationwide. He also was the first vice president to succeed to the presidency and then win his party's nomination to a new term of his own. From 1912 on, vice presidents were routinely nominated to serve a second term. As the changes began to attract more qualified candidates, vice presidents also began to assume greater responsibilities.

Beginning with Franklin D. Roosevelt's administration, presidents began to include their vice presidents in cabinet meetings, use them as a liaison with Congress, and send them on missions to foreign countries. President Harry S. Truman began the practice of making the vice president a member of the National Security Council (to keep the vice president abreast of national security issues), and President Dwight D. Eisenhower named the first vice president to head a commission (a now common practice).

Today, vice presidents are expected to be fully prepared to take over the president's duties in the event the president dies or becomes incapacitated. They are kept informed about matters of state, offer advice to the president, act as advocates of administration policy, and handle various ceremonial functions and special tasks assigned by the president. In recent years especially, presidents have been willing to give their vice presidents a more active role in the administration.

Q **220. Can the vice president declare the president unfit to perform the presidential duties?**

A The Twenty-fifth Amendment, ratified in 1967, assigned the vice president an important new power, that of declaring the president unfit or unable to perform the duties of office. Although the vice president cannot act alone, and there is little likelihood this power will ever be exercised, the vice president is nevertheless the central figure in the process: the vice president and a majority of the principal officers of the executive departments have only to inform Congress in writing that the president is unable to perform the duties of the office. The vice president then takes over as acting president.

This amendment also confirmed the established practice of the vice president becoming president—not acting president—when succeeding to office after the death of a president *(see next question)*.

Q **221. What precedent did Vice President John Tyler set in 1841?**

A When President William Henry Harrison died in 1841 soon after taking office, Vice President John Tyler was immediately called to take over the president's duties. No president had ever died in office before, and although the Constitution made it clear the vice president was to act as successor, it said nothing about whether the vice president was to serve out the deceased president's full term or was to serve only as acting president until a new one was chosen in a special election. Some members of Congress even introduced a resolution in the House of Representatives stating that Tyler was only acting president. The bill failed, and Tyler decided the issue by announcing he intended to serve out Harrison's term and then moving into the White House. He refused to answer official correspondence addressed to him as acting president, endured being called "His Accidency" in the press, and otherwise resisted efforts to treat him as anything less than the president. His determination succeeded and set the precedent for future vice presidents.

(See 26 Which amendments to the Constitution deal with the presidency? 60 Has the office of the vice president ever been vacant?)

Q **222. How many vice presidents have succeeded to the presidency?**

A As of mid-2000, nine of the forty-five vice presidents had succeeded to the presidency, eight of them on the death of the president and one after a resignation. Four vice presidents succeeded when the president died of natural causes; the four others, after the president was assassinated. Vice presidents who succeeded were:

Succeeded a president who died of natural causes:

John Tyler (succeeded William Henry Harrison, 1841)
Millard Fillmore (succeeded Zachary Taylor, 1850)
Calvin Coolidge (succeeded Warren G. Harding, 1923)
Harry S. Truman (succeeded Franklin D. Roosevelt, 1945)

Succeeded a president who was assassinated:

Andrew Johnson (succeeded Abraham Lincoln, 1865)
Chester A. Arthur (succeeded James A. Garfield, 1881)
Theodore Roosevelt (succeeded William McKinley, 1901)
Lyndon B. Johnson (succeeded John F. Kennedy, 1963)

Succeeded a president who resigned:

Gerald R. Ford (succeeded Richard M. Nixon, 1973)

(See 55 Which presidents died in office? 58 Which president resigned from office? 60 Has the office of the vice president ever been vacant?)

▶ *Why was the Twenty-fifth Amendment necessary? See 54 What happens if the president dies or is disabled while in office?*

▶ *Has there ever been an acting president? See 57 Who was the first acting president?*

▶ *How many vice presidents have been members of Congress? See 142 Have any political offices served as stepping-stones to the vice presidency?*

Q 223. Which vice president made the first goodwill trip abroad on behalf of the president?

A John Nance Garner, President Franklin D. Roosevelt's first vice president, made the first trip abroad in 1935. He traveled first to the Philippines for the inauguration of the new president there and then went to Mexico on the second leg of the tour. Since then vice presidents have traveled abroad regularly on the president's behalf, mainly on goodwill missions and to attend ceremonial functions, but from time to time they have been given some more important missions to carry out overseas. It was not until Richard M. Nixon held the office, however, that vice presidents began traveling extensively as a regular part of the job.

Q 224. What did Vice President George Bush mean when he said, "You die, I fly"?

A Among the many ceremonial duties that fall to the vice president is that of representing the president at the funerals of foreign dignitaries, and this chore can be a frequent one. George Bush, who served two terms as vice president during the Reagan administration, flew overseas so many times to attend funerals that he coined the grimly humorous expression, "You die, I fly."

▶ *Why did the Framers of the Constitution give the job of president of the Senate to the vice president? See 25 How did the vice presidency come about?*

Q 225. Which vice president cast the most tie-breaking votes in the Senate?

A The record for most tie-breaking votes belongs to John Adams, the first vice president, who cast twenty-nine during his two terms of office. John C. Calhoun, who was vice president under both John Quincy Adams and Andrew Jackson, came in a close second with twenty-eight. More recent vice presidents cast far fewer votes because as the Senate membership grew larger, the number of ties dropped off sharply. Since Schuyler Colfax's thirteen tiebreakers between 1869 and 1873, no vice president has been called on to cast more than eight.

Vice President	Tie-Breaking Votes
John Adams	29
Thomas Jefferson	3
Aaron Burr	3

Vice President	Tie-Breaking Votes
George Clinton	11
Elbridge Gerry	8
Daniel D. Tompkins	5
John C. Calhoun	28
Martin Van Buren	4
Richard M. Johnson	14
John Tyler	0
George M. Dallas	19
Millard Fillmore	3
William R. King	0
John C. Breckinridge	10
Hannibal Hamlin	7
Andrew Johnson	0
Schuyler Colfax	13
Henry Wilson	1
William A. Wheeler	5
Chester A. Arthur	3
Thomas A. Hendricks	0
Levi P. Morton	4
Adlai E. Stevenson	2
Garret A. Hobart	1
Theodore Roosevelt	0
Charles W. Fairbanks	0
James S. Sherman	4
Thomas R. Marshall	4
Calvin Coolidge	0
Charles G. Dawes	2
Charles Curtis	3
John Nance Garner	3
Henry A. Wallace	4
Harry S. Truman	1
Alben W. Barkley	7
Richard M. Nixon	8
Lyndon B. Johnson	0
Hubert H. Humphrey	4
Spiro T. Agnew	2

Vice President	Tie-Breaking Votes
Gerald R. Ford	0
Nelson A. Rockefeller	0
Walter F. Mondale	1
George Bush	7
Dan Quayle	0
Al Gore (as of late 1999)	4

THE PRESIDENT AND CONGRESS

(See also The President and Foreign Policy)

Q 226. Who has the power to make laws, Congress or the president?

A Only Congress can pass legislation, but the president has a pivotal role in the process—except for certain situations, the president's signature is required on a bill before it becomes law. A president who opposes a bill passed by Congress can veto—refuse to sign—the measure and return it to Congress. The Framers of the Constitution gave the president this check on Congress's lawmaking power to prevent abuses—legislative tyranny—and presidents regularly use vetoes (or veto threats) to force Congress to reconsider its position in legislative battles.

Presidents influence legislation in other ways too. They command the attention of the media and the public and so can pressure Congress to pass specific legislative programs. In fact today presidents are looked upon as the nation's "chief legislator." They are expected to take the lead in proposing new legislation to Congress and use their annual State of the Union addresses to propose wholesale legislative agendas for Congress to adopt. (Congress can and often does refuse to follow the president's lead, though). Presidents and their assistants even deliver drafts of proposed legislation to Congress. Other ways in which presidents influence the legislative process include lobbying members of Congress directly on specific bills, offering support for other legislation favored by members, and patronage (including the president's help in campaigning).

(See 202 How do presidents turn patronage and pork-barrel projects to their advantage? 231 Who usually wins veto battles, Congress or the president? 233 What is the source of the president's power as legislative leader? 234 How does the president lobby Congress? 235 Can the president sway Congress by appealing directly to the public? 261 How do the media and the president interact?)

Q 227. What is a veto?

A A president who opposes legislation passed by Congress can prevent the measure from becoming law by vetoing it—that is, once Congress has sent him a bill for his signature, he can veto it by returning it unsigned to either the House or Senate, depending on where the bill originated. The president must act within ten days (not counting Sundays), however, or the bill automatically becomes law (unless Congress is not in session). Usually the president includes a veto message along with the unsigned bill, citing the objectionable parts of the bill.

Congress then has three options: revise the bill, override the president's veto, or do nothing and let the measure die. Because congressional leaders find it is difficult to muster the necessary two-thirds vote in both houses to override a presidential veto, Congress only rarely manages an override. For that reason, presidents are often able to force Congress to rewrite legislation.

Although the Constitution says only that two-thirds of the members of each house must vote to override a presidential veto, the Supreme Court decided in 1919 that Congress needed only two-thirds of a quorum to override. In each house a quorum is the bare majority—fifty-one of the one hundred senators, for example. Even so, Congress is rarely able to rally the support needed for an override.

(See 229 What is a line-item veto? 231 Who usually wins veto battles, Congress or the president?)

Q 228. How does a pocket veto differ from a regular veto?

A Ordinarily, when the president refuses to sign a bill and does not return it to Congress within ten days (excluding Sundays), the bill automatically becomes law. But if Congress adjourns before the ten days are up and the president has not signed or returned the bill, the measure dies because Congress could not reconsider the measure if the president did return it. This is called a pocket veto.

Pocket vetoes can be controversial, however, because of disagreements over the meaning of adjournment. Congress defines adjournment narrowly—the final adjournment of a two-year session—but presidents have tried to impose a broader interpretation that includes recesses and interim adjournments during a session. The Supreme Court ruled in the 1920s that presidents could apply the pocket veto during a long recess of Congress. But by the 1970s the Court had ruled against pocket vetoes during congressional recesses and during adjournments between sessions of the same Congress. Moreover, Congress has devised procedures for recesses and short adjournments designed to preclude a president from using a pocket veto.

Q 229. What is a line-item veto?

A When presidents veto a bill, they must reject the entire bill—even if they disagree with only a small part of it. A line-item veto would allow presidents to sign a bill into law while vetoing only the objectionable parts. Many presidents since Ulysses S. Grant, who became the first to call for a line-time veto in 1873, have asked Congress for this modified veto power. Supporters have argued that the line-item veto would allow presidents to cut some of the congressional district-friendly spending items often attached to the appropriations bills that must be passed if government agencies are to be funded.

Republicans in Congress finally did pass a line-item veto measure in 1996, and President Bill Clinton used it to veto parts of eleven acts passed by Congress. But court challenges to the law resulted in a 1998 ruling by the Supreme Court, which found the line-item veto unconstitutional. The Court said it gave the president what amounted to the power to approve bills in a form that Congress had never passed.

Q 230. Which presidents vetoed the most and fewest bills?

A Franklin D. Roosevelt, who served longer than any other president, vetoed the most bills—635 between 1933 and 1945. Congress managed to override his veto only nine times. Grover Cleveland's veto record was second highest—584 bills—but he served eight years, not twelve. His yearly average for vetoes was seventy-three, well above Roosevelt's average of fifty-three a year.

Seven presidents vetoed no bills at all during their terms. The seven, all of whom served during the 1800s, were: John Adams, Thomas Jefferson, John Quincy Adams, William Henry Harrison, Zachary Taylor, Millard Fillmore, and James A. Garfield.

President	Regular	Pocket Vetoes	Overrides Vetoes
George Washington	2	0	0
John Adams	0	0	0
Thomas Jefferson	0	0	0
James Madison	5	2	0
James Monroe	1	0	0
John Quincy Adams	0	0	0
Andrew Jackson	5	7	0
Martin Van Buren	0	1	0

President	Regular	Pocket Vetoes	Overrides Vetoes
William Henry Harrison	0	0	0
John Tyler	6	4	1
James K. Polk	2	1	0
Zachary Taylor	0	0	0
Millard Fillmore	0	0	0
Franklin Pierce	9	0	5
James Buchanan	4	3	0
Abraham Lincoln	2	5	0
Andrew Johnson	21	8	15
Ulysses S. Grant	45	48	4
Rutherford B. Hayes	12	1	1
James A. Garfield	0	0	0
Chester A. Arthur	4	8	1
Grover Cleveland	304	110	2
Benjamin Harrison	19	25	1
Grover Cleveland	42	128	5
William McKinley	6	36	0
Theodore Roosevelt	42	40	1
William Howard Taft	30	9	1
Woodrow Wilson	33	11	6
Warren G. Harding	5	1	0
Calvin Coolidge	20	30	4
Herbert Hoover	21	16	3
Franklin D. Roosevelt	372	263	9
Harry S. Truman	180	70	12
Dwight D. Eisenhower	73	108	2
John F. Kennedy	12	9	0
Lyndon B. Johnson	16	14	0
Richard M. Nixon	26	17	7
Gerald R. Ford	48	18	12
Jimmy Carter	13	18	2
Ronald Reagan	39	39	4
George Bush	27	19	1
Bill Clinton (through late 1999)	27	0	4
Total	1,473	1,069	103

Q 231. Who usually wins veto battles, Congress or the president?

A Because it takes a two-thirds vote in both houses of Congress to override a president's veto, Congress rarely manages to win veto battles. Of the 2,542 bills presidents vetoed between 1789 and 1999, only 103 were overridden. President Andrew Johnson, who faced a hostile Congress dominated by Radical Republicans, suffered the most veto overrides, fifteen in all, and thus had only a 28.6 success rate. Harry S. Truman and Gerald R. Ford each had twelve of their vetoes overridden, for success rates of 93.3 percent and 75.0 percent, respectively. President Franklin D. Roosevelt, who vetoed more bills than any other president (635 during three-plus terms), had only nine overridden, for a 97.6 percent success rate. Nearly all other presidents had either no overrides or just a few. In fact, Congress did not succeed in overriding its first bill until the 1840s, during the Tyler administration.

▶ *What checks on executive power does Congress have? See 22 Does the Constitution impose checks and balances on presidential powers? 23 What checks on powers of the other branches does the president have?*

Q 232. Who was the last president to be present in Congress during a floor debate?

A President George Washington was the first and the last. Hoping to win quick approval for a treaty concluded with Native American tribes, he decided to deliver it personally to Congress one day in 1789. But when he remained in the chamber to await action on the treaty, senators clearly became uneasy and put off deliberations. Washington never again visited Congress in person, except to deliver his State of the Union addresses. But he did send Treasury Secretary Alexander Hamilton and Secretary of State Thomas Jefferson to the Capitol for private meetings with members of Congress on fiscal and foreign policy concerns. Presidents since Washington have used this method of sending surrogates to meet with congressional leaders. They also invite members to the White House for face-to-face meetings.

(See 234 How does the president lobby Congress? 240 Why do presidents give the State of the Union address each year?)

233. What is the source of the president's power as legislative leader?

A Presidents today have far more influence over the legislative process than the Framers of the Constitution originally envisioned. The Constitution gives the president the power to veto legislation, certainly a potent weapon, but beyond that it says only that the president shall "from time to time give to the Congress Information of the State of the Union, and recommend to their Consideration such Measures as he shall judge necessary and expedient." During the 1800s Congress was the dominant legislative force in the government, and presidents did not routinely propose legislation. But that changed in the twentieth century. Today, presidents not only recommend specific legislation, but also are expected to propose national policy agendas and use their considerable powers of persuasion to push the enabling legislation through Congress.

Part of the president's power as national legislative leader stems from the nature of the presidency. As the single most powerful and most visible member of the government, the president is a national figure who often can sway public sentiment and bring a wide array of interest groups to bear on reluctant members of Congress. The growing power of the news media since the late 1800s also has at times helped presidents, who use it to broadcast their appeals to voters. Some events play into the president's hands as well. For example, people look to the president, not Congress, in national crises such as the Great Depression. Congress also has helped empower the president by delegating additional powers, such as responsibility for drafting the annual budget. That responsibility has given the president the lead in planning for taxing and spending.

(See 238 What precedent did President Franklin D. Roosevelt's "Hundred Days" set?)

234. How does the president lobby Congress?

A When presidents want a bill passed, they lobby Congress by various means, including by making personal appeals and sending surrogates, such as cabinet members, to meet with members of Congress. The president's staff is an important resource in the lobbying process. Staffers provide policy advice, meet with members of Congress, and help the president track votes in Congress for and against administration bills. Even the vice president gets into the act when it comes to lobbying Congress. (John Nance Garner, President Franklin D. Roosevelt's first vice president, originated the idea of weekly meetings between the president and congressional leaders.)

Presidents since Dwight D. Eisenhower also have included an Office of Congressional Relations in their staff organization. The personnel in this office work directly with all factions in Congress and prepare weekly reports on the status of administration bills. They also act as liaison between Congress and the executive branch agencies.

Personal appeals by the president—a telephone call or a face-to-face meeting at the White House—can have a powerful effect on a reluctant member of Congress. But presidents have other weapons at their disposal when lobbying Congress, notably patronage. For example, they can offer to support the member's reelection campaign or push for a bill that favors the member's district. They also can pressure Congress by making public appeals in behalf of the legislation *(see next question)*.

(See 202 How do presidents turn patronage and pork-barrel projects to their advantage?)

Q 235. Can presidents sway Congress by appealing directly to the public?

A Presidents regularly resort to public appeals to put pressure on Congress to enact legislation. As the single most visible government leader, the president can use speeches and other means to sway public opinion on a given issue, and that often has a powerful effect on Congress. The electronic mass media have only enhanced the president's ability to reach national audiences when need be. President Franklin D. Roosevelt took office during the heyday of broadcast radio and skillfully used the airwaves with his now-legendary "fireside chats" to build public support for himself and his legislative programs. Presidents from John F. Kennedy on have likewise used television to great advantage. Lyndon B. Johnson's televised speech in 1965 helped push his landmark Voting Rights Act through Congress. President Ronald Reagan, a former actor, used the media to win wide support for his dramatic budget and tax cuts in 1981.

(See 261 How do the media and the president interact? 334 What have presidents done in the battle for the public's favor?)

Q 236. Do presidents have an easier time with Congress when their party has a majority in Congress?

A Presidents promote a nonpartisan image whenever possible and usually get at least some members of the opposing party to vote for administration bills in Congress. But the success of their legislative programs often turns on the strength of their own party in Congress. When the other party controls one or two chambers of Congress, presidents and Congress can deadlock, making passage of important legislation very difficult. Moreover, if presidents become embroiled in a fight with factions of their own party (which happened to President Jimmy Carter, for example), their legislative programs will face tough sledding.

Until the 1960s, the president's party had controlling majorities in Congress more often than not. Since then, however, divided government has become more common.

(See 291 When has the president's party held a majority in Congress?)

Q 237. What presidents have had the most success in dealing with Congress?

A The most successful were Thomas Jefferson, Theodore Roosevelt, Woodrow Wilson, Franklin D. Roosevelt, and Lyndon B. Johnson. All had firm ties with party and committee leaders in Congress, and their parties held majorities in one or, usually, both houses.

Q 238. What precedent did President Franklin D. Roosevelt's "Hundred Days" set?

A Roosevelt's first one hundred days in office, during which his administration pushed a torrent of New Deal legislation through Congress, established the president's role as the nation's legislative leader. Until the crisis of the Great Depression in the 1930s, presidents were not always expected to propose legislation—Congress formulated and enacted the laws; the president carried them out. But the sheer magnitude of the economic collapse during the 1930s and the widespread hardship it created demanded new approaches.

Taking office in 1933 when the economic depression was at its worst, President Franklin Roosevelt pioneered the new approach. During the Hundred Days, he sent Congress a flood of proposed legislation to ease the suffering and restore the economy, including such New Deal programs as public welfare and public works. In doing that, he upstaged Congress's hold on the legislative agenda and, more than ever before, made setting national government policy the responsibility of presidents.

Franklin Roosevelt was not the first president to make a formal presentation of a draft bill to Congress, however. That distinction fell to President William Howard Taft. And President Woodrow Wilson used the State of the Union address to introduce a legislative program. But until Franklin Roosevelt, Congress clearly controlled the legislative agenda.

(See 226 Who has the power to make laws, Congress or the president? 233 What is the source of the president's power as legislative leader? 243 What was FDR's Court-packing plan?)

Q 239. Have the president and Congress ever been deadlocked?

A When the president's party does not control Congress, chances are greater that partisan battles will escalate into legislative gridlock. But it does not happen all the time. Since 1968, for example, the president's party has been out of power in Congress for all but two brief periods—during the Carter administration in the late 1970s and during the first two years of Bill Clinton's first term in the early 1990s. Republican presidents have often found themselves at odds with Democratic majorities in one or both houses of Congress, but on many issues the two sides found ways to compromise. Battles between President Ronald Reagan and Congress over the federal budget boiled over, however, leading to deadlocks that shut down the government altogether for brief periods (the first in 1981). The Bush and Clinton administrations also experienced shutdowns during budget battles with Congress.

Political battles between the president and Congress are not a strictly modern phenomenon, however. President John Tyler, the first vice president to succeed to the presidency, fought with leaders of his Whig Party and was effectively disowned by it in the 1840s. After the Civil War, President Andrew Johnson fought with Radical Republicans who controlled Congress and barely escaped being removed from office when their attempt at impeaching him failed.

(See 64 Why was President Andrew Johnson impeached? 65 What brought about President Bill Clinton's impeachment?)

Q 240. Why do presidents give the State of the Union address each year?

A The Constitution set the requirement for an annual report to Congress on the state of the nation. Presidents George Washington and John Adams delivered their annual addresses in person before Congress, but President Thomas Jefferson believed written reports were more dignified. Jefferson's successors followed suit by delivering written reports until Woodrow Wilson revived the practice of delivering annual addresses before joint sessions of Congress. Today, the State of the Union address is among the president's most important ceremonial duties and offers him the opportunity to announce new programs and policies (for example, Lyndon B. Johnson announced his Great Society program during a State of the Union address).

The president also is required to prepare and submit to Congress hundreds of other reports, including annual budget messages and economic reports. In addition, Congress can request special reports on the activities of specific agencies in connection with its oversight and investigative powers.

► *Can the president call Congress into session? See 23 What checks on powers of the other branches does the president have?*

THE PRESIDENT AND THE COURTS

Q **241. Did the Supreme Court rule against expansion of presidential powers in the last century?**

A The Court has generally ruled in favor of presidents expanding their economic, diplomatic, and war powers, and has rejected attempts by Congress and the states to limit presidential powers. But it did hand down several rulings in the twentieth century that curbed presidential powers, including four especially important ones: several rulings in the mid-1930s striking down key parts of Franklin D. Roosevelt's New Deal; its ruling that Harry S. Truman's seizure of steel mills in 1952 was unconstitutional; its decision forcing Richard M. Nixon to turn over tapes of Oval Office conversations related to the Watergate scandal (while granting the president the power of executive privilege in many other cases); and its ruling against the president's line-item veto.

(See 203 What is executive privilege? 322 What reason did Truman give for seizing the steel mills?)

► *What constitutional checks and balances are there between the executive branch and the courts? See 22 Does the Constitution impose checks and balances on presidential powers? 23 What checks on powers of the other branches does the president have?*

Q **242. Which president had the largest number of Supreme Court rulings against him?**

A The Supreme Court ruled against President Richard M. Nixon twenty-five times, including his Court challenge on executive privilege, for a total far above that of any other president. Only President Franklin D. Roosevelt came close, with eight unfavorable rulings. The Court ruled against President Abraham Lincoln five times, and all other presidents lost no more than three decisions. Eighteen presidents had no rulings against them at all. In all, as of 1997 the Court had ruled against the president just seventy-six times, an indication of the Court's reluctance to rule against the nation's chief executive.

Q 243. What was FDR's Court-packing plan?

A Although Congress passed the legislation needed to create and run President Franklin D. Roosevelt's New Deal programs, the idea of giving federal agencies so much power to regulate the economy was revolutionary for its time and produced the expected court challenges. In 1935 and 1936 the Supreme Court handed down several key rulings against the administration.

President Roosevelt was furious, especially since a group of four conservative justices had been involved in all the unfavorable rulings. In early 1937 the president counterattacked by proposing passage of a "judicial reorganization" act by Congress that would add as many as six more justices to the Supreme Court. Opponents called it a thinly disguised plan to pack the Court with justices who would support New Deal programs and roundly criticized Roosevelt's challenge of the Court's independence.

The public outcry forced Roosevelt to abandon the idea. But amid all the furor one of the conservative justices switched sides, and in subsequent rulings the Court reversed itself. From the late 1930s on, Roosevelt was able to appoint more liberal-minded justices to replace retiring conservatives and further cement his support on the high court.

Q 244. What precedent did *United States v. Curtiss-Wright Export Corp.* set?

A This 1936 Supreme Court ruling, which upheld the president's right to act alone in matters concerning foreign affairs, was a landmark decision on the president's constitutional powers in this area. The case itself revolved around the challenge posed by an aircraft company, Curtiss-Wright, to President Franklin D. Roosevelt's arms embargo against Bolivia, then at war with neighboring Paraguay. As it happened, Congress had passed a law giving Roosevelt the right to stop arms sales to any warring nation. But the Court held that even without the law, the president by necessity had the power to act independently in foreign affairs, because an individual executive (as opposed to a legislative body) was better able to deal with foreign powers.

(See 20 What are the enumerated powers of the presidency?)

Q 245. Have presidents ever ignored Supreme Court rulings?

A Although they rarely do so, presidents have defied Court decisions. Andrew Jackson flatly refused to enforce an 1832 Court ruling that the state of Georgia had no jurisdiction over Cherokee Indians within its borders. And during the Civil War, President Abraham Lincoln let stand his emergency order suspending the writ of habeas corpus, even though the Supreme Court had ruled the order unconstitutional. In fact, the Supreme Court has no mechanism for enforcing its orders, other than the president, who is responsible for enforcing the law. The broad public support for the authority of the Court can make defying its rulings politically costly for a president, however.

Q 246. What factors do presidents consider when making a Supreme Court nomination?

A A nominee's judicial experience is a key consideration, of course, but presidents must weigh other factors as well. Usually they try to find candidates from within their own party, whose political and legal philosophies are compatible with their own. In that way, presidents use their appointment power to influence the overall direction of the Court—if their nominees rule as expected after reaching the bench. Not all of them have, as President Dwight D. Eisenhower, a Republican conservative, discovered after naming Earl Warren chief justice. Warren presided over a period of judicial activism that ushered in many liberal reforms during the 1950s and 1960s.

Presidents also have tended to respect the idea of traditional seats on the bench. There has been a Catholic seat since 1894, a Jewish seat since 1916, and a seat for an African American since 1967. President Ronald Reagan appointed the first woman, Sandra Day O'Connor, to the high court in 1981.

(See 181 Is the president's power to appoint important?)

Q 247. Which presidents have had the greatest success in using appointments to influence the direction of Supreme Court rulings?

A Five presidents are regarded as having been especially successful in their Supreme Court appointments—Andrew Jackson, Abraham Lincoln, Franklin D. Roosevelt, Richard M. Nixon, and Ronald Reagan. President Jackson's six appointees shifted the Court's direction from one of backing the national government to staunch support for states' rights. Lincoln's early appointees, especially, helped to swing the Court in favor of the extraordinary emergency measures the president and Congress had enacted to deal with the Civil War. Decades later, Roosevelt's eight appointees provided broad support on the bench for his New Deal programs, which greatly expanded the powers of the federal government. (Earlier decisions had found key New Deal programs unconstitutional.) Nixon had campaigned against the Warren Court's many liberal rulings on criminal procedures. His four Court appointees formed a new majority that halted further expansion of the Warren Court's criminal procedure rulings, but stopped short of reversing them. Reagan's four appointees, including conservative chief justice William H. Rehnquist, moved the Court distinctly to the right. The Court proved willing to examine controversial issues and modified the Court's position in some areas, such as majority-minority legislative districts (districts deliberately drawn to include a majority of black voters) and affirmative action (programs designed to give blacks and other disadvantaged groups preference in hiring, college enrollment, and other areas).

Q 248. Which president appointed the most Supreme Court justices? The fewest?

A During his two terms in office, President George Washington appointed eleven Supreme Court justices, more than any other president. The fact that in 1789 he appointed the entire first panel of justices—five in all—markedly increased his total. In numbers, President Franklin D. Roosevelt was not far behind. He appointed eight justices (and elevated another to chief justice) during his three-plus terms in office. William Howard Taft, who became a Supreme Court justice himself after leaving office, appointed six in his one term.

Just four presidents did not make any appointments to the Court—William Henry Harrison, Zachary Taylor, Andrew Johnson, and Jimmy Carter. Both Harrison and Taylor died early in their terms and so had little opportunity to make appointments. Andrew Johnson nominated a justice in 1866, but the Senate refused to act. As for Carter, no vacancies opened up on the Court during his one term in office, making him the first full-term president who named no justice to the Court.

Q 249. Do presidents become involved in judicial nominations to lower federal courts?

A Presidents are responsible for nominating federal appeals and district court judges. Because this task involves making such a large number of nominations to these courts, presidents generally turn the selection process over to the attorney general and others at the Justice Department. Once named, nominees must be approved by the Senate, where the tradition of "senatorial courtesy" comes into play. By this practice, senators who are members of the president's party and who represent the state in which the judge will serve can request the Senate to reject any nominee they oppose.

Q 250. Does the Senate always confirm the president's Supreme Court nominations?

A Although most Court nominees are approved, from time to time the Senate has rejected a candidate on political or ethical grounds. Of the 148 nominations presidents have made to the Supreme Court, the Senate has rejected or not acted on just twenty-eight. Three candidates had better luck on their renomination, but one other candidate, Edward B. King, was forced to give up after the Senate rebuffed him twice, in 1844 and 1845.

Probably the most controversial confirmation hearing in modern times involved President Ronald Reagan's nominee, Robert H. Bork, whose conservative legal philosophy aroused stiff opposition in the Democratic-controlled Senate and resulted in the most recent outright rejection by that body. President George Bush's nominee, Clarence Thomas, survived highly publicized hearings into allegations he had sexually harassed a former employee when she worked for him at the Equal Opportunity Commission and at the Education Department. Thomas narrowly won Senate confirmation.

Q 251. Which Supreme Court case upheld the president's pardon power?

A While the courts have generally ruled in favor of the president's power to pardon, the Supreme Court handed down what is probably the most important ruling on the matter in 1867. Two years earlier, in 1865, Congress had passed the Test Oath Act of 1865 to bar former Confederates and their supporters from practicing law after the Civil War. President Andrew Johnson, who was at odds with Radical Republicans in Congress over their harsh treatment of the defeated Confederate states, pardoned a Confederate sympathizer to allow him to practice law.

Challenged in court, the pardon case reached the Supreme Court as *Ex parte Garland* (1867). The high court not only upheld the pardon, but also found that the president could issue the pardon before, during, or after a trial for any offense "known to the law." Furthermore, the Court said the pardon had the effect of completely restoring the criminal's prior legal status.

Q 252. Do presidents have the constitutional authority to recognize foreign governments?

A Presidents can and do recognize the governments of foreign countries, but that power is not specifically mentioned in the Constitution. Instead, presidents base their recognition power on the fact that the Constitution grants them the authority to send and receive ambassadors. Implied in the act of receiving an ambassador, presidents have said, is recognition that the foreign government sending the diplomat is legitimate. That argument has allowed presidents to claim exclusive control over deciding which countries to recognize officially and when to cut off relations with a country.

Q 253. Why is the president's power to appoint ambassadors important?

A Because the diplomatic skills and personalities of ambassadors can affect the outcome of foreign policy, presidents must be able to appoint and remove ambassadors as they see fit. For the most important ambassadorships, where diplomatic experience is essential, presidents often rely on career foreign service officials.

Presidents traditionally have also used their appointment power to reward political allies and major campaign contributors, often by naming them ambassador to a small country. In addition, appointments are sometimes used to make political statements or to carry out a desired policy by putting in place a political ally.

Q 254. How many foreign embassies does the United States have?

A The United States maintains diplomatic missions in over 170 countries around the world to provide lines of communication between foreign governments and the president on matters of mutual concern. The only countries with which the United States currently does not have diplomatic relations are Cuba, Iran, Iraq, Libya, Liechtenstein, North Korea, and Taiwan.

Q 255. Does the Constitution grant the president or Congress greater powers to conduct foreign affairs?

A The Constitution grants the president and Congress about equal powers over foreign affairs. For example, the president has the authority to negotiate treaties and to appoint ambassadors, but the Senate must approve in both cases. The president can deploy American troops overseas, but only Congress can declare war. And when the president proposes sending foreign aid to nations in need, Congress decides whether to approve the funds because it has the power of the purse. Nevertheless, presidents have other advantages beyond those powers granted explicitly in the Constitution, and those advantages have allowed them to dominate foreign policy, especially in modern times *(see next question)*.

Q 256. What advantages does the president have over Congress in conducting foreign affairs?

A Chief among presidents' advantages is the fact that they head the country's foreign affairs bureaucracy—information from diplomats, the military, and intelligence agencies comes through their office, giving them firsthand knowledge about the governments that must be dealt with. Also, because the president is a single individual—not a legislative body like Congress—he can negotiate with foreign governments quickly and secretly. Using their position as the country's most visible government leader, presidents are better able to win the confidence of foreign leaders and rally support at home for foreign policies.

Because of these advantages, presidents dominate foreign policy, especially when it comes to formulating and setting policies in motion. Congress has the power to delay or modify the president's policies, but its actions are almost always in response to the administration's foreign affairs initiatives. Still, the president usually needs the support of Congress to succeed in the foreign policy arena.

Q 257. How does the president conclude a treaty?

A The treaty process begins with negotiations between representatives of the president and the foreign government. Only the president or a designated representative has the power to enter into treaty negotiations on behalf of the United States, and Congress cannot prevent the president from doing so.

Once the terms of a treaty have been drafted, the president then decides whether to submit the document to the Senate for approval (presidents have sometimes abandoned an agreement when approval seemed unlikely). For its part, the Senate can amend the agreement before approving it. In this situation the president can either drop the treaty or renegotiate the terms with the foreign government.

After the Senate approves the treaty, the president (and the leader of the foreign country) must ratify it. Once both leaders have ratified the treaty by signing the document, the president officially proclaims the treaty to be the law of the United States.

(See 260 Are there limits to treaty terms?)

Q 258. Has the Senate ever rejected a treaty?

A The Senate has approved without changes over two-thirds of all treaties presidents have submitted and has rejected only twenty-three of them. These rejections do not include the treaties that presidents withdrew or did not submit because the political embarrassment of a Senate rejection seemed likely.

The most famous rejection occurred in 1920 when the Senate refused to approve the Treaty of Versailles. In addition to formally ending World War I, the treaty also included a provision establishing the League of Nations, which President Woodrow Wilson had proposed. The Senate's first treaty rejection came in 1825, when it killed a pact with Colombia to suppress the slave trade. The most recent rejection was the Comprehensive Test Ban Treaty submitted by President Bill Clinton in 1999.

Q 259. Why have executive agreements become so important?

A The president can use executive agreements to conclude trade agreements, exchanges of territory, defense pacts, and anything else a treaty can do. The only difference is that provisions of an executive agreement may not supersede any conflicting federal laws.

The advantage of executive agreements for presidents is that they do not require Senate approval, which a formal treaty does. Thus presidents can negotiate terms with a foreign power without having to worry about what would be politically acceptable to the Senate and the political embarrassment of a rejection by the Senate.

Because of these advantages, presidents in recent times have favored executive agreements over formal treaties. Between 1981 and 1996, for example, they concluded only 289 treaties as opposed to 5,327 executive agreements. In 1972 Congress responded to the sudden rise in executive agreements by passing the Case Act, which requires the president to notify Congress of any executive agreement within sixty days.

(See 279 Which president concluded the first executive agreement?)

Q 260. Are there limits to treaty terms?

A Article VI of the Constitution states that treaties "shall be the supreme Law of the Land"—that is, treaty provisions have the force of federal law within the United States and are binding on the states as well. That last provision provoked a Supreme Court test, but in *Foster* v. *Neilson* (1829) the Court ruled the federal government has the power to make treaties with provisions that supersede state laws.

Once ratified, treaties remain in force until one or the other party violates the treaty terms or both parties agree to terminate it. The Constitution is silent on whether the president or Congress has the power to terminate a treaty, but in 1979 the Supreme Court ruled that the president can revoke a treaty without Senate approval.

THE PRESIDENT AND THE PRESS

Q 261. How do the media and the president interact?

A The news media serve a dual purpose when it comes to the presidency. On the one hand, they serve as a watchdog of the government, broadcasting nationwide any news of its successes and failures and closely examining the president's actions minutely on an almost daily basis. On the other hand, the news media have helped make the president the most watched and talked about figure in government, thereby enabling him to reach mass audiences through the media and rally considerable public support for administration policies.

All modern presidents have had to become adept at handling the media, and various methods have evolved to help them control the flow of information from the White House to the public via the various news outlets. The presidential press secretary, the administration's spokesperson, plays an important role in handling the news media and shaping the president's image through them. Presidents and their staffs control the flow of information from the White House to the public by holding daily press briefings, background briefings, and news conferences; by making strategic public announcements; and by granting or withholding exclusive interviews for specific reporters.

Q 262. Which modern presidents have been effective communicators?

A Probably the two most effective communicators to hold the office of president in the twentieth century were Franklin D. Roosevelt and Ronald Reagan. Both used the media masterfully to present themselves to the public and build support for their agendas. Other presidents made effective use of the media as well. Theodore Roosevelt was the first president to actively pursue newspaper coverage, and John F. Kennedy was the first president to use television effectively. Bill Clinton, whose relations with the press were not always the best, nevertheless raised to new levels the art of "going public" to win support for himself and his policies.

Q 263. About how many reporters are there in the White House press corps?

A About seventy-five reporters representing the major television networks, daily newspapers, news services, and other media are assigned to the White House full time to cover the president and his policies. The members of the White House press corps are just a small part of the thousands of journalists who are based in Washington and who sometimes cover the president.

Q 264. Why did President John Adams support passage of the Sedition Act?

A Early in John Adams's term, newspapers published by supporters of Thomas Jefferson, leader of the emerging Democratic-Republican Party, virulently attacked Adams and his Federalist Party. Adams was deeply offended by the attacks. But they were nothing new—newspapers, pamphlets, and similar publications in the late 1700s and early 1800s were routinely written with deliberate bias in order to advance the interests of a particular faction or cause, at times even becoming outright propaganda. (The idea of reporting information objectively did not become a journalistic standard until later in the 1800s.) To counter the anti-Federalist attacks, the Federalist-dominated Congress passed, and Adams signed into law, the Alien and Sedition Acts in 1798—four laws designed to stifle criticism of federal officeholders and to prevent conspiracies against the government. Ten of Jefferson's supporters were fined and jailed under the acts. But the acts created a major political backlash against the Federalists, and Jefferson's supporters asserted that they had violated freedom of the press. Kentucky and Virginia declared the acts null and void in those states. Ultimately, objections to the acts helped Jefferson defeat Adams in the 1800 election and brought on the collapse of the Federalist Party. Once in control of Congress, Democratic-Republicans repealed one act and let lapse all but one other. The Logan Act, which bars negotiations between private citizens and the enemy during wartime, was left in force.

Q 265. How did President Lincoln handle the press during the Civil War?

A Abraham Lincoln handled newspapers with a carrot and a stick. On the one hand, he worked more closely with reporters than any previous president. On the other, he made wide use of his wartime powers to censor and suppress newspapers that printed stories opposing the war. Lincoln's successor, Andrew Johnson, became the first president to grant newspaper reporters interviews on a regular basis.

266. How did President Theodore Roosevelt deal with the press?

A The first president to actively cultivate press coverage and to maintain direct contact with reporters, Roosevelt gave journalists far greater access to the White House than any previous president. That and Roosevelt's dynamic personality won him wide coverage in newspapers of his day. During the Roosevelt administration, relations with the press were informal (later presidents introduced structured press conferences), but Roosevelt did try to control White House coverage. He did not hesitate to criticize particular news stories and opposed what he believed to be irresponsible investigative journalism in his day. Roosevelt called it "muckraking," a term he coined.

Q **267. Which president held the first formal news conferences?**

A Woodrow Wilson staged the first formal presidential press conference on March 15, 1913, shortly after his inauguration, and he continued the practice until 1915. Before him, President Theodore Roosevelt had met regularly with reporters, but only on an informal basis. Wilson, who required reporters to submit their questions beforehand in writing, was unhappy with the idea of press conferences from the very beginning. Although he halted the practice two years into his term, every president since him has held them.

▶ *When was the office of presidential press secretary established? See 36 When did presidents begin to rely on press secretaries to handle the media?*

Q **268. Which president held the most news conferences?**

A Franklin D. Roosevelt holds the record for both the most news conferences (998) and the highest average per year (almost 83) while in office. Roosevelt in fact used news conferences as an important tool for communicating his policy goals to the public. The president's comments at these informal Oval Office sessions could be attributed to the president, but not quoted directly.

No president since has even come close to Roosevelt's record on news conferences. Truman managed 41 a year for a total of 324 during his nearly two terms in office. Richard M. Nixon, who had poor relations with the press, held only 37 news conferences while in office.

Q 269. Who was the first woman to serve as White House press secretary?

A President Bill Clinton named the first woman press secretary, Dee Dee Myers, in 1993. Because Myers was outside the loop of top Clinton advisers, the White House press corps became suspicious about her knowledge and credibility. Clinton's relations with the press suffered as a result, and after he replaced her with Michael McCurry in 1994, he made a point of including McCurry in the information loop.

THE PRESIDENTS AND SPECIAL INTERESTS

Q 270. How many interest groups are there?

A About 1,700 interest groups have offices in Washington, D.C., so that they can lobby the federal government. The groups represent a broad spectrum of special interests, including businesses, unions, professionals such as doctors and lawyers, public interest organizations concerned with the environment, education, and other issues, and even groups representing state governments.

Interest groups have been active in one form or another since the government's earliest days, but they have enjoyed new power and importance since the New Deal. Their rise was a reaction to the federal government's expansion of its regulatory authority into areas of the economy and society previously beyond its reach. Suddenly, private individuals and specific groups found they could protect their interests and even reap huge benefits by influencing what rules the government did or did not impose. That knowledge, in turn, spawned hundreds of new interest groups created for the sole purpose of lobbying the federal government.

Q 271. What can interest groups do for the president?

A In modern times especially, interest groups have become an important source of campaign funds—and votes—for presidential candidates. But their support does not stop there. Once in office, the president can use interest groups to lobby Congress for sought-after legislation and to provide expertise on policy issues, such as Social Security and health care. And because interest groups represent specific blocs of voters, coalitions of groups can help the president mobilize broad public support for new or controversial policies.

Q 272. Which interest groups usually support Democrats? Republicans?

A Democrats usually win broad support from interest groups representing labor, minorities, women's rights organizations, and environmental groups. Interest groups that usually back Republicans include those representing business and the financial sector, conservative social and religious organizations, and farm groups.

Q 273. Why do interest groups tend to work more closely with Congress and cabinet officials?

A Practical concerns tend to dictate where interest groups establish their closest ties. Members of Congress and cabinet officials are more accessible than the president and top White House staff—the president simply does not have enough time to meet with each and every lobbyist concerned about a specific regulatory or technical issue. Also, such matters often are more relevant to the operations of a particular agency or the economy of a particular state, and so are of greater concern to cabinet officials and members of Congress. Lobbyists' ties tend to be longer lasting with members of Congress, especially senior members who eventually head committees and career officials in the cabinet. Presidents, on the other hand, come and go after a term or two.

Q 274. What does the White House Office of Public Liaison do?

A Created during the Nixon and Ford administrations, this office handles relations between interest groups and the president. Staffers keep track of each group's concerns, what the president has done to help the groups, and what the groups have done for the president. The office also works to build coalitions of interest groups to support specific policy proposals the president wants to pursue.

(See 455 How is the White House staff organized?)

FOR THE RECORD

Q 275. How many presidents have served more than one term?

A Just twelve of the forty two presidents have been elected to and served out two full terms (Franklin D. Roosevelt served a third and part of a fourth). Another seven served at least one full term and part of another, either because they succeeded to the presidency or because they failed to complete the second full term. Of these, Abraham Lincoln and William McKinley were assassinated shortly after beginning their second term; Richard M. Nixon was forced to resign early in his second term; and Theodore Roosevelt, Calvin Coolidge, Harry S. Truman, and Lyndon B. Johnson succeeded presidents who died in office.

Presidents who served two full terms were: George Washington, Thomas Jefferson, James Madison, James Monroe, Andrew Jackson, Ulysses S. Grant, Grover Cleveland (two nonconsecutive terms), Woodrow Wilson, Franklin D. Roosevelt (served three-plus terms), Dwight D. Eisenhower, Ronald Reagan, and Bill Clinton.

Q 276. Who was the first presidential appointee?

A President George Washington named his first appointee in June 1789, soon after becoming president. He appointed William Short as the chargé d'affaires to France.

Q 277. How many presidential cabinet appointments has the Senate rejected?

A Nine separate cabinet appointees have been rejected by the Senate—some more than once. The first ever rejected was Roger B. Taney, President Andrew Jackson's choice for secretary of the Treasury in 1834. John Tower, President George Bush's nominee for secretary of defense, suffered the most recent rejection, in 1989.

President John Tyler endured the most rejections, four nominees in all, including two different nominees for secretary of the Treasury, and one each for secretary of the navy and secretary of war. The Senate was especially hard on Tyler's first nominee for secretary of the Treasury, Caleb Cushing. It rejected him three times in one day in 1843.

(See 181 Is the president's power to appoint important? 464 What does the president's cabinet do?)

Q 278. When were the first veto and pocket veto? The first veto override?

A President George Washington vetoed the first bill on April 5, 1792 (it was a congressional reapportionment bill) and ultimately vetoed only one other bill during his two terms. His immediate successors followed his policy of restricting use of the veto power to legislation they believed to be unconstitutional. James Madison became the first president to pocket veto a bill in 1812 (two of his seven vetoes were pocket vetoes). Congress did not succeed in overriding the first veto until 1845, during the administration of President John Tyler. Tyler vetoed the bill on February 20, and both houses of Congress voted to override on March 3.

(See 227 What is a veto? 228 How does a pocket veto differ from a regular veto? 230 Which presidents vetoed the most and fewest bills? 231 Who usually wins veto battles, Congress or the president?)

Q **279. Which president concluded the first executive agreement?**

A President Thomas Jefferson became the first when he concluded an agreement in 1803 to effect the Louisiana Purchase. As with all later executive agreements, Jefferson made this one without congressional approval.

(See 259 Why have executive agreements become so important? 287 Which president oversaw the largest territorial expansion of the continental United States?)

Q **280. Who was the first president to hold televised news conferences?**

A Dwight D. Eisenhower gave the first one on January 19, 1955, although the event was filmed first and edited before broadcast. The first president to give live televised news conferences was John F. Kennedy, beginning January 25, 1961.

(See 149 Who were the first presidents heard on radio and seen on television?)

PRESIDENTIAL COMMISSIONS

Q **281. What purpose do presidential commissions serve?**

A Presidential commissions provide policy advice and information on subjects that are beyond the expertise of the president's White House staff and the cabinet. Forming a commission can help focus public attention on a specific issue, or, as some critics claim, give presidents a way to divert attention from a problem or delay action on it. Studies have found that presidents usually do follow a commission's recommendations, however.

Commissions can be permanent and provide the president with ongoing policy advice about a basic public concern, such as the Presidential Commission on Mental Retardation. Or they may be temporary, ad hoc groups organized to study specific issues and recommend policy, such as the President's Commission on the space shuttle *Challenger* accident. White House conferences, to which hundreds of experts on a specific topic are invited, are a second type of temporary advisory commission. Usually they meet only for a few days before reporting their findings and recommendations to the president.

President George Washington organized the first presidential commission (to study the Whiskey Rebellion). But it was not until the twentieth century that presidents began using them with any regularity—forty-five presidential commissions were active in the mid-1990s.

(See 301 What happened during the Whiskey Rebellion?)

Q 282. Who was the first vice president appointed to head a presidential commission?

A President Dwight D. Eisenhower began the practice of naming the vice president as head of presidential commissions, both to lend prestige to the commission and to provide his vice president, Richard M. Nixon, with added responsibility. Nixon's first post as commission chairman came in 1953 when he headed a commission organized to end racial discrimination in federal contracting. Nixon later chaired another commission, the Cabinet Committee on Price Stability for Economic Growth. The only vice president since Nixon who did not chair a commission was Walter F. Mondale. He specifically asked President Jimmy Carter to be spared from commission duties, so that he could devote his time to acting as a presidential adviser and troubleshooter.

Q 283. Which first lady was first to head a presidential commission?

A Hillary Rodham Clinton was the first; early in his first term President Bill Clinton asked her to head his commission on health care reform. The first lady oversaw the formulation of the commission's recommendations and advocated passage of reform legislation before congressional committees. Ultimately, however, Congress refused to pass the legislation.

(See 180 What does the first lady do?)

Q 284. What notable commissions have presidents created?

A In the twentieth century, presidents established both permanent and temporary commissions to study a wide variety of issues and provide advice on them. As of the mid-1990s forty-five permanent presidential commissions were in place, ranging from the Committee to Preserve the White House to the National Commission on Alcoholism and Alcohol-Related Problems. Modern presidents also have formed high-profile ad hoc commissions, including the Aldrich Commission (1908–1912), which recommended creation of the Federal Reserve System; the President's Committee on Administrative Management (Brownlow Committee, 1936–1937), which led to creation of the Executive Office of the President; two Hoover Commissions (1947, 1953), which recommended further reorganization; the Warren Commission (1963–1964), which investigated President John F. Kennedy's assassination; and the Tower Commission (1986–1987), which investigated the Iran-contra affair.

FOR FURTHER INFORMATION

For more information on the powers and duties of the presidency, as well as its historical development, see first the mainstays: *Congressional Quarterly's Guide to the Presidency* (2d ed.), *The Presidency A to Z* (2d ed.), or the *Encyclopedia of the American Presidency*. At least one of these three should be available in most libraries. Also listed below are books that focus on more specific topics covered in this chapter. See, for example, *Powers of the Presidency, Presidential Vetoes and Public Policy,* and *Ten Presidents and the Press.*

Auei, Lisa B. *Tokens and Treasures: Gifts to Twelve Presidents.* Washington, D.C.: National Archives and Records, 1996.

Diamond, Edwin, and Robert Silverman. *White House to Your House: Media and Politics in Virtual America.* Cambridge: MIT Press, 1995.

Edwards, George C., III. *At the Margins: Presidential Leadership of Congress.* New Haven: Yale University Press, 1990.

Ellis, Richard J. *Presidential Lightning Rods: The Politics of Blame Avoidance.* Lawrence: University Press of Kansas, 1994.

Epstein, Lee, and Thomas G. Walker. *Constitutional Law for a Changing America: A Short Course.* 2d ed. Washington, D.C.: CQ Press, 2000.

Florig, Dennis. *The Power of Presidential Ideologies.* Westport, Conn.: Greenwood Press, 1992.

Graf, Henry F. *The Presidents: A Reference History.* New York: Macmillan, 1996.

Hess, Stephen. *Organizing the Presidency.* Washington, D.C.: Brookings, 1988.

Historic Documents on the Presidency, 1776–1989. Ed. Michael Nelson. Washington, D.C.: Congressional Quarterly, 1989.

Kellerman, Barbara, and Ryan J. Barilleaux. *The President as World Leader.* New York: St. Martin's Press, 1991.

Kernell, Samuel. *Going Public: New Strategies of Presidential Leadership.* 3d ed. Washington, D.C.: CQ Press, 1997.

LeLoup, Lance T., and Steven Shull. *Congress and the President: The Policy Connection.* Orlando, Fla.: Harcourt Brace, 1992.

Levy, Leonard W., and Louis Fisher. *Encyclopedia of the American Presidency.* New York: Simon and Shuster, 1993.

Nelson, Michael. *The Presidency and the Political System.* 6th ed. Washington, D.C.: CQ Press, 2000.

———, ed. *Congressional Quarterly's Guide to the Presidency.* 2d ed. Washington, D.C.: Congressional Quarterly, 1996.

———, ed. *The Evolving Presidency: Addresses, Cases, Essays, Letters, Reports, Resolutions, Transcripts, and Other Landmark Documents, 1787–1998.* Washington, D.C.: CQ Press, 1998.

———, *Powers of the Presidency.* 2d ed.Washington, D.C.: Congressional Quarterly, 1997.

———, *The Presidency A to Z.* 2d ed. Michael Nelson, advisory editor. Washington, D.C.: Congressional Quarterly, 1998.

Ragsdale, Lyn. *Vital Statistics on the Presidency: Washington to Clinton.* Rev. ed. Washington, D.C.: Congressional Quarterly, 1998.

Rejai, Mostafa, and Kay Phillips. *Demythologizing an Elite: American Presidents in Empirical, Comparative, and Historical Perspective.* Westport, Conn.: Greenwood Press, 1993.

Rivals for Power: Presidential-Congressional Relations. Ed. James A. Thurber. Washington, D.C.: CQ Press, 1996.

Rossiter, Clinton. *The Supreme Court and the Commander in Chief.* Ithaca: Cornell University Press, 1976.

Rozell, Mark J., and Clyde Wilcox. *Interest Groups in American Campaigns: The New Face of Electioneering.* Washington, D.C.: CQ Press, 1999.

Small, Norman J. *Some Presidential Interpretations of the Presidency.* New York: De Capo, 1970.

Suru, William D. *Presidential Cars and Transportation.* Iola, Wis.: Krause Publications, 1995.

The Supreme Court A to Z. 2d ed. Ed. Kenneth Jost. Washington, D.C.: Congressional Quarterly, 1998.

Thomas, Norman C., and Joseph A. Pika. *Politics of the Presidency.* Rev. 4th ed. Washington, D.C.: CQ Press, 1997.

Thompson, Kenneth W. *Ten Presidents and the Press.* Lanham, Md.: University Press of America, 1983.

Warshaw, Shirley A. *Powersharing: White House-Cabinet Relations in the Modern Presidency.* Albany: State University of New York Press, 1996.

Watson, Richard A. *Presidential Vetoes and Public Policy.* Lawrence: University Press of Kansas, 1993.

Wetterau, Bruce. *Congressional Quarterly's Desk Reference on the Federal Budget.* Washington, D.C.: CQ Press, 1998.

IV
THE PRESIDENCIES

IN GENERAL

Q 285. Which presidents served the longest and shortest periods of time?

A President Franklin D. Roosevelt spent just over twelve years in office—three full terms and part of a fourth. Sworn in on March 4, 1933, he served until his death on April 12, 1945. Before Roosevelt, the longest any president had served was eight years (two terms). The Twenty-second Amendment, ratified in 1951, now limits presidents to two terms.

William Henry Harrison holds the record for the shortest term of office, just one month. Harrison caught a severe cold while delivering his inaugural address on March 4, 1841, and died of pneumonia on April 4, 1841.

(See 178 Why was the two-term limit imposed on the presidency?)

▶ *Who were the oldest and youngest presidents? Vice presidents? See 145.*

Q 286. Has any president served nonconsecutive terms?

A President Grover Cleveland, a Democrat, was the first and, to date, only president to serve nonconsecutive terms. Elected to his first term by a narrow margin, 60,000 popular votes and 37 electoral votes, he served from 1885 to 1889. In the election of 1888 Cleveland polled 100,000 more popular votes than Republican Benjamin Harrison, but lost to him in the electoral college.

Cleveland practiced law in New York City after losing his reelection bid and then four years later again faced Harrison. This time Cleveland won both the popular and electoral votes, but an economic depression marred his second term, which ran from 1893 to 1897. The Democratic Party refused to renominate him in 1896.

Q **287. Which president oversaw the largest territorial expansion of the continental United States?**

A By authorizing his representatives to negotiate the Louisiana Purchase for $15 million in 1803, President Thomas Jefferson ultimately became responsible for doubling the size of the United States, adding more land (828,000 square miles) than any subsequent president. The huge tract purchased from France stretched from the Mississippi River to the Rocky Mountains and from the Gulf of Mexico to Canada. Even the vast territories the United States won during the Mexican War (1846–1848)—California, Arizona, New Mexico, and other western states—amounted to only 522,000 square miles.

President Jefferson, who had concluded the deal by executive agreement, was deeply concerned about the constitutionality of his actions, but the Senate ratified the treaty for the purchase in October 1803.

(See 279 Which president concluded the first executive agreement?)

▶ *Which presidents received the Nobel Peace Prize? See 147 Which two presidents won Nobel Prizes?*

Q **288. Where can I find presidential papers and speeches?**

A The best published source for modern presidents is the series *Public Papers of the Presidents of the United States Since Hoover,* published by the U.S. Government Printing Office and available in many libraries. Various collections of official papers and speeches have been published for earlier presidents, one of which is the Government Printing Office's *A Compilation of the Messages and Papers of the Presidents, 1789–1897.* Also, every president since Herbert Hoover has had a presidential library, which houses original copies of presidential papers. *(For addresses of the presidential libraries, see 166 Do all of the presidents have presidential libraries?)*

Q **289. When did the executive mansion become known as the "White House"?**

A "White House" did not become the official name of the executive mansion until 1901, when President Theodore Roosevelt issued an executive order to that effect. The name had been used informally for almost two centuries, however. President George Washington, who had much to do with the building of the executive mansion, gave the building its original—and thoroughly republican-sounding—name, the "President's House."

The mansion itself conspired to change Washington's designation, however. Its sandstone walls were naturally a light brown color, and in 1798, while construction was still under way, workers applied the first coat of whitewash, producing a bright white finish. That unmistakable feature of the huge building eventually led to the informal name "White House," which was used at least as early as 1809 (by Secretary of War Henry Dearborn) and was firmly entrenched by the 1820s. During the 1850s, "President's House" was officially abandoned altogether for the more formal-sounding "Executive Mansion." That remained the formal designation until President Roosevelt finally changed it.

Q 290. Who was the first president to live in the White House?

A President John Adams was the first. He arrived in the fall of 1800 to find work on the White House far from complete, and when First Lady Abigail Adams arrived two weeks later, things were not much improved. Only a few rooms were livable, and over a month passed before the first family had an outdoor privy available for their use. Nevertheless, the special meaning of the White House impressed itself on Adams, as it did on the presidents who succeeded him. On his second night there he composed a prayer, which he included in a letter to Abigail. Later engraved on the mantel over the fireplace in the State Dining Room, the prayer reads: "I Pray to Heaven to Bestow the Best of Blessings on THIS HOUSE, and on All that shall hereafter Inhabit it. May none but Honest and Wise Men ever rule under this Roof."

Q 291. When has the president's party held a majority in Congress?

A The president's party has held a majority in Congress more often than not—out of 106 Congresses, the White House and Congress have been controlled by the same party sixty-nine times, or 65 percent. Since 1945, however, the White House and Congress have been controlled by the same party only twenty-eight times, or 39 percent.

While a majority in Congress can provide smooth sledding for a president's legislative program, it is no guarantee. Feuding between factions of the party can cost the president the deciding votes needed for passage of favored legislation, or the president's party may have such a slim majority that just a few defections of party members can spell defeat for a bill.

Even though presidents may have a harder time when they face a Congress dominated by the opposition party—as all Republican presidents since Dwight D. Eisenhower have—the administration can still win legislative battles. But presidents must be more careful to build working coalitions with at least some legislators in the opposition party. Recent presidents and their party's standings in Congress are listed below (D–Democrat; R–Republican). The majority party in each chamber is listed first.

President	House	Senate
Herbert Hoover (R)		
1929–1931	R 267/D 167	R 56/D 39
1931–1933	D 220/R 214	R 48/D 47
Franklin D. Roosevelt (D)		
1933–1935	D 310/R 117	D 60/R 35
1935–1937	D 319/R 103	D 69/R 25
1937–1939	D 331/R 89	D 76/R 16
1939–1941	D 261/R 164	D 69/R 23
1941–1943	D 268/R162	D 66/R 28
1943–1945	D 218/R 208	D 58/R 37
Harry S. Truman (D)		
1945–1947	D 242/R 190	D 56/R 38
1947–1949	R 245/D 188	R 51/D 45
1949–1951	D 263/R 171	D 54/R 42
1951–1953	D 234/R 199	D 49/R 47
Dwight D. Eisenhower (R)		
1953–1955	R 221/D 211	R 48/D 47
1955–1957	D 232/R 203	D 48/R 47
1957–1959	D 233/R 200	D 49/R 47
1959–1961	D 283/R 153	D 64/R 34
John F. Kennedy (D)		
1961–1963	D 263/R 174	D 65/R 35
Kennedy/Johnson (D)		
1963–1965	D 258/R 177	D 67/R 33
Lyndon B. Johnson (D)		
1965–1967	D 295/R 140	D 68/R 32
1967–1969	D 247/R 187	D 64/R 36

President	House	Senate
Richard M. Nixon (R)		
1969–1971	D 243/R 192	D 57/R 43
1971–1973	D 254/R 180	D 54/R 44
Nixon/Ford (R)		
1973–1975	D 239/R 192	D 56/R 42
1975–1977	D 291/R 144	D 60/R 37
Jimmy Carter (D)		
1977–1979	D 292/R 143	D 61/R 38
1979–1981	D 276/R 157	D 58/R 41
Ronald Reagan (R)		
1981–1983	D 243/R 192	R 53/D 46
1983–1985	D 269/R 165	R 54/D 46
1985–1987	D 252/R 182	R 53/D 47
1987–1989	D 258/R 177	D 55/R 45
George Bush (R)		
1989–1991	D 259/R 174	D 55/R 45
1991–1993	D 267/R 167	D 56/R 44
Bill Clinton (D)		
1993–1995	D 258/R 176	D 57/R 43
1995–1997	R 230/D 204	R 53/D 47
1997–1998	R 227/D 207	R 55/D 45

(See 236 Do presidents have an easier time with Congress when their party has a majority in Congress?)

Q 292. Who became president without having been elected to the office?

A Vice President Gerald R. Ford became president in 1974, even though he had not been elected to either the vice presidency or the presidency. The Republican Party's minority leader in the House of Representatives, Ford was appointed to the vice presidency in late 1973 under the Twenty-fifth Amendment (1967). The elected vice president, Spiro T. Agnew, resigned over charges he had received bribes during his years in state government.

At the time, President Richard M. Nixon and his White House staff also were being investigated for abuses of power related to the Watergate affair. Nixon was eventually forced to resign, and on August 9, 1974, Ford succeeded to the presidency. In December 1974 Ford appointed former New York governor Nelson A. Rockefeller to fill the vacancy in the vice presidency.

(See 58 Which president resigned from office? 59 Have any vice presidents resigned from office? 373 What happened in the Watergate scandal?)

Q **293. What have presidents said about the presidency?**

A While the nation's highest office has never wanted for suitors, those who serve as president sometimes come away with a decidedly less enthusiastic view of the job. The never-ending pressures of responsibility and power, the incessant intrusions into their personal lives, as well as the sheer volume of work clearly weigh on presidents. Here is what some presidents have said about the job:

John Adams. "No man who ever held the office of President would congratulate a friend on obtaining it. He will make one man ungrateful, and a hundred men his enemies, for every office he can bestow."

Thomas Jefferson. "To myself, personally, [the presidency] brings nothing but unceasing drudgery and daily loss of friends."

Andrew Jackson. "I am engaged preparing for [the meeting of Congress], and this with my other labors, employs me day and night. I can with truth say mine is a situation of dignified slavery."

James A. Garfield. ". . . the last person in the world to know what the people really want and think [is the president]."

Theodore Roosevelt. "Oh, if I could only be president and Congress too, for just ten minutes."

Herbert Hoover. "There are only two occasions when Americans respect privacy, especially in presidents. Those are fishing and prayer."

Harry S. Truman. "Well all the president is, is a glorified public relations man who spends his time flattering, kissing, and kicking people to get them to do what they are supposed to do anyway."

John F. Kennedy. "I had plenty of problems when I came into office. But wait until the fellow who follows me sees what he will inherit."

Lyndon B. Johnson. "A president's hardest task is not to do what is right but to know what is right."

Q 294. What is the "twenty-year jinx" on the presidency?

A Like all superstitions, the twenty-year jinx on the presidency is a matter of unfortunate coincidence, not an unnatural force directed at presidents. Nevertheless, presidents who were elected at every twenty-year interval from 1840 to 1960 wound up dead while in office, either by assassination or by natural causes. Not every president died immediately after being elected at one of the twenty-year intervals, however. President Ronald Reagan, who was elected in 1980, broke the jinx by surviving an assassination attempt against him in 1981 to serve out two full terms.

The seven presidents who were elected at twenty-year intervals and who then died while in office were: William Henry Harrison, elected 1840, died 1841; Abraham Lincoln, elected 1860, assassinated 1865; James A. Garfield, elected 1880, assassinated 1881; William McKinley, elected 1900, assassinated 1901; Warren G. Harding, elected 1920, died 1923; Franklin D. Roosevelt, elected 1940, died 1945; John F. Kennedy, elected 1960, assassinated 1963.

▶ *How many presidents died while in office? See 55 Which presidents died in office?*

Q 295. Which presidents and first ladies died in the White House?

A Two presidents and three first ladies died there. Presidents William Henry Harrison and Zachary Taylor both died of natural causes soon after moving into the White House (1841 and 1850, respectively). President John Tyler's wife Letitia (died 1842) was the first of the first ladies to pass away in the White House. The victim of a stroke in 1839, she was already an invalid when Tyler succeeded to the presidency after William Henry Harrison's untimely death. She died at the White House a few months after her daughter Elizabeth's White House wedding. Caroline Harrison, wife of President Benjamin Harrison, died of tuberculosis in 1892, during her husband's unsuccessful reelection bid. The last first lady to die in the White House was Woodrow Wilson's wife Ellen, who succumbed to a kidney ailment in 1914.

(See 55 Which presidents died in office? 132 Which presidents' wives died prematurely? 133 Which presidents' children died while their fathers were in office? 135 Where are the presidents' wives buried? 173 When did the presidents and vice presidents die?)

296. Which presidents were assassinated?

A The nation has been shocked four times by assassinations of presidents. Abraham Lincoln, James A. Garfield, William McKinley, and John F. Kennedy all fell to assassins' bullets.

Abraham Lincoln. The Civil War had just ended when, on the evening of April 14, 1865, President Lincoln and the first lady attended a play, *Our American Cousin,* at Ford's Theater in Washington, D.C. Actor John Wilkes Booth had been planning to kill the president for some time. That night he gained access to Lincoln's booth at the theater and shot him from behind at point-blank range. Mortally wounded, Lincoln was taken across the street to a boardinghouse, where he died the next morning. Soldiers trapped Booth on a Virginia farm and shot him dead on April 26.

James A. Garfield. In office only four months, President Garfield arrived at the Washington, D.C., train station on July 2, 1881, to begin a tour of New England. At the station, a disgruntled office-seeker named Charles J. Guiteau walked up to Garfield and shot him twice, shouting, "I am a Stalwart; now Arthur is president!" With a bullet lodged near his spine, Garfield remained alive for two months before finally dying, probably of blood poisoning. Guiteau, who may have been insane, was tried and convicted of the slaying and hanged on June 30, 1882.

William McKinley. Invited to speak at the Pan-American Exposition in Buffalo, New York, on September 6, 1901, McKinley was greeting people in a receiving line when an anarchist named Leon Czolgosz walked up and shot him in the stomach. Doctors were unable to find the bullet, but McKinley appeared to recover over the next few days. Fever and gangrene eventually set in, however, and on September 14 McKinley died. Czolgosz, who had been captured at the scene, was convicted and executed.

John F. Kennedy. Visiting Dallas, Texas, on November 22, 1963, President Kennedy was riding in a motorcade through the downtown area with First Lady Jacqueline Kennedy at his side. Suddenly shots rang out from the Texas School Book Depository, a building along the route, and Kennedy was struck in the neck and head. Rushed to the hospital, he died at 1:15 p.m. Lee Harvey Oswald, a maladjusted worker at the book depository who had once defected to the Soviet Union, was arrested as the assassin. Two days later he was shot and killed by Dallas nightclub owner Jack Ruby.

(See 154 Did President Garfield's doctors contribute to his death from an assassin's bullet? 161 What medical condition left John F. Kennedy near death before he became president?)

Q 297. Which presidents survived assassination attempts?

A Five presidents were victims of attempted assassinations—Andrew Jackson, Franklin D. Roosevelt, Harry S. Truman, Gerald R. Ford, and Ronald Reagan. All were the targets of gun-wielding, would-be assassins.

Andrew Jackson escaped almost certain death on January 30, 1835, at the Capitol Building when an insane house painter, Richard Lawrence, fired two pistols at the president while standing just a few feet away. Luck was with the shocked president, however, because both pistols misfired and the would-be assassin was apprehended.

Franklin Roosevelt, while president-elect, was shot at by anarchist Joseph Zangara on February 15, 1933, in Miami, Florida. The bullets missed Roosevelt, but Chicago mayor Anton J. Cermak was killed in the attack.

Harry Truman was the intended victim of two Puerto Rican nationalists. On November 1, 1950, they tried to enter Blair House in Washington, D.C., where the Trumans were staying while the White House was being renovated. In the gunfight that erupted, one policeman and one would-be assassin were killed. Police caught the other assailant.

Gerald Ford escaped two attempts while visiting California in September 1975. The first occurred in Sacramento on September 5 when Lynette "Squeaky" Fromme approached Ford with a gun before being wrestled to the ground. Soon after, on September 22, a self-styled revolutionary named Sara Jane Moore fired a single shot while Ford was walking to his car from a San Francisco hotel. Ford was rushed away from the scene.

Ronald Reagan was seriously wounded on March 30, 1981, outside a Washington, D.C., hotel by would-be assassin John W. Hinckley Jr. Hinckley also seriously wounded Reagan's press secretary, James Brady, and a police officer. President Reagan lost a considerable amount of blood, but was rushed to the hospital where emergency treatment saved his life. Reagan was the first president to be wounded by an assassin and survive.

(See 162 How seriously was Ronald Reagan wounded during the 1981 assassination attempt?)

Q 298. Which president's son was on the scene of three presidential assassinations?

A Abraham Lincoln's oldest son, Robert Todd Lincoln, did not witness the shootings themselves, but in each of three assassinations he had the misfortune of arriving shortly afterward. When his father was shot on April 15, 1865, Todd was brought to the boardinghouse across the street from Ford's Theater, where his father lay dying. Sixteen years later, on July 2, 1881, he was serving as James A. Garfield's secretary of war and went to the Washington railroad station to deliver a message to the president. The unfortunate Lincoln arrived on the scene just after Garfield had been shot. Then two decades later, President William McKinley invited Lincoln to attend a speech he planned to give at the Pan-American Exposition in Buffalo, New York. Lincoln arrived there on September 6, 1901, just minutes after McKinley had been fatally wounded by an assassin.

Q **299. Who was the first president to have a bodyguard?**

A President Franklin Pierce was the first to have a full-time bodyguard, a federal employee named Thomas O'Neil. Although Pierce left no record of why he wanted the protection, it was at his request. Perhaps it was because he had witnessed the attempted assassination of Andrew Jackson and was besieged daily by office-seekers at the White House. Or perhaps it was because the presidency in Pierce's time conferred more of a celebrity status than had been known before. Pierce's appearances in public invariably drew hordes of well-wishers who pushed and shoved for the opportunity to shake his hand.

Bodyguards were used routinely by later presidents. Because of tensions between the North and South in 1860, for example, President Abraham Lincoln was regularly surrounded by bodyguards, even during his election campaign. Among them was the founder of the Pinkerton detective agency, Alan Pinkerton.

WORDS AND DEEDS

Q **300. What did President George Washington mean when he said, "I walk on untrodden ground"?**

A As the first president under the Constitution, Washington was well aware that his actions would set the direction and tone of the presidency. "I walk on untrodden ground," he said. "There is scarcely any part of my conduct which may not hereinafter be drawn into precedent." He knew that having suffered under British rule, Americans still distrusted executive power and that "the first transactions of a nation . . . make the deepest impression." His enormous popularity had helped make the presidency possible, but a key task as president was to make executive power consistent with representative democracy. To that end, he favored the republican title "President of the United States" over more regal-sounding alternatives and established a tradition (which has not survived) of meeting personally with the public at the executive mansion on a regular basis.

During his first term, President Washington established the precedent that executive authority belonged only to the president. In keeping with that precedent, he won passage of a bill giving him the sole power to dismiss executive officers, even though Senate confirmation was required to appoint them in the first place. But in keeping with his firm belief in the separation of powers, he left the legislative process to Congress. He recommended legislation to Congress from time to time but did not actively push for its passage (which presidents do today). As for his veto power, Washington used it sparingly, only when he believed a bill was unconstitutional and not because he disagreed with the measure.

Washington also tried to set the precedent that the president would be above partisan politics and would act only for the good of the nation. Despite his efforts, however, political parties did begin to develop, and during the presidency of his successor, John Adams, party conflict became a permanent feature of the government.

(See 226 Who has the power to make laws, Congress or the president?)

Q 301. What happened during the Whiskey Rebellion?

A A tax revolt by farmers in western Pennsylvania known as the Whiskey Rebellion became the first real test of strength for President George Washington and the newly formed federal government he led. For many years farmers had converted their excess corn into whiskey, which they sold. Beginning in 1791, though, many of them refused to pay a hefty federal excise tax on the whiskey, and in western Pennsylvania attacks on revenue agents became a serious problem. When the Pennsylvania governor refused President Washington's order to use the militia to quash the rebellion in 1794, Washington turned out the militias of the surrounding states—some 15,000 strong—and took personal command. That put an end to the rebellion without so much as a shot being fired. Washington later pardoned the rebels convicted after the revolt.

(See 206 Can the president pardon criminals? 207 What does the president do as commander in chief?)

Q 302. What effect did the Jay Treaty have on Washington's administration?

A The 1794 treaty with Britain, called the Jay Treaty, averted a war but aroused the first serious partisan opposition to Washington's administration. John Jay, Washington's

Federalist administration, and even Washington himself became targets of partisan attacks because of it (Jay was burned in effigy).

The threat of war had loomed in the 1790s because the British had failed to evacuate posts in the Old Northwest as agreed and their agents were encouraging Indians to attack American settlers. In addition, by 1794 the British navy had seized some three hundred American ships bound for France, then at war with Britain.

To avert war, President Washington sent the chief justice of the United States, John Jay, to Britain to negotiate a treaty (Washington broke with his own precedent by not informing Congress beforehand of the terms he sought). The Jay Treaty called for evacuation of the Old Northwest, creation of a commission to adjust shipping claims, establishment of the border between the United States and Canada, and settlement of pre-Revolutionary War debts and claims of British Loyalists.

Thomas Jefferson's Democratic-Republican supporters believed the treaty was a sellout and openly criticized the administration for it. Among other things, they complained that the treaty infringed on U.S. neutral rights and allowed the British to impress (seize) American sailors. The Senate ratified the treaty on June 24, 1795, by a vote of 20–10.

(See 257 How does the president conclude a treaty?)

Q 303. How did Thomas Jefferson describe the two parties into which people naturally divide?

A Thomas Jefferson and his followers in the Democratic-Republican Party railed against the aristocratic tendencies they saw in the Federalist administrations of Washington and Adams. So, when President Jefferson took office in 1801, he deliberately set the presidency on a more republican course (among other things, at the White House he replaced the custom of bowing with a simple, republican handshake). For Jefferson, the divide between Federalists and his Democratic-Republican Party was simple: "Men by their constitutions are naturally divided into two parties: 1. Those who fear and distrust the people, and wish to draw all powers from them into the hands of the higher classes. 2. Those who identify themselves with the people, have confidence in them, cherish and consider them as the most honest and safe, although not the most wise depository of the public interests . . ." (letter to Henry Lee, August 10, 1824).

Q 304. How did "Mr. Madison's War" begin?

A When President James Madison took office in 1809, pressure for war against Britain was building. Britain, at war with France, was interfering with American trade, and British navy ships were impressing (seizing) American sailors on the high seas. Hoping to convince the British of American resolve, Madison asked Congress to approve war preparedness measures in November 1811. But the War Hawks in Congress wanted war and finally forced Madison to ask for a declaration of war in June 1812.

The War of 1812 became "Mr. Madison's War" when troops were needed for a preemptive strike into British Canada. With a national standing army of only a few thousand troops, Madison had little choice but to use the state militias. He turned first to the New England states, which had opposed going to war in the first place. The Massachusetts and Connecticut governors refused outright to take part in what they denounced as "Mr. Madison's War," forcing Madison to look to other states for troops.

Q 305. Why did the British burn the White House in 1814?

A The burning of the White House during the War of 1812 was in retaliation for an earlier American attack on the British colonial city of Toronto, Canada. The British invasion force landed some distance from Washington, D.C., in late August 1814 with the prime objective of burning the American capital. By August 24 they had overwhelmed the last American forces outside Washington, and President James Madison, who was observing the battle, sent word to First Lady Dolley Madison to leave the White House for safer territory.

Meanwhile, Dolley bravely tried to follow the normal White House routine as nearly as possible to keep from starting a panic in the city. She even had the usual midafternoon dinner prepared and the table set, in case President Madison should return from the battlefield. Against the worst, however, she had one coach filled with as many state papers as it would hold.

The messenger from President Madison arrived about three in the afternoon and in the final minutes before her hasty departure, Dolley had the Gilbert Stuart portrait of George Washington taken down and removed to safety. She also took along some silver, ornaments, and red velvet curtains that had been packed away.

The British soldiers arrived in the city about seven-thirty that evening. After setting fire to the Capitol Building, they headed to the White House. The officers helped themselves to the president's dinner that Dolley had laid out, while their troops made preparations to burn the mansion. About an hour later they lit the fires and watched as the White House, enveloped in smoke and fire, was gutted. The marauding British then burned the executive offices as well.

Q 306. Which president introduced the "spoils system"?

A Patronage—the practice of rewarding loyal party members with appointive offices in the government—began during President George Washington's second term. Washington was responding to the rise of partisan opposition from the followers of Thomas Jefferson and refused to appoint anyone who did not support the Federalist Party. When he took office, Jefferson too limited his appointments to fellow Democratic-Republicans.

But this was a far cry from President Andrew Jackson's theory of "rotation in office." Jackson enthusiastically embraced the idea of wholesale replacement of political opponents with loyal party followers. Indeed, he defended the notion as a means of reforming the government, but initially carried out the reshuffling in such a heavy-handed fashion that it aroused considerable protest. Jackson's campaign manager, Martin Van Buren, was more experienced in such matters and took over the process.

Van Buren's only mistake was in deliberately barring Vice President John C. Calhoun's followers from office. They complained bitterly that Van Buren was corrupting the public service. When the matter came up before the Senate, Democratic senator William Marcy of New York defended Van Buren by saying he saw nothing wrong with the rule "to the victor belong the spoils." That gave Jackson's system of "rotation" a name that has been used ever since—the spoils system. Patronage declined in importance—but did not disappear—after enactment of the Pendleton Act (Civil Service Reform Act) in 1883.

(See 202 How do presidents turn patronage and pork-barrel projects to their advantage?)

Q 307. How did President Jackson test Vice President Calhoun's loyalties?

A The 1830s were a time of increasing tensions between the North and South over slavery and other issues. Vice President John C. Calhoun, born into a family of wealthy South Carolina planters, had backed the national government's interests earlier in his career, but by the late 1820s he was changing his mind.

President Andrew Jackson noticed Calhoun's shift from nationalist to states' rights sentiments. Deciding to see exactly where Calhoun's loyalties lay, Jackson delivered a pointed toast at a Jefferson Day dinner on April 13, 1830. Looking directly at Calhoun, Jackson offered the salutation, "Our Union—it must be preserved." Calhoun accepted the challenge and responded, "The Union, next to our liberties, most dear."

With that, Calhoun effectively cast his lot with the South. Two years later, in 1832, Calhoun's home state of South Carolina sparked what became known as the "Nullification Crisis" by declaring federal tariffs invalid within its borders. But when President Jackson threatened to use 200,000 troops to enforce the law, South Carolina officials agreed to a compromise tariff. Calhoun, meanwhile, was dropped from Jackson's reelection ticket in 1832. He then resigned from office in December 1832, becoming the first vice president to do so.

(See 59 Have any vice presidents resigned from office?)

▶ *How did Vice President Tyler deal with the constitutional uncertainty over his succession to office? See 221 What precedent did Vice President John Tyler set in 1841?*

Q 308. How did the explosion onboard the U.S.S. *Princeton* change President Tyler's life?

A Eager to show his support for the military, President John Tyler attended the test firing of a new 12-inch super cannon, the Peacemaker, aboard the warship U.S.S. *Princeton* on February 28, 1844. Unlike conventional cannons, this one was made of wrought iron and was so powerful that it could fire balls weighing several hundred pounds.

The huge cannon was fired twice with Tyler and other admiring dignitaries standing nearby. Tyler was heading back up to the deck for the third shot when his son-in-law delayed him briefly by singing a short military song. The ditty took just long enough for the president to miss the firing—and the tragic explosion of the gun's breech that killed eight onlookers.

Among the dead were Tyler's secretary of state, secretary of the navy, and his friend David Gardiner, who was the father of Julia Gardiner, a young woman he had been seeing since a short time after his wife's death in 1842. Just four months after the *Princeton* explosion, Tyler shocked the country again by marrying Julia, a beautiful twenty-four-year-old who was less than half his age.

(See 130 Which presidential family had the most children? The fewest? 164 Did any presidents run for political office after leaving the presidency?)

Q 309. What was "Manifest Destiny"?

A By this popular doctrine Americans justified the rapid westward expansion of the country during the mid-1800s, including the annexation of Texas, the conquest of the Southwest and West, and eventually even the acquisition of Alaska and Hawaii. "Manifest destiny" was meant to imply that Americans had an almost sacred duty to push westward to provide new opportunities and more room for the country's growing population. The term was first used in mid-1845 by newspaper editor John L. O'Sullivan, who was writing in favor of annexing Texas.

Q 310. Who preached peace while waging war?

A To wrest California and the present-day southwestern United States from Mexican control, President James K. Polk deliberately provoked a war with Mexico in 1846. By adroit maneuvering, however, he billed the war he had ignited as a defensive fight against Mexican belligerence, and in his annual message to Congress on December 8, 1846, he proclaimed, "The war will continue to be prosecuted with vigor as the best means of securing peace."

The annexation of Texas in 1845, which Mexico regarded as a hostile act, was the burr that helped drive Mexico to war. After the annexation, President Polk sent U.S. troops into disputed territory along the Texas border, hoping the Mexicans would attack the troops and provide him with an excuse for declaring war. (He had been willing to offer over $30 million for the disputed territory, New Mexico, and California, but the Mexicans refused to even talk to his emissary.) By the spring of 1846, Polk had lost almost all patience and was about to declare war without any provocation when the Mexicans finally attacked the troops. Wasting no time, Polk immediately asked Congress for a declaration of war. Successful American invasions of Mexico ended the war in early 1848 and gained Polk all the territory he had wanted.

Q 311. How did Abraham Lincoln and Jefferson Davis frame the opposing objectives of the North and South in the Civil War?

A The years of bitter debate between North and South over slavery had left the South primed and ready to fight, and Abraham Lincoln's election as president in 1860 was the spark that ignited the Civil War. Lincoln was not an abolitionist, and, even though he campaigned against extending slavery into new territories, neither he nor his newly formed Republican Party called for an end to it in states where it existed. Nevertheless, the South refused to accept his presidency and a few weeks after his election seceded from the Union.

For Lincoln, even after a year of fighting between North and South, slavery was not the central issue of the conflict. Writing to newspaper publisher Horace Greeley on August 22, 1862, he said, "My paramount object in this struggle is to save the Union, and is not either to save or to destroy slavery. If I could save the Union without freeing any slave, I would do it; and if I could save it by freeing all the slaves, I would do it; and if I could save it by freeing some and leaving others alone, I would also do that." Lincoln did make ending slavery a part of the war, however, when he issued his Emancipation Proclamation on January 1, 1863.

Jefferson Davis gave an equally succinct assessment of the South's reasons for fighting. In his inaugural address as Confederate president on February 18, 1861, he said simply, "All we ask is to be let alone."

Q 312. Which famous speech did President Lincoln begin with the words "Four score and seven years ago . . ."?

A Abraham Lincoln's Gettysburg Address, among the most famous ever delivered by a president, begins with those memorable words. Expected to deliver only a brief speech at the dedication of a national cemetery at Gettysburg, Pennsylvania, on November 19, 1863, Lincoln took the podium after a two-hour address by the famous orator Edward Everett. He then delivered his brief speech to the audience of 15,000 gathered on Cemetery Ridge, where only a few months earlier Confederate troops had been defeated and the tide of the war had turned. Because his speech was so short and the audience's reaction was merely polite applause, Lincoln felt the speech had gone badly. Newspaper reports were mixed, but over the years Lincoln's brief address has gained its rightful place as a remarkable expression of the democratic ideal.

GETTYSBURG ADDRESS

Four score and seven years ago our fathers brought forth on this continent, a new nation, conceived in Liberty, and dedicated to the proposition that all men are created equal.

Now we are engaged in a great civil war, testing whether that nation or any nation so conceived and so dedicated, can long endure. We are met on a great battle-field of that war. We have come to dedicate a portion of that field, as a final resting place for those who here gave their lives that that nation might live. It is altogether fitting and proper that we should do this.

But, in a larger sense, we can not dedicate—we can not consecrate—we can not hallow—this ground. The brave men, living and dead, who struggled here, have consecrated it, far above our poor power to add or detract. The world will little note, nor long remember, what we say here, but it can never forget what they did here. It is for us the living, rather, to be dedicated here to the unfinished work which they who fought here have thus far so nobly advanced. It is rather for us to be dedicated here to the great task remaining before us—that from these honored dead we take increased devotion to that cause for which they gave the last full measure of devotion—that we here highly resolve that these dead shall not have died in vain—that this nation, under God, shall have a new birth of freedom—and that government of the people, by the people, for the people, shall not perish from the earth.

▶ *What was the "stolen election"? See 440 What deal was made to win Republican Rutherford B. Hayes the presidency in 1876?*

313. Did President McKinley want the war against Spain?

Though some denounced President William McKinley as a weakling, he resisted the war fever overtaking the country early in 1898 as sentiment for the Spanish-American War mounted. "I have been through one war," the Civil War veteran said, "I have seen the dead piled up and I do not want to see another." Even after the U.S. battleship *Maine* inexplicably exploded February 15, 1898, while tied up in the harbor at Havana, Cuba, McKinley opposed declaring war against Spain until all efforts at negotiating had been exhausted. In early April 1898, however, he finally yielded to the pressure and asked Congress to declare war. American forces quickly gained control of Cuba, Puerto Rico, the Philippines, and Guam, which became U.S. possessions.

314. What was President Theodore Roosevelt's "Square Deal"?

Speaking out in 1902 against the mighty business trusts in industries such as the railroads, steel, and oil, President Theodore Roosevelt proclaimed, "We demand that big business give people a square deal." The monopolistic trusts, he declared, had become so powerful that small businesses and workers could not hope to stand up to them. Roosevelt's Square Deal sought to level the playing field, and he did so by using federal antitrust laws to attack the trusts' monopolistic business practices in the courts.

The first big success for Roosevelt's "trust-busting" program came in 1902 when the government won its antitrust suit against Northern Securities Company, a railroad conglomerate run by J. P. Morgan and John D. Rockefeller. The victory popularized the Square Deal, and over the next seven years the Roosevelt administration hauled forty-three other big corporations into court. Roosevelt pushed Congress to strengthen the Interstate Commerce Commission, the first federal regulatory commission, and by pressing for passage of the Pure Food and Drug Act of 1906, he helped to introduce the idea of federal responsibility for consumer protection.

Q 315. Which proverb did President Theodore Roosevelt like to quote?

A Speaking of the best way to handle foreign affairs, Roosevelt once said, "Speak softly and carry a big stick, [and] you will go far." That sentiment regularly revealed itself in his actions as president, but nowhere was it more evident than in his foreign policy. Roosevelt's "big stick"—the threat of force—was the U.S. Navy. By badgering Congress for new battleships at every opportunity, he managed to build the navy into the world's second most powerful (behind Britain), and he used it to intervene militarily in the Caribbean and elsewhere.

Perhaps the best example of his "big stick" tactics was his acquisition of U.S. rights to the land for the Panama Canal. When Colombia rejected an offer of $10 million, Roosevelt simply encouraged a revolt in Panama, which was then under Colombian control. To make sure the revolt succeeded, he sent the warship *Nashville* to Panama, where it turned back a Colombian attempt to attack the Panamanian capital from the sea. Thus established as a republic, Panama agreed to lease the United States a canal zone six miles wide for $10 million and an annual fee. Construction of the canal itself then began. The canal remained under U.S. control until 1999, when it was turned over to the Panamanian government.

Q 316. What did President Wilson say when he called for America's entry into World War I?

A Insisting that the "world must be made safe for democracy," on April 2, 1917, President Woodrow Wilson called on Congress to declare war against Germany. With World War I already under way, Wilson's address came shortly after Germany announced it would resume unrestricted submarine warfare. Underscoring America's major aim, Wilson went on to say that the world's peace "must be planted upon the tested foundations of political liberty. We have no selfish ends to serve. We desire no conquest, no dominion. . . ."

At war's end, Wilson remained true to his original declaration. His famous "Fourteen Points," which in 1918 outlined his proposals for the treaty to end World War I, sought no territory for the United States. And one key provision proposed creation of an international body (the League of Nations) to promote peace and make the world "safe for democracy." President Wilson's idea for the League of Nations was included in the Treaty of Versailles, which ended World War I, but the U.S. Senate refused to ratify the treaty. The U.S. refusal to participate in the league was among the reasons for the organization's failure in the 1930s.

Q 317. Did President Warren G. Harding suspect his friends in office were up to no good?

A Warren Harding was a well-intentioned, easygoing president who liked playing poker with friends but who was far too trusting of them. Some of those he appointed to his administration took advantage of their positions. By most accounts, though, Harding himself was personally honest and had no involvement in his friends' scandalous behavior, which eventually plagued his presidency, notably in the Teapot Dome scandal.

While he probably did not know exactly what his friends were up to, Harding apparently suspected something. He once reportedly lamented, "My God, this is a hell of a job! I have no trouble with my enemies. I can take care of my enemies all right. But my damn friends, my goddamn friends. . . . They're the ones that keep me walking the floor nights!"

(See 372 What happened in the Teapot Dome scandal?)

Q 318. What were "Hoovervilles"?

A By the election of 1932, Republican President Herbert Hoover was bearing the brunt of the blame for the Great Depression. Although his policies had not caused the stock market crash of 1929 or the depression that followed, both happened on his watch and many Americans blamed him for them. His fiscal conservatism and feeble efforts at easing the suffering of millions of jobless Americans confirmed that impression for many people and became political fodder for the Democrats, who actively played to the resentment by heaping abuse on Hoover.

Shantytowns were nothing new in America, but by 1931 the rude shacks appearing in places like New York City's Riverside Park were being called "Hoovervilles." Shoes with holes in them became "Hoover shoes," and the newspapers hobos covered themselves with at night were called "Hoover blankets."

Q 319. What did President Roosevelt mean when he said, "The only thing we have to fear is fear itself"?

A When Franklin D. Roosevelt took office in March 1933, there was indeed much to fear. After the stock market crash of 1929 the nation sank into the Great Depression; 25 percent of American workers were jobless and thousands were losing their homes, businesses, and farms. As if that were not enough, a banking crisis in 1933 threatened to start a panic that would destroy the banking system.

With the economy in a shambles, President Roosevelt began his inaugural address by reminding Americans that the nation was fundamentally strong and would recover. "The only thing we have to fear," he warned, "is fear itself—nameless, unreasoning, unjustified terror which paralyzes needed efforts to convert retreat into advance." He went on to describe in broad terms what could be done and how. By using his emergency powers as president and by introducing legislation in Congress, his administration would begin actively working to end the depression. The New Deal programs he established did not actually end the depression, but they did much to ease the suffering of millions and wrought fundamental changes in American society.

(See 336 What effect did FDR's "fireside chats" have?)

Q 320. What did FDR do after learning about the Pearl Harbor attack?

A On the morning of December 7, 1941, President Franklin D. Roosevelt remained closeted in his Oval Office. The night before he had read decoded copies of the Japanese government's secret instructions to its ambassador in Washington. On seeing them, the president said, "This means war." The fact that Japan was planning an attack was already known, but the attack was expected in Asia. That Sunday morning the navy base at Pearl Harbor in Hawaii had let down its guard, and it proved a disastrous mistake.

President Roosevelt received the first news of Japan's sneak attack on Pearl Harbor at 1:40 Sunday afternoon, via a telephone call from Navy Secretary Frank Knox. After consulting with his top military advisers that afternoon, Roosevelt went before Congress the next day to ask for a declaration of war. Calling December 7, 1941, "a date which will live in infamy," Roosevelt told Congress, "America was suddenly and deliberately attacked by naval and air forces of the Empire of Japan. We will gain the inevitable triumph, so help us God." Congress voted the declaration of war that day, and three days later also formally declared war on Germany, Japan's ally.

Q 321. What convinced President Truman to order the atom bomb dropped on Japan?

A Thrust into office by Franklin D. Roosevelt's death in 1945, Harry S. Truman soon confronted not only the ongoing war in Europe and the Pacific, but also the dilemma posed by the nation's newest weapon, the atom bomb. The bomb, which had cost $2 billion to build, was so powerful and so daunting that Truman's top advisers believed it would "shock" the Japanese into unconditional surrender without any further bloodshed.

This was an important consideration. Japan had lost the war a year earlier and yet continued to fight on resolutely. On the Japanese island of Okinawa, tens of thousands of Japanese soldiers had fought to the death, long after there was any hope of winning. Twelve thousand Americans had been killed and thirty-six thousand wounded for that one small island. Now the Japanese were arming the civilian population on the main islands for another suicidal last stand to repulse the coming American invasion—this in the face of devastating nightly American firebombing raids that were decimating Japanese cities and killing hundreds of thousands at a clip.

For Truman, the atom bomb was "the most terrible bomb in the history of the world," but he had little doubt about the decision to use it. This was war and the bomb provided an alternative to an invasion by American troops. He wrote later with his characteristic directness, "It occurred to me that a quarter of a million of the flower of our young manhood were worth a couple of Japanese cities, and I still think they were and are."

Q 322. What reason did Truman give for seizing the steel mills?

A President Harry S. Truman justified his seizure of the steel plants on April 9, 1952, by saying an interruption in steel production would hurt the Korean War effort. The thousands of U.S. troops fighting in Korea were depending on U.S.-made arms and supplies from the United States. Thus when the steelworkers' unions announced plans to strike, Truman seized control of the mills to keep them operating. He based his action on his emergency powers as commander in chief and noted that Congress could countermand the order.

Congress did not, but the Supreme Court did. Ruling in a suit (*Youngstown Sheet and Tube Co. v. Sawyer*) brought by the steel mills in 1952, the Court said only Congress, not the president, had the authority to order the seizure. It noted that Congress had in fact specifically excluded government seizures to prevent strikes in the Taft-Hartley Act of 1947. The Court's ruling was one of the few in this century to curb the expansion of presidential powers.

(See 241 Did the Supreme Court rule against expansion of presidential powers in the last century?)

Q 323. What did President Eisenhower propose as "The Chance for Peace"?

A In perhaps the best speech of his presidency, Dwight D. Eisenhower in April 1953 publicly called on the Soviet Union to agree to end the nuclear arms race. Called "The Chance for Peace," the president's address noted that the arms race was draining money away from the poor who needed food, clothing, and shelter. Continuing it would have no good end: "The worst to be feared and the best to be expected can be simply stated," he said. "The worst is atomic war. The best would be this: a life of perpetual fear and tension; a burden of arms draining the wealth and labor of all peoples." Eisenhower's overture to the Soviet Union came in the wake of Soviet dictator Joseph Stalin's death in 1953, but the Soviets did not respond. They also ignored a follow-up proposal aimed at easing cold war tensions. Under Eisenhower's 1955 Open Skies plan, U.S. and Soviet aircraft would have been allowed to overfly each other's countries.

(See 356 What cold war policies did the Truman Doctrine establish?)

Q 324. What did JFK hope to inspire when he said, "Ask not what your country can do for you . . . "?

A As a presidential candidate, John F. Kennedy campaigned on the Democratic platform of shaking the country out of its complacency, with the idea of inspiring Americans to take on the challenges of a new era. A key element of what became President Kennedy's New Frontier program was to encourage Americans to get more involved in building a better nation by helping others, a concept he expressed so eloquently in his inaugural speech on January 20, 1961: ". . . ask not what your country can do for you—ask what you can do for your country." Probably the most familiar embodiment of this theme was Kennedy's Peace Corps program, established in 1961.

Q 325. What was President Johnson's vision for his Great Society program?

A Succeeding to the presidency after John F. Kennedy's assassination in 1963, Lyndon B. Johnson put forward a series of sweeping social programs aimed at improving American society. He outlined his vision of the Great Society in a commencement speech given May 22, 1964: "For in your time we have the opportunity to move not only toward the rich society and the powerful society, but upward to the Great Society." His programs, he said, would focus on rebuilding the nation's cities, expanding civil rights, restoring the environment, and improving schools. Aided by his legislative skills and by a Democratic-controlled Congress, Johnson succeeded in getting eighty Great Society bills enacted in 1965 alone. Among those passed were Medicare and Medicaid, the Voting Rights Act of 1965, the Elementary and Secondary Education Act, and the War on Poverty. They put in place the most wide-ranging social reform program enacted since Roosevelt's New Deal.

326. How did President Johnson defend American involvement in the Vietnam War?

A Just months after being elected to his first full term, President Lyndon B. Johnson began a massive buildup of American forces in South Vietnam. His decision eventually committed hundreds of thousands of Americans to the fight against communist North Vietnam, and created a moral and political quagmire that even Johnson, the adroit politician, could not escape. All that was yet to come, however. At an April 27, 1965, news conference, President Johnson defended direct American involvement by invoking the "domino theory" and by warning, "Defeat in South Vietnam would deliver a friendly nation to terror and repression. It would encourage and spur on those who seek to conquer all free nations that are within their reach." Johnson, who had lived through World War II, the communist victory in China, and the Korean War, went on to say, "This is the clearest lesson of our time. From Munich until today we have learned that to yield to aggression brings only greater threats and brings even more destructive war."

Over the next years he poured more troops, more firepower, and billions of dollars into the escalating war against North Vietnam, trying to force the communists to the bargaining table. "I know the other side is winning," he said, "so they do, too. No man wants to trade when he's winning." In Vietnam Johnson kept upping the ante, but the costs in terms of casualties, social unrest at home, and the drain on the economy finally became too great.

(See 328 How did President Nixon propose to end the war in Vietnam?)

Q 327. What did President Johnson say about the race riots that plagued the civil rights movement?

A While signing the Civil Rights Act of 1968, which banned discrimination in housing, President Lyndon B. Johnson called for an end to the increasingly frequent and destructive riots by blacks in the name of civil rights. "We all know the roots of injustice run deep," he said in April 1968, "but violence cannot redress a solitary wrong or remedy a single unfairness." Just a few days earlier, rioting had erupted in several cities in response to the assassination of civil rights leader Martin Luther King Jr. The riots provided yet another example of the violence that had become part of the civil rights movement during the mid-1960s.

Q **328. How did President Nixon propose to end the war in Vietnam?**

A Richard M. Nixon entered office in 1969 committed to achieving "peace with honor" in Vietnam. Although the majority of Americans still supported the war, the antiwar protest movement had gained considerable strength by demonstrating against President Lyndon B. Johnson's troop buildup in Vietnam and by calling attention to the rising death toll. President Nixon planned to "Vietnamize" the war by training and equipping South Vietnamese soldiers so that they could fight the North Vietnamese communist troops themselves. At the same time, Nixon planned to slowly withdraw U.S. troops and eventually end American involvement in Vietnam.

While Vietnamization of the war resulted in the gradual withdrawal of American troops, the revamped South Vietnamese units still were no match for their North Vietnamese and Viet Cong counterparts. In January 1973, however, the Nixon administration negotiated a peace agreement with North Vietnam, committing the United States to the withdrawal of the last of its troops. With American troops out of the picture, Vietnamese communist forces overran the country and in 1975 claimed complete victory.

Q **329. What was President Nixon's "silent majority"?**

A Confronted by mass protests against the war in Vietnam, President Richard M. Nixon gave a televised address on November 3, 1969, in which he defended his policies and asked for the support of "the great silent majority of my fellow Americans" against "a vocal minority" that threatened to prevail "over reason and the will of the majority." Although that was not the first use of "silent majority" (Vice President Spiro T. Agnew had included it in a speech six months earlier), Nixon's speech popularized the term and made it a rallying cry for those who supported the war and opposed antiwar protesters. Later, the term was used to refer to the mass of average, middle-class Americans.

Q **330. Did President Nixon try to cover up the Watergate affair?**

A At a meeting on March 22, 1973, as the Watergate investigators began closing in, President Richard M. Nixon called a meeting of his top aides. He told them emphatically, "I want you all to stonewall it, let them [the Watergate burglars] plead the Fifth Amendment, cover-up or anything else, if it'll save it—save the plan. That's the whole point." Over the next few months Nixon publicly denied having any involvement in the June 1972 burglary at the Democratic National Committee headquarters in the

Watergate complex in Washington, D.C., or the cover-up, even as he dismissed those same top aides because of the scandal. But Nixon had been secretly recording conversations in his offices, and tapes of meetings like that on March 22 became the so-called "smoking gun" that finally tripped up the president. After the Supreme Court ordered the tapes released to investigators, Nixon had no choice but to publicly admit his involvement in the affair. He resigned from office on August 9, 1974.

(See 345 What was Nixon's "Checkers speech" about? 373 What happened in the Watergate scandal?)

Q 331. Why did President Carter say, "The insiders have had their chance, and they have not delivered"?

A Democrat Jimmy Carter was a dark-horse candidate in the 1976 presidential campaign. A southerner and faithful Christian, the former Georgia governor presented himself as the alternative to establishment politicians. He believed the mistakes of the imperial-style presidency—the Vietnam War and Watergate scandal—had alienated voters, leaving them distrustful of establishment politicians. His answer was to campaign as a new, down-to-earth, populist-style leader, who would make the presidency more responsive to the people.

As president, however, Carter found that his outsider approach worked against him. He had no ties with the Democratic Party's established powers or with the interest groups, such as those representing labor and minorities, that usually supported Democrats. Carter also found himself at odds with Democratic liberals in Congress. Failures in his domestic and foreign policy efforts only led to further disaffection among voters and cost him his reelection bid in 1980.

(See 362 Why were the Camp David accords so important? 363 What was the Iranian hostage crisis?)

Q 332. How did President Reagan propose to make you "better off than you were four years ago"?

A Campaigning on a conservative platform in 1980, Ronald Reagan promised to restore American power and credibility, reduce taxes, increase defense spending, and balance the budget by cutting wasteful government spending. He also wanted to "get the government off the backs of the people" by deregulating whole industries and shifting federal social welfare programs to the states. Reagan offered all this as an antidote to the frustration and disappointment created by the domestic and foreign policy failures of the Carter years, and it won him the presidency. Four years later, with the economy booming, Reagan was able to win reelection by again asking, "Are you better off than you were four years ago?"

Q 333. What change did President Clinton's statement that "the era of big government is over" signal?

A Almost a decade of mushrooming federal deficits and partisan battling between conservatives and liberals over how much the federal government should and could afford to do preceded Bill Clinton's arrival to the presidency. His predecessor, conservative Republican George Bush, had succinctly stated the problem of the limits faced by the federal government: "We have more will than wallet."

After bitter fights with Congress over his ill-fated health care program and balancing the budget, Clinton signaled a change. During his 1996 State of the Union address, he declared, "We know big government does not have all the answers. We know there's not a program for every problem. We have worked to give the American people a smaller, less bureaucratic government in Washington. . . . The era of big government is over. But we cannot go back to the time when our citizens were left to fend for themselves. . . . Self-reliance and teamwork are not opposing virtues; we must have both."

President Clinton did not abandon his belief that the federal government had a responsibility to do all that it could, however. Instead, his later budgets proposed modest expansions of existing programs and numerous new programs that were smaller and less costly than those in earlier years.

PRESIDENTS AND PUBLIC OPINION

Q 334. What have presidents done in the battle for the public's favor?

A Presidents keep themselves in the public eye and try to build support for their programs by holding news conferences, making public appearances, and delivering major speeches. In fact, presidents attach so much importance to these efforts to woo the public that they spend one-third of their time in office, by one estimate, on public appearances. But each president has had his own style, placing more or less emphasis on one or another means of getting the message out. Also, events such as a war or domestic emergency may dictate the need for more or fewer news conferences and major speeches.

Q 335. How have the mass media helped presidents shape public opinion?

A The mass media—newspapers, radio, and television—keep the public informed about important events and issues. And by reaching so many millions of Americans every day, the media also provide government leaders with a means of turning voters' attention to specific issues and convincing them which policies are best. Presidents especially have benefited from the attention the media, particularly television, lavish on them. Today, presidents can "go public" by appealing directly to voters for support on policies, instead of working with members of Congress or interest groups to build support. And because the media feature what presidents say and do so prominently, they have an immediate advantage over their critics, whose counterproposals tend to get second billing. The disadvantage, of course, is that the media can and do find fault with presidents and their policies, criticism that can be politically damaging.

Q 336. What effect did FDR's "fireside chats" have?

A The timing for Franklin D. Roosevelt's now-famous Sunday evening radio addresses, his fireside chats, could not have been better. The nation had already endured three years of severe unemployment and economic depression, and in March 1933 a banking crisis—bank closures and runs on banks—swept the country. On Sunday evening, March 12, President Roosevelt broadcast his first fireside chat, reassuring his listeners and urging them to trust the banks. His personal, conversational approach proved a tremendous success and led to a series of twenty-seven fireside chats during his twelve years in office. The addresses not only helped him explain many of his New Deal policies to the public at large, but also boosted his popularity and helped him pressure Congress to enact new programs.

Q 337. Who was the first president to use public opinion surveys to gauge reactions to his policies?

A President Franklin D. Roosevelt used them regularly for the first time in the late 1930s to help measure public response to his positions on possible U.S. involvement in World War II. Pollster George Gallup provided the survey data.

Lyndon B. Johnson took public opinion polling a step further, becoming the first president to include a full-time pollster on his White House staff. Since then, presidents have relied heavily on public opinion polls to help determine their positions on specific issues and set their overall agendas.

Q **338. Does the president's popularity follow a pattern through his administration?**

A Since 1945 the Gallup Poll has conducted a monthly survey to determine the president's approval rating, and some clear patterns have emerged. As one might expect, presidents tend to enjoy a "honeymoon" of high approval ratings early in their first term, but over the full four years their ratings tend to decline. One reason is that voters become disappointed when bold campaign promises go unfulfilled. Presidents' popularity can rise dramatically when they confront an international crisis (voters rally around the flag during emergencies), but the increase is usually temporary. Presidents' handling of domestic issues also can improve their standing over the longer term, but here the economy is the deciding factor. If the economy is sluggish or in a recession, a president's approval rating is sure to drop.

(See 379 Is the economy a factor in presidential elections?)

Q **339. Which modern president had the lowest popularity rating? The highest?**

A By the time he resigned in 1974 over the Watergate affair, President Richard M. Nixon's yearly average for approval ratings had sunk to about 26 percent, lower than any other president's in modern times. President Harry S. Truman's yearly average rating late in his second term was not much better, about 28 percent, because of the stalemated Korean War and his firing of Gen. Douglas MacArthur. But Truman also enjoyed the highest average approval rating to date—just over 80 percent—when he took office after Franklin D. Roosevelt's death. Lyndon B. Johnson came closest to that in 1963 (about 78 percent approval) when he succeeded to the presidency after John F. Kennedy's assassination.

Q **340. Who are considered the greatest presidents? The weakest?**

A According to a famous poll of historians conducted by Harvard professor Arthur M. Schlesinger Sr. in 1948, the six greatest presidents were, in descending order, Abraham Lincoln, George Washington, Franklin D. Roosevelt, Woodrow Wilson, Thomas Jefferson, and Andrew Jackson. The poll ranked four others as near great—Theodore Roosevelt, Grover Cleveland, John Adams, and James K. Polk.

Only two presidents were considered outright failures, Ulysses S. Grant and Warren G. Harding. Historians ranked the rest as average or below average. Harry S. Truman, who was president at the time of the poll, was not considered in the survey.

Q 341. Who were regarded as the hardest-working presidents?

A Until modern times, most presidents did not have to work long hours. They usually took care of official business in normal workday hours or less—President Benjamin Harrison, for example, routinely spent no more than three hours a day at his desk. But as the federal government became more involved in American society, demands on the president grew. Most recent presidents have cultivated the image of a hard worker—Lyndon B. Johnson, Richard M. Nixon, Gerald R. Ford, Jimmy Carter, George Bush, and Bill Clinton all burned the midnight oil in the Oval Office. By contrast, Dwight D. Eisenhower, John F. Kennedy, and Ronald Reagan arranged their workloads so that they routinely had some of their afternoons off.

President James K. Polk was among the hardest-working presidents before the modern era. A compulsive worker, he never took days off.

VICE PRESIDENTS

Q 342. Which vice president served the shortest term?

A William R. King, President Franklin Pierce's vice president, died just twenty-five days after taking office. King was already ill with tuberculosis when nominated by the Democrats in 1852, and after the election he went to Cuba seeking a milder climate to cure it. With special permission from Congress, he took the oath of office on March 24, 1853, in Cuba, but then died on April 18 after returning home to Alabama. He is the only top official of the executive branch to have taken the oath on foreign soil.

(See 12 What is the president's oath of office? The vice president's? 60 Has the office of the vice president ever been vacant?)

Q 343. Has anyone ever served as vice president for more than one president?

A Two vice presidents, George Clinton and John C. Calhoun, each served under two different presidents. George Clinton, a seven-term governor of New York and a Democratic-Republican, served first under President Thomas Jefferson (1805–1809). Then after losing his bid for the Democratic-Republican presidential nomination to James Madison, he again accepted the vice-presidential slot. Already seventy years old, he served as Madison's vice president from 1809 until his death in 1812. Clinton was the first vice president to die in office.

Calhoun served as vice president under John Quincy Adams, a Democratic-Republican, from 1825 to 1829. After relations between Calhoun and Adams soured, Calhoun openly supported Adams's opponent, Andrew Jackson, in the 1828 election. Jackson in turn named Calhoun as his vice-presidential running mate. Calhoun served as Jackson's vice president from 1829 to 1832, but he and Jackson also had a falling-out. Calhoun resigned just before the end of his term, having been dropped from Jackson's reelection ticket. Calhoun was the first vice president to resign.

(See 59 Have any vice presidents resigned from office? 60 Has the office of the vice president ever been vacant? 307 How did President Jackson test Vice President Calhoun's loyalties?)

Q 344. Which vice president served as a Confederate general after leaving office?

A Vice President John C. Breckinridge, a Kentucky Democrat, served under President James Buchanan in the years just before the Civil War. When he left office with Buchanan in 1861, he had already been elected to the U.S. Senate from Kentucky. Breckinridge took his seat in Congress that summer (Kentucky voted not to secede) and opposed President Abraham Lincoln's preparations for war against the Confederacy. Late in 1861, Breckinridge joined the Confederacy, was expelled from the Senate, and eventually served in the western campaigns as a brigadier general. In the last months of the war, he became the Confederate secretary of war.

Q 345. What was Nixon's "Checkers speech" about?

A Late in the 1952 presidential campaign, newspapers headlined a story accusing the Republican vice-presidential candidate, Richard M. Nixon, of having a secret "slush fund" financed by campaign contributions from California businessmen. Nixon denied any wrongdoing. The fund, he said, was not secret; it had been set up to cover routine expenses, such as travel, telephone calls, and postage. Nevertheless, the flap became a major embarrassment for Republican presidential candidate Dwight D. Eisenhower.

When newspapers called for Nixon's resignation from the ticket, he made a last-ditch effort to save his political career by giving an emotional speech in his own defense. During the nationwide broadcast on September 23, 1952, Nixon denied doing anything illegal and charged that Democratic candidates also had similar expense funds. But he did admit to accepting a cocker spaniel puppy named Checkers from a Texas supporter. His children loved the puppy, Nixon told television viewers, and he intended to keep it no matter what anybody thought. Nixon's appeal, remembered today as the "Checkers speech," turned the tide of public opinion and saved his candidacy.

(See 373 What happened in the Watergate scandal?)

Q 346. When did the vice president get an official residence?

A Vice presidents were expected to provide their own living quarters until 1974, when Congress authorized funds for a permanent vice-presidential residence. The change became necessary because the cost of devising security arrangements for each vice president and family in their own residence had long surpassed the cost of maintaining an official residence.

A Queen Anne–style brick mansion, the residence is located on the grounds of the U.S. Naval Observatory on Massachusetts Avenue. The six-bedroom house has an enclosed patio on the second floor, one of the vice president's offices, an outdoor swimming pool, a putting green, and tennis courts. Living quarters for the vice president's family are on the second and third floors.

Q 347. Who was the first vice president to live in the vice president's official residence full time?

A Vice President Walter F. Mondale became the first when he and his family moved there at the start of his term in 1977. The house had been available to Vice President Gerald R. Ford, but he succeeded to the presidency in August 1974. Vice President Nelson A. Rockefeller, who filled the vacancy in the vice presidency, lived in a mansion owned by his family during his term, which began in late 1974. Rockefeller oversaw the continuing renovation and redecoration of the official residence while in office but did not live there.

▶ *Which vice presidents went on to become president? See 222 How many vice presidents have succeeded to the presidency?*

▶ *Which vice presidents resigned from office? See 59 Have any vice presidents resigned from office?*

▶ *Have any vice presidents died in office? See 60 Has the office of the vice president ever been vacant?*

▶ *Have any vice presidents committed impeachable offenses? See 66.*

▶ *What was the Burr conspiracy about? See 143 Which former vice president was tried for treason?*

FOR THE RECORD

Q **348. When did the presidents and vice presidents serve?**

A Presidents and their vice presidents (in italics) are listed below, accompanied by their term and party affiliation (D–Democratic; DR–Democratic-Republican; F–Federalist; R–Republican; W–Whig). The eight vacancies in the vice presidency resulting from the vice presidents succession are indicated. For more information on why the vacancies occurred and on the presidents whose terms were cut short by assassination, death from natural causes, or resignation, see the questions listed at the end of the table.

President (Party)/*Vice President*	*Term*
George Washington (F)	April 30, 1789–March 4, 1793
John Adams	April 30, 1789–March 4, 1793
George Washington (F)	March 4, 1793–March 4, 1797
John Adams	March 4, 1793–March 4, 1797
John Adams (F)	March 4, 1797–March 4, 1801
Thomas Jefferson	March 4, 1797–March 4, 1801
Thomas Jefferson (DR)	March 4, 1801–March 4, 1805
Aaron Burr	March 4, 1801–March 4, 1805
Thomas Jefferson (DR)	March 4, 1805–March 4, 1809
George Clinton	March 4, 1805–March 4, 1809
James Madison (DR)	March 4, 1809–March 4, 1813
George Clinton	March 4, 1809–April 12, 1812
James Madison (DR)	March 4, 1813–March 4, 1817
Elbridge Gerry	March 4, 1813–November 23, 1814
James Monroe (DR)	March 4, 1817–March 4, 1821
Daniel D. Tompkins	March 4, 1817–March 4, 1821
James Monroe (DR)	March 4, 1821–March 4, 1825
Daniel D. Tompkins	March 4, 1821–March 4, 1825
John Quincy Adams (DR)	March 4, 1825–March 4, 1829
John C. Calhoun	March 4, 1825–March 4, 1829

President (Party)/*Vice President*	Term
Andrew Jackson (D)	March 4, 1829–March 4, 1833
John C. Calhoun	March 4, 1829–December 28, 1833
Andrew Jackson (D)	March 4, 1833–March 4, 1837
Martin Van Buren	March 4, 1833–March 4, 1837
Martin Van Buren (D)	March 4, 1837–March 4, 1841
Richard M. Johnson	March 4, 1837–March 4, 1841
William Henry Harrison (W)	March 4, 1841–April 4, 1841
John Tyler	March 4, 1841–April 6, 1841
John Tyler (W)	April 6, 1841–March 4, 1845
Vice presidency vacant	
James K. Polk (D)	March 4, 1845–March 4, 1849
George M. Dallas	March 4, 1845–March 4, 1849
Zachary Taylor (W)	March 4, 1849–July 9, 1850
Millard Fillmore	March 4, 1849–July 10, 1850
Millard Fillmore (W)	July 10, 1850–March 4, 1853
Vice presidency vacant	
Franklin Pierce (D)	March 4, 1853–March 4, 1857
William R. King	March 24, 1853–April 18, 1853
James Buchanan (D)	March 4, 1857–March 4, 1861
John C. Breckinridge	March 4, 1857–March 4, 1861
Abraham Lincoln (R)	March 4, 1861–March 4, 1865
Hannibal Hamlin	March 4, 1861–March 4, 1865
Abraham Lincoln (R)	March 4, 1865–April 15, 1865
Andrew Johnson	March 4, 1865–April 15, 1865
Andrew Johnson (R)	April 15, 1865–March 4, 1869
Vice presidency vacant	
Ulysses S. Grant (R)	March 4, 1869–March 4, 1873
Schuyler Colfax	March 4, 1869–March 4, 1873
Ulysses S. Grant (R)	March 4, 1873–March 4, 1877
Henry Wilson	March 4, 1873–November 22, 1877
Rutherford B. Hayes (R)	March 4, 1877–March 4, 1881
William A. Wheeler	March 4, 1877–March 4, 1881
James A. Garfield (R)	March 4, 1881–September 19, 1881
Chester A. Arthur	March 4, 1881–September 20, 1881
Chester A. Arthur (R)	September 20, 1881–March 4, 1885
Vice presidency vacant	

President (Party)/*Vice President*	Term
Grover Cleveland (D)	March 4, 1885–March 4, 1889
Thomas A. Hendricks	March 4, 1885–November 25, 1889
Benjamin Harrison (R)	March 4, 1889–March 4, 1893
Levi P. Morton	March 4, 1889–March 4, 1893
Grover Cleveland (D)	March 4, 1893–March 4, 1897
Adlai E. Stevenson	March 4, 1893–March 4, 1897
William McKinley (R)	March 4, 1897–March 4, 1901
Garret A. Hobart	March 4, 1897–November 21, 1901
William McKinley (R)	March 4, 1901–September 14, 1901
Theodore Roosevelt	March 4, 1901–September 14, 1901
Theodore Roosevelt (R)	September 14, 1901–March 4, 1905
Vice presidency vacant	
Theodore Roosevelt (R)	March 4, 1905–March 4, 1909
Charles W. Fairbanks	March 4, 1905–March 4, 1909
William Howard Taft (R)	March 4, 1909–March 4, 1913
James S. Sherman	March 4, 1909–October 30, 1913
Woodrow Wilson (D)	March 4, 1913–March 4, 1917
Thomas R. Marshall	March 4, 1913–March 4, 1917
Woodrow Wilson (D)	March 4, 1917–March 4, 1921
Thomas R. Marshall	March 4, 1917–March 4, 1921
Warren G. Harding (R)	March 4, 1921–August 2, 1923
Calvin Coolidge	March 4, 1921–August 3, 1923
Calvin Coolidge (R)	August 3, 1923–March 4, 1925
Vice presidency vacant	
Calvin Coolidge (R)	March 4, 1925–March 4, 1929
Charles G. Dawes	March 4, 1925–March 4, 1929
Herbert Hoover (R)	March 4, 1929–March 4, 1933
Charles Curtis	March 4, 1929–March 4, 1933
Franklin D. Roosevelt (D)	March 4, 1933–January 20, 1937
John Nance Garner	March 4, 1933–January 20, 1937
Franklin D. Roosevelt (D)	January 20, 1937–January 20, 1941
John Nance Garner	January 20, 1937–January 20, 1941
Franklin D. Roosevelt (D)	January 20, 1941–January 20, 1945
Henry A. Wallace	January 20, 1941–January 20, 1945
Franklin D. Roosevelt (D)	January 20, 1945–April 12, 1945
Harry S. Truman	January 20, 1945–April 12, 1945

President (Party)/*Vice President*	*Term*
Harry S. Truman (D)	April 12, 1945–January 20, 1949
Vice presidency vacant	
Harry S. Truman (D)	January 20, 1949–January 20, 1953
Alben W. Barkley	January 20, 1949–January 20, 1953
Dwight D. Eisenhower (R)	January 20, 1953–January 20, 1957
Richard M. Nixon	January 20, 1953–January 20, 1957
Dwight D. Eisenhower (R)	January 20, 1957–January 20, 1961
Richard M. Nixon	January 20, 1957–January 20, 1961
John F. Kennedy (D)	January 20, 1961–November 22, 1963
Lyndon B. Johnson	January 20, 1961–November 22, 1963
Lyndon B. Johnson (D)	November 22, 1963–January 20, 1965
Vice presidency vacant	
Lyndon B. Johnson (D)	January 20, 1965–January 20, 1969
Hubert H. Humphrey	January 20, 1965–January 20, 1969
Richard M. Nixon (R)	January 20, 1969–January 20, 1973
Spiro T. Agnew	January 20, 1969–January 20, 1973
Richard M. Nixon (R)	January 20, 1973–August 9, 1974
Spiro T. Agnew	January 20, 1973–October 10, 1973
Gerald R. Ford	December 6, 1973–August 9, 1974
Gerald R. Ford (R)	August 9, 1974–January 20, 1977
Nelson A. Rockefeller	December 19, 1974–January 20, 1977
Jimmy Carter (D)	January 20, 1977–January 20, 1981
Walter F. Mondale	January 20, 1977–January 20, 1981
Ronald Reagan (R)	January 20, 1981–January 20, 1985
George Bush	January 20, 1981–January 20, 1985
Ronald Reagan (R)	January 20, 1985–January 20, 1989
George Bush	January 20, 1985–January 20, 1989
George Bush (R)	January 20, 1989–January 20, 1993
Dan Quayle	January 20, 1989–January 20, 1993
Bill Clinton (D)	January 20, 1993–January 20, 1997
Al Gore	January 20, 1993–January 20, 1997
Bill Clinton (D)	January 20, 1997–
Al Gore	January 20, 1997–

(See 55 Which presidents died in office? 58 Which president resigned from office? 59 Have any vice presidents resigned from office? 60 Has the office of the vice president ever been vacant? 296 Which presidents were assassinated?)

Q 349. Which president proclaimed the first national holiday?

A George Washington had that honor. He proclaimed the first national holiday to be Thanksgiving, declaring it should be observed on November 26, 1789. Congress had recommended President Washington make the proclamation, and since then Thanksgiving has become one of the nation's most important national holidays. Presidential proclamations alone cannot officially establish national holidays, however. They must be backed up by acts of Congress.

Q 350. When was the first White House wedding?

A Sixteen weddings have been held at the White House, the first in March 1812. The first White House bride was First Lady Dolley Madison's sister, Lucy Payne Washington, the widow of George Washington's nephew. Lucy married Supreme Court Justice Thomas Todd. In March 1820 the first president's child, President James Monroe's daughter Maria, was married in the White House. (Another president's daughter, Tricia Nixon, had the most recent White House wedding, in June 1971.)

The only president and first lady married in the White House were President Grover Cleveland and Frances Folsom, who wed on June 2, 1886. At age twenty-one, Frances also was the youngest first lady. President William Henry Harrison's wife, Anna, was the oldest first lady. She was sixty-five when her husband took office.

▶ *Who was the first president to be photographed? See 148.*

▶ *Who were the first presidents heard on radio and seen on television? See 149.*

Q 351. Who was the first president to fly in an airplane?

A Ever the adventurer, Theodore Roosevelt was the first president to ride in a car (1902) and submerge in a submarine (1905), but it was not until 1910, after he left office, that he became the first to go aloft in an airplane. Franklin D. Roosevelt was the first president to have a presidential plane, but that did not come about until 1945. Roosevelt's plane, the forerunner of today's *Air Force One*, was a propeller-driven Douglas DC-4 Skymaster, nicknamed the *Sacred Cow*.

Andrew Jackson was the first president to ride on a train (June 6, 1833).

(See 185 Why is the president's plane called Air Force One?*)*

Q **352. Who was the first president to open a baseball season by throwing out a baseball?**

A The time-honored tradition of the president tossing out the first baseball of the new professional baseball season began in 1910 with William Howard Taft. On April 14 he opened the American League season by throwing out a ball at the start of the game between the Washington Senators and the Philadelphia Athletics. The Senators went on to win 3–0.

BEYOND OUR SHORES

Q **353. How did the Monroe Doctrine come about?**

A During the 1820s the Monroe administration became concerned about a threatened invasion of South America by a joint French and Spanish force, as well as by Russian claims to the Oregon Territory. Most of Spain's Latin American colonies had revolted and gained independence earlier in the 1800s, but now it seemed European powers had new designs on the Western Hemisphere. To counter the threat, Secretary of State John Quincy Adams recommended that President James Monroe announce American opposition to any such intrusion. To that end, President Monroe enunciated the now-famous Monroe Doctrine to Congress on December 2, 1823, declaring that the United States would resist European intervention in the affairs of independent nations in the Western Hemisphere. The doctrine, which had the tacit support of the British, soon discouraged both French and Russia interest in the Americas.

Years later, President Theodore Roosevelt expanded on the Monroe Doctrine, announcing that the United States intended to intervene in any Latin American country to restore order or topple any government engaging in "chronic wrongdoing." This was called the Roosevelt Corollary.

(See 315 Which proverb did President Theodore Roosevelt like to quote?)

Q **354. Who was the first president to travel abroad while in office?**

A President Theodore Roosevelt became the first in 1906, when he traveled to Panama. Work on the Panama Canal, which Roosevelt helped make possible, had already begun, but the massive construction project would not be complete until 1914.

Presidents did not begin to travel abroad to any significant degree until the 1950s, when Dwight D. Eisenhower spent a total of fifty days abroad during his second term, making 115 public appearances. President Bill Clinton holds the record for most days devoted to foreign travel during his two terms—242 days as of mid-2000. President George Bush is second, with 86 days during his one term.

Q **355. What was "dollar diplomacy"?**

A President William Howard Taft instituted this foreign policy strategy, in which he sought to expand U.S. influence in South America and elsewhere by increasing U.S. foreign trade and investment. Taft's dollar diplomacy relied primarily on financial incentives, but he was not afraid to use troops to protect U.S. interests when necessary. Like President Theodore Roosevelt before him, he sent troops to Central America on more than one occasion: U.S. Marines landed in Nicaragua twice when unrest threatened (1910 and 1912) and during a revolution in Honduras (1911). Taft's dollar diplomacy generated considerable ill feelings in South America and had only limited success at stimulating American investment in South America.

▶ *What was the aim of President Wilson's Fourteen Points? See 316 What did President Wilson say when he called for America's entry into World War I?*

Q **356. What cold war policies did the Truman Doctrine establish?**

A President Harry S. Truman proclaimed this famous foreign policy doctrine in a speech in March 1947 as a direct response to communist expansionism in Greece and Turkey. The Truman Doctrine pledged that the United States would help free peoples resist communist takeovers, and it established the cold war policy objective of "containing" communism to prevent its spread. In his speech, Truman asked for $400 million in military aid for Turkey and Greece. This aid helped to thwart the communists and established the cold war pattern of using foreign aid to fight communism. The Truman administration further promoted the Truman Doctrine's basic objectives through the Marshall Plan, which provided U.S. loans to help the Western European countries rebuild after World War II, and by establishing the North Atlantic Treaty Organization. Truman's Point Four program, begun in 1950, expanded the aid program to underdeveloped nations around the world.

Q **357. What are summit conferences?**

A Meetings between the heads of the major governments are called summit conferences or *summits*—a word coined by Winston Churchill in 1953. During the cold war era especially, summit conferences were an important part of the president's foreign policy duties. They enabled presidents to meet face to face with their Soviet counterparts and to form personal ties that lessened tensions between the countries. Presidents also enjoyed increased public approval ratings from the publicity stemming from the summits. Since the end of World War II and the start of the cold war, every president has met with a Soviet (since 1990, Russian) leader in a summit conference, often to discuss arms control agreements.

Since the end of the cold war in the early 1990s, economic summits between the major industrialized nations have gained prominence over political summits. Leaders of the Group of Eight nations (United States, Britain, Canada, France, Germany, Italy, Japan, and Russia) meet each year to discuss economic and trade matters. The annual conferences began in 1975 (Russian leaders began attending in 1998).

Listed below are the political (as opposed to economic) summit conferences held with Soviet leaders in the cold war years:

Potsdam, July–August 1945—President Harry S. Truman, Soviet leader Joseph Stalin, British prime minister Winston Churchill, and others discussed post–World War II partition of Germany.

Geneva, July 1955—President Dwight D. Eisenhower, Soviet leader Nikolai Bulganin, British prime minister Anthony Eden, and others discussed reunification of Germany, disarmament, and European security.

Camp David, Md., September 1959—President Eisenhower and Soviet leader Nikita Khrushchev discussed the Berlin problem.

Paris, May 1960—President Eisenhower, Soviet leader Khrushchev, French president Charles de Gaulle, and British prime minister Harold Macmillan discussed the U-2 incident.

Vienna, June 1961—President John F. Kennedy and Soviet leader Khrushchev discussed the Berlin problem.

Glassboro, N.J., June 1967—President Lyndon B. Johnson and Soviet leader Aleksei Kosygin discussed the Middle East.

Moscow, May 1972—President Richard M. Nixon and Soviet leader Leonid Brezhnev discussed SALT I, antiballistic missile limitations.

Washington, D.C., June 1973—President Nixon and Soviet leader Brezhnev discussed détente.

Moscow and Yalta, June–July 1974—President Nixon and Soviet leader Brezhnev discussed arms control.

Vladivostok, November 1974—President Gerald R. Ford and Soviet leader Brezhnev discussed arms control.

Vienna, June 1979—President Jimmy Carter and Soviet leader Brezhnev discussed SALT II.

Geneva, November 1985—President Ronald Reagan and Soviet leader Mikhail Gorbachev discussed arms control, U.S.-Soviet relations.

Reykjavik, October 1986—President Reagan and Soviet leader Gorbachev discussed arms control.

Washington, D.C., December 1987—President Reagan and Soviet leader Gorbachev discussed Intermediate Nuclear Force (INF) Treaty and Afghanistan.

Moscow, May 1988—President Reagan and Soviet leader Gorbachev discussed arms control and human rights.

New York, December 1988—President Reagan and Soviet leader Gorbachev discussed U.S.-Soviet relations.

Malta, December 1989—President George Bush and Soviet leader Gorbachev discussed arms control and Eastern Europe.

Washington, D.C., May–June 1990—President Bush and Soviet leader Gorbachev discussed arms control.

Helsinki, September 1990—President Bush and Soviet leader Gorbachev discussed Middle East crisis.

Moscow, July 1991—President Bush and Soviet leader Gorbachev discussed arms control and Soviet economic and political future.

Q 358. What was "rocket rattling"?

A Every president from Harry S. Truman on understood that nuclear war was all but unthinkable. Limited engagements—brushfire wars fought with conventional weapons—became the norm for the cold war era, but that did not preclude calculated threats to use nuclear missiles—rocket rattling—to force the other side to back down.

President Dwight D. Eisenhower developed the strategy of threatening "massive retaliation" with nuclear missiles during the 1950s. Soon after taking office, he deliberately leaked word to the Chinese that he was prepared to use extreme measures against them if the stalled talks on the Korean War did not produce an end to the fighting. When talks suddenly resumed and quickly produced a truce in July 1953, President Eisenhower credited his implied threat of nuclear strikes against China.

From this developed the concept of massive retaliation—the United States would not necessarily respond to every communist takeover, but would respond where and when it wanted with massive retaliation. The idea was to use the threat of nuclear retaliation somewhere as a deterrent to communist aggression on all fronts.

By most accounts, the closest the United States has come to nuclear war was during the Cuban missile crisis of 1962, when the Kennedy administration, according to Secretary of State Dean Rusk, stood "eyeball to eyeball" with the Soviets. Soon after receiving aerial photographs of Soviet missile launchers being installed in Cuba, Kennedy decided to force their removal by establishing a naval blockade of Cuba. Kennedy also announced publicly that American military forces were being put on alert.

The Soviets in Cuba could be seen speeding up their work, and a few days into the crisis an American reconnaissance plane was shot down. War with the Soviets now seemed likely. In the end, though, the Soviets "blinked," and secret talks between Kennedy and Soviet leader Nikita Khrushchev quickly produced an agreement, along with a new concern about avoiding nuclear war through better relations.

Q 359. Who was involved in the "Kitchen Debate"?

A Widely publicized, this impromptu debate took place between Vice President Richard M. Nixon and Soviet premier Nikita Khrushchev on July 24, 1959. Nixon was in Moscow for the formal opening of the American National Exhibition, which included the model American kitchen that became the namesake of the debate. As the two leaders inspected the kitchen, they pressed their points with determination and a bit of one-upmanship while reporters looked on. They ranged over such diverse subjects as the merits of capitalism and communism, summit meetings, rockets, the free exchange of ideas, and even washing machines. The cold war was little altered, but the dialogue put it in more human terms.

Q 360. Why did President Kennedy's "Ich bin ein Berliner" speech cause such a sensation?

A In the postwar years, defections of East Germans and other communist nationals to the more prosperous West Berlin were politically embarrassing to communist East Germany. In 1961 the East German regime tried solving the problem by building a 100-mile-long wall, dubbed the Berlin Wall. Patrolled by armed guards with orders to shoot anyone trying to escape, the wall quickly became a hated symbol of communist oppression.

President John F. Kennedy declared America's continuing commitment to the defense of West Berlin, but otherwise could not prevent the wall from being built. When he traveled to West Berlin on June 26, 1963, however, he stood at the wall before a huge crowd of cheering West Germans. To them he said, "Today, in the world of freedom, the proudest boast is "Ich bin ein Berliner" [I am a Berliner].

► *Why did President Johnson commit American troops to the Vietnam War? See 326 How did President Johnson defend American involvement in the Vietnam War?*

► *What was President Nixon's formula for ending the Vietnam War? See 328 How did President Nixon propose to end the war in Vietnam?*

Q 361. What was President Nixon's China card?

A Richard M. Nixon, who had built his political career on attacking communism, entered office in 1969 with a plan to fundamentally alter the cold war status quo. He actively pursued better relations with America's longtime enemy, the Soviet Union, instituting a policy of détente (relaxation of tensions) in the hope of securing agreements to limit the arms race. To help bring the Soviets to the bargaining table, Nixon played his China card. Well aware of a rift between communist China and the Soviet Union, he took the unprecedented step of pursuing better relations with China. The so-called "Ping-Pong diplomacy"—a highly publicized exchange of table tennis teams in 1971—and Nixon's trip to China in 1972 revealed a sea change in Sino-American relations. The budding U.S.-China friendship put pressure on the Soviets, and in 1972 they agreed to the first Strategic Arms Limitation Treaty, which limited antiballistic missile systems and capped the number of missile launchers each side could have.

Q 362. Why were the Camp David accords so important?

A Like presidents before him, President Jimmy Carter sought a solution to the long-standing hostility between Arabs and Israelis. Certainly the oil that Arabs controlled was one of Carter's concerns, but so too were the survival of Israel and Middle East stability. After Egyptian president Anwar Sadat made a historic visit to Israel in 1977, negotiations between Egypt and Israel stalled. To restart the talks, President Carter invited Sadat and Israeli prime minister Menachem Begin to his presidential retreat at Camp David, Maryland, in September 1978. There, with his help, Sadat and Begin finally agreed to "frameworks"—the Camp David accords—for a peace treaty between their countries and for a more general peace in the Middle East as well. As a direct result of the Camp David talks, Egypt and Israel signed a historic formal peace treaty in Washington, D.C., on March 26, 1979. Egypt was thus the first Arab state to sign a peace treaty with Israel.

Q 363. What was the Iranian hostage crisis?

A The Carter administration's most troublesome foreign policy dilemma, the hostage crisis, came about when Iranian militants seized the American embassy and fifty-two American hostages in Tehran, Iran, on November 4, 1979. They did so with the blessings of Ayatollah Ruholla Khomeini, Iran's revolutionary Islamic leader, who had seized power from pro-American shah Mohammad Reza Pahlavi of Iran earlier that year. Over the next fifteen months, the Carter administration tried to negotiate with the militants and even launched a rescue attempt in 1990 that not only failed but also caused the death of eight American soldiers. The protracted crisis humiliated the United States abroad and seriously undermined Carter's administration at home. No agreement was reached until January 19, 1981, well after Carter had lost his reelection bid. But the Iranians waited until January 20, the day Carter's successor, President Ronald Reagan, took office, to release the hostages.

Q 364. When have U.S. troops been deployed in foreign countries?

A Since World War II, the United States, for the first time in its history, has maintained a large standing army. The relative weakness of the former European powers after World War II and the cold war with the Soviet Union helped force that decision. Presidents from Truman on have deployed American naval vessels, warplanes, and troops to foreign shores for various purposes, ranging from outright war to peacekeeping and humanitarian activities. The deployments, by administration, since World War II are:

Harry S. Truman: 1946, Trieste and Bosporus Strait; 1948–1949, China; 1950–1953, Korean War; 1950–1955, Formosa (Taiwan)

Dwight D. Eisenhower: 1954–1955, Tachen Islands; 1956, Suez crisis; 1957, Indonesia and Quemoy (Taiwan); 1958, Indonesia and Lebanon; 1959–1960, Cuba

John F. Kennedy: 1962, Cuban missile crisis and Thailand; 1963, Haiti

Lyndon B. Johnson: 1964, Congo; 1964–1973, Vietnam War; 1965, Dominican Republic; 1967, Congo

Richard M. Nixon: 1970, Cambodia

Gerald R. Ford: 1975, Vietnam, Cambodia, and *Mayaguez* (ship); 1976, Lebanon and Korea

Jimmy Carter: 1978, Zaire; 1980, Iran

Ronald Reagan: 1981, El Salvador and Libya; 1982, Sinai and Lebanon; 1983, Chad and Grenada; 1986, Libya

George Bush: 1989, Panama; 1990–1991, Persian Gulf War; 1992–1993, Somalia

Bill Clinton: 1993, Bosnia and Iraq; 1994, Haiti, Kuwait; 1998, Sudan, Iraq; 1999, Kosovo

SCANDALS

Q 365. Which presidents have been accused of having affairs?

A Accusations of sexual affairs have been lodged against eleven presidents, including seven of the seventeen presidents who served in the twentieth century. To be sure, some of the accusations were mere suspicions circulated by the president's enemies, but in other cases presidents either admitted to the affairs or their conduct was such public knowledge that there was little room left for doubt. Among those presidents known to have had affairs were James A. Garfield, Grover Cleveland (who was unmarried at the time), Woodrow Wilson, Warren G. Harding, Franklin D. Roosevelt, John F. Kennedy, Lyndon B. Johnson, and Bill Clinton. George Washington and Dwight D. Eisenhower were rumored to have had affairs but no proof exists.

Thomas Jefferson has been identified as a possible father of children by a slave, Sally Hemmings.

(See 85 Which presidents fathered illegitimate children?)

▶ *What did the Burr conspiracy hope to achieve? See 143 Which former vice president was tried for treason?*

Q **366. Why did the Senate censure President Jackson?**

A The Senate took the unusual step of censuring President Andrew Jackson on March 28, 1834, for allegedly abusing his power. Jackson had squared off against Whigs in Congress and vetoed a bill to recharter the Second Bank of the United States in 1832. He even campaigned against the bank in the presidential election of 1832, which he won decisively. Jackson then decided to move the national bank's funds into state banks, but Treasury Secretary Louis McLane thought it unwise and refused to do so (Congress had given him, not the president, authority for that decision). After McLane was moved to the position of secretary of state, his replacement, William J. Duane, also refused, provoking Jackson to fire him and appoint Attorney General Roger B. Taney as Treasury secretary. Taney then transferred the funds, and in the wake of this action, the Senate voted to censure Jackson. It also refused to confirm Taney's appointment. Jackson complained the censure was unconstitutional, but had to wait until Democrats gained a majority in the Senate to get the censure resolution expunged.

(See 123 What was the Eaton affair about?)

Q **367. What was the Roorback forgery scandal?**

A Negative campaign tactics in the 1800s sometimes took a vicious turn, and the Roorback forgery provides a good example. Democrat James K. Polk's 1844 campaign started the mudslinging by claiming that Whig opponent Henry Clay was living in a Washington, D.C., brothel and that he had broken all Ten Commandments. Whigs tried to turn abolitionists in the Democratic Party against Polk by accusing him of being a cruel slave owner. As if to confirm the accusations, in August 1844 excerpts from a book by a German tourist, Baron von Roorback, appeared in a New York newspaper run by abolitionists. One paragraph talked about a Tennessee slave trader's camp, in which forty slaves had supposedly been bought by Polk and cruelly branded with his initials. The damning excerpt was making the rounds of other abolitionist newspapers when Democrats discovered the text had been faked. Abolitionist newspapers immediately headlined the story, and the forgery backfired on Calhoun, who was called a hypocrite because he owned slaves himself. The forgery gave rise to the term *roorback*, a false story circulated to achieve political ends.

Q 368. What happened in the scandal over the Gold Panic of 1869?

A In 1869 two financial speculators, Jay Gould and James Fisk Jr., tried to drive up the price of gold by convincing President Ulysses S. Grant to halt federal sales of surplus gold (the government had been selling about $2 million a month in gold to help keep the price stable). During the summer the conspirators talked with Grant personally and assumed they had convinced him to halt the sales. Thinking gold prices would surely rise, Gould and Fisk bought contracts for gold, which helped drive up the price even further. Meanwhile, they tried to use Grant's brother-in-law, who was involved in the scheme as an investor, to influence Grant's decision on gold sales. But in late September President Grant wrote to his sister, warning her that her husband should sell off his gold contracts. Two days later Grant ordered the sale of $4 million in government gold, and gold prices plunged $20 an ounce inside of an hour. Fisk and other speculators lost millions in the panic that followed, remembered as Black Friday. Congress investigated the affair (James A. Garfield chaired the committee), but found no evidence of wrongdoing by the president.

Q 369. What was the Crédit Mobilier scandal about?

A This famous scandal in the late 1800s involved millions of dollars in corporate fraud, as well as the alleged bribery of members of Congress, including House Speaker Schuyler Colfax and Rep. James A. Garfield. Colfax had become vice president under Ulysses S. Grant by the time the scandal came to light in 1872, and Garfield later became president.

Construction of the Union Pacific's share of the first transcontinental railroad, in which the federal government had a financial stake, provided the vehicle for the fraud. Contracts for laying Union Pacific's tracks went to the Crédit Mobilier corporation, which in 1865 was owned by a Union Pacific vice president. Two years later, Rep. Oakes Ames, a Republican from Massachusetts who was also Union Pacific's president, took over Crédit Mobilier and set up the swindle—between 1867 and 1869 his Union Pacific railroad paid Crédit Mobilier for inflated construction costs with cash and Union Pacific stock. This effectively siphoned Union Pacific's assets to

Crédit Mobilier, eventually earning Ames and his partners at Crédit Mobilier almost $20 million.

Meanwhile, to keep Congress from investigating the swindle, Representative Ames sold $33 million in shares to members of the Senate and House (including Colfax and Garfield), as well as to the federal railroad director. One of Ames's disgruntled associates blew the whistle on the scheme in 1872. The House considered impeaching Colfax but decided his actions were not impeachable. It censured Ames and took no action against Garfield.

Q 370. What happened in the Whiskey Ring scandal?

A Probably the worst scandal of President Ulysses S. Grant's administration, the Whiskey Ring conspiracy began about 1870 as a scheme to divert federal liquor taxes to the Republican Party. Treasury officials, Internal Revenue officials, and distillers were drawn into the scheme, which became so profitable that the conspirators began keeping some of the millions it produced for themselves. Ultimately hundreds of officials were involved, including Grant's personal secretary, Orville Babcock, and numerous prominent Republicans.

When the scandal was exposed in 1874 by Treasury Secretary Benjamin H. Bristow, about 240 officials were arrested and President Grant's son and brother were implicated. Grant at first supported the investigation but eventually halted the prosecution by ordering his attorney general to stop offering grants of immunity in exchange for testimony. As a result, Babcock and many of the other officials were acquitted.

Q 371. What was the Star Route scandal about?

A Because the U.S. postal system expanded so rapidly in the West after the Civil War, the government began using private contractors, including the Pony Express and stagecoach lines, to help deliver the mail there. Routes handled by private contractors were indicated by a star on postal service maps, giving rise to the name Star Routes.

In the 1870s Second Assistant Postmaster Thomas J. Brady conspired with Star Route contractors to defraud the post office. He approved rate increases for nonexistent service improvements, and contractors kicked back part of the fraudulent profits. The conspirators included the secretary of the Republican National Committee and prominent Republicans in the Post Office and Treasury Department.

President James A. Garfield ordered an investigation of the Star Routes soon after taking office in 1881, and in late June the president ordered the investigation speeded up. He was shot and mortally wounded four days later by a rejected office-seeker.

Prosecution continued under President Chester A. Arthur, but after two trials the key figures were acquitted.

(See 296 Which presidents were assassinated?)

Q 372. What happened in the Teapot Dome scandal?

A Teapot Dome was a complex scandal involving President Warren G. Harding's secretary of the interior, Albert B. Fall, oil leases allowing exploitation of U.S. Navy oil reserves, and bribes given to Fall by two wealthy oil magnates. While many people were outraged that Fall had let contracts to exploit the navy's oil reserves, some of the contracts were perfectly legal. But in the case of Teapot Dome oil reserve in Wyoming, Fall had assigned the contract in April 1922 without competitive bidding—to oil magnate Henry F. Sinclair, owner of Mammoth Oil.

President Harding died of natural causes in 1923 as the Teapot Dome scandal was beginning to unfold, but months passed before the bribery and corruption finally came to light. After Fall left office in March 1923, Sinclair gave him $233,000 in bonds and $36,000 in cash. Edward Doheny, who owned an oil company holding contracts to exploit Elk Hills, California, oil reserve, loaned Fall $100,000 in cash late in 1921. Fall was eventually convicted of bribery and was sentenced to a year in jail and a $100,000 fine, making him the first cabinet member ever convicted for a crime committed while in office. Both Sinclair and Doheny were found innocent of bribery charges. Sinclair. however, was convicted of jury tampering during a conspiracy trial related to the scandal. He was sentenced to six months in jail.

▶ *Why was Vice President Spiro T. Agnew forced to resign? See 59 Have any vice presidents resigned from office?*

Q 373. What happened in the Watergate scandal?

A A June 17, 1972, break-in at the Democratic National Committee headquarters in Washington, D.C., which President Richard M. Nixon's press secretary characterized as a "third-rate burglary," became the thread that unraveled the Watergate scandal, perhaps the worst political scandal in U.S. history. Because earlier in 1972 President Nixon had been deeply concerned about winning reelection, certain of his White House staffers and campaign committee workers had begun to engage in illegal activities, including the burglary at the Democratic headquarters at the Watergate office and apartment complex.

Nixon went on to win the November election by a landslide, but the ripples caused by the Watergate burglary began to widen. In February 1973 the Senate established the Senate Watergate committee to investigate the 1972 campaign, and in March James McCord, a Nixon reelection campaign worker arrested in the case, began talking. He charged that presidential counsel John Dean and Nixon reelection committee head John Mitchell had told him to commit perjury to cover up his connection to the burglary.

With the scandal now spreading to the upper echelons of the Nixon White House, the president fired Dean (who had refused to take the fall for the cover-up) and announced on April 30, 1973, that three of his top staffers had resigned. President Nixon also denied any knowledge of the attempted cover-up, including reported payments of hush money. Dean challenged that assertion, however, when he testified before the newly appointed special prosecutor some weeks later and before the Senate committee. In July 1973 the committee learned that Nixon had secretly taped conversations in the White House.

The special prosecutor subpoenaed the tapes, beginning a legal battle in which Nixon refused to give them up on grounds of executive privilege. But it was a losing effort, and on August 5 the Supreme Court forced Nixon to turn over the tapes to the special prosecutor. With impeachment all but certain, President Nixon resigned on August 9, 1973, and Vice President Gerald R. Ford was sworn in as his successor. A few weeks later, on September 8, President Ford granted Nixon a full pardon for any crimes he may have committed while in office.

(See 58 Which president resigned from office? 203 What is executive privilege? 206 Can the president pardon criminals? 330 Did President Nixon try to cover up the Watergate affair?)

Q 374. How did the Iran-contra scandal come about?

A The contras of the Iran-contra scandal were rebels fighting against the leftist Sandinista government in Nicaragua. The Reagan administration had been covertly supporting the contras in the early 1980s, both to undermine a communist regime it did not want in Central America and to discourage the Sandinistas from meddling in the civil war in nearby El Salvador. In 1984, however, the Democratic-controlled Congress decided to stop any further U.S. aid to the contras (the Boland Amendment). But Reagan administration officials proceeded to circumvent the aid cutoff by soliciting donations for the contras from private individuals and friendly governments (about $48 million in two years). Lt. Col. Oliver North, a member of Reagan's National Security Council staff, ran the aid network.

North also ran another covert program for the Reagan administration—the secret sale of arms to Iran. Under pressure to win the return of hostages held by pro-Iranian terrorists in Lebanon, the Reagan administration ignored a U.S. ban on the sale of weapons to Iran and in 1985 began selling that country arms in return for its help in winning release of the hostages. Profits from the arms sales flowed to North, who in 1985 illegally diverted $3.8 million to the contras. North maintained that he had been authorized to do so, but his boss, Adm. John Poindexter, said he had never informed President Reagan of the diversion, which was the crux of the scandal. Meanwhile, just before the scandal was revealed, Congress reversed itself and again approved aid to the contras.

The scandal was investigated by the administration's Tower Commission, a congressional committee, and a special prosecutor, Lawrence Walsh, spent six and a half years and $47.9 million on his investigation. President Reagan was roundly criticized for his hands-off administrative style, but no direct involvement was ever proved. North and Poindexter were convicted of wrongdoing, but they had their convictions overturned on appeal because Congress had earlier granted them immunity during its investigation. President George Bush pardoned six others who had been implicated in the affair.

(See 462 Why was the National Security Council formed?)

Q 375. What was the Whitewater scandal?

A The complicated Whitewater scandal began unfolding in 1989, after the failure of the Madison Guaranty Savings and Loan Association in Little Rock, Arkansas, which was owned by Jim McDougal, a friend of then-governor Bill Clinton. After the bank collapsed because of personal loans to Arkansas political insiders and risky real estate loans—at a cost to taxpayers of $64 million—the Justice Department began to investigate whether the bank's assets had been illegally diverted to the political insiders. Bill and Hillary Clinton had invested in one of the failed real estate ventures, the Whitewater development scheme, and Hillary Clinton was a member of the Rose Law Firm in Little Rock, which had represented McDougal's failed bank.

President Clinton steadfastly denied any wrongdoing, but a special prosecutor was appointed in 1994 to see if any funds from McDougal's bank had been diverted to the Clintons' Whitewater account or had been used to repay his 1984 gubernatorial campaign debts. The president and first lady were forced to give testimony, but as of early 2000 neither had been convicted of any criminal acts. In 1996 McDougal and his wife, Susan, were convicted of arranging fraudulent loans, and Arkansas governor Jim Guy Tucker was convicted on charges related to Whitewater.

376. Who brought the Monica Lewinsky scandal to light?

A The prestige and powers of the presidency are such that if presidents really want to keep something secret, they have a good chance of doing so. But just one whistle-blower can upset everything. In President Bill Clinton's case, that person was Linda Tripp, a former White House staffer, whose tape recordings of her conversations with Clinton girlfriend Monica Lewinsky brought to light the sex scandal.

Between 1995 and 1997 Clinton had had an illicit sexual relationship with Lewinsky, a young White House intern. During that time, Lewinsky talked about the affair with friend Linda Tripp, who began secretly taping the conversations. Meanwhile, on January 17, 1998, President Clinton was compelled to testify in the long-running Paula Jones civil lawsuit (Jones claimed Clinton had sexually harassed her when he was Arkansas governor). During testimony he was asked about extramarital affairs, including any with Lewinsky. He denied under oath having sexual relations with her.

Tripp took her tapes to Whitewater special prosecutor Kenneth W. Starr, who was granted jurisdiction to investigate further. When news of Starr's investigation broke in January 1998, President Clinton went on television and flatly denied the affair. But Lewinsky told Starr about a dress she had worn during a sexual encounter with Clinton, and months later DNA tests confirmed Lewinsky's story. In August Clinton finally admitted the sexual relationship publicly and apologized for his conduct.

Clinton was impeached in December 1998 by the Republican-controlled House, but in early 1999 he was acquitted after the Senate tried his case. However, in early 2000 the judge in the Paula Jones civil suit ruled that Clinton had intentionally lied about his sexual relations with Lewinsky during testimony given in the Jones suit.

(See 65 What brought about President Bill Clinton's impeachment?)

FOR FURTHER INFORMATION

Among the best one-volume sources for detailed information on the policies, programs, and events of presidential administrations is Henry F. Graff's *The Presidents: A Reference History*. Each president's administration is described in highly readable narratives, which are broken down into various subsections about important aspects of the president's time in office. Other standard sources, arranged by topic instead of by president, include *Congressional Quarterly's Guide to the Presidency* (2d ed.), *The Presidency A to Z* (2d ed.), and the *Encyclopedia of the American Presidency*. For more detailed information on individual administrations, libraries usually have at least a book or two (sometimes sets of them) on each of the presidents—large libraries will probably have dozens on the major presidents. These are too numerous to list, but a wide selection of sources relating to the topics covered in this chapter is listed below. For those who prefer researching by the Internet, both the White House (http://www. whitehouse.gov) and the White House Historical Association (http://www. whitehousehistory.org) maintain Web sites.

Boller, Paul F. *Presidential Anecdotes.* New York: Oxford University Press, 1996.

Campbell, Karlyn, and Kathleen H. Jamieson. *Deeds Done in Words: Presidential Rhetoric and the Genres of Governance.* Chicago: University of Chicago Press, 1990.

Carpenter, Glenn J. *From George to George: A Book of Anecdotes, Facts, and Other Trivia about Our Forty-one Presidents.* Fargo, N.D.: Prairie House, 1992.

Connolly, Thomas, and Michael Senegal. *Almanac of the American Presidents.* New York: Facts on File, 1991.

Couch, Ernie. *Presidential Trivia.* New York: Routledge, 1996.

Cunningham, Noble E. *Popular Images of the Presidency: From Washington to Lincoln.* Columbia: University of Missouri Press, 1991.

Dallek, Robert. *Hail to the Chief: The Making and Unmaking of American Presidents.* Westport, Conn.: Hyperion, 1996.

Diller, Daniel C., and Stephen L. Robertson. *The Presidents, First Ladies and Vice Presidents: White House Biographies.* Washington, D.C.: Congressional Quarterly, 1996.

Ellis, Richard J. *Presidential Lightning Rods: The Politics of Blame Avoidance.* Lawrence: University Press of Kansas, 1994.

Fields, Wayne. *Union of Words: A History of Presidential Eloquence.* New York: Free Press, 1995.

Florig, Dennis. *The Power of Presidential Ideologies.* Westport, Conn.: Greenwood Press, 1992.

Frost, Elizabeth. *The World Almanac of Presidential Quotations.* Rahway, N.J.: World Almanac, 1993.

Garrison, Webb. *A Treasury of White House Tales.* Nashville: Rutledge Hill Press, 1996.

Gelderman, Carol. *All the Presidents' Words: The Bully Pulpit and Creation of the Virtual Presidency.* New York: Walker, 1997.

Graff, Henry F. *The Presidents: A Reference History.* New York: Macmillan, 1996.

Historic Documents on the Presidency: 1776–1989. ed. Michael Nelson. Washington, D.C.: Congressional Quarterly, 1989.

Kane, Joseph Nathan. *Presidential Fact Book.* New York: Random House, 1998.

Kellerman, Barbara, and Ryan J. Barilleaux. *The President as World Leader.* New York: St. Martin's Press, 1991.

Kernell, Samuel. *Going Public: New Strategies of Presidential Leadership.* 3d. ed. Washington, D.C.: CQ Press, 1997.

Laird, Archibald. *The Near Great: Chronicle of the Vice Presidents.* North Quincy, Mass.: Christopher Publishing House, 1980.

Levy, Leonard W., and Louis Fisher. *Encyclopedia of the American Presidency.* New York: Simon and Shuster, 1993.

Murray, Robert E., and Tim H. Blessing. *Greatness in the White House: Rating the Presidents.* University Park: Pennsylvania State University Press, 1993.

Nacos, Brigitte L. *The Press, Presidents, and Crises.* New York: Columbia University Press, 1990.

Nelson, Michael, ed. *Congressional Quarterly's Guide to the Presidency.* 2d ed. 2 vols. Washington, D.C.: Congressional Quarterly, 1996.

———, ed. *The Presidency and the Political System.* 6th ed. Washington, D.C.: CQ Press, 2000.

Plischke, Elmer. *Diplomat in Chief: The President at the Summit.* New York: Praeger, 1986.

Powers of the Presidency. 2d ed. Washington, D.C.: Congressional Quarterly, 1997.

The Presidency A to Z. 2d ed. Washington, D.C.: Congressional Quarterly, 1998.

The President, the Public, and the Parties. 2d ed. Washington, D.C.: Congressional Quarterly, 1997.

Presidential Polls and the News Media. Boulder: Westview Press, 1996.

Purcell, Edward L., ed. *The Vice Presidents: A Biographical Dictionary.* New York: Facts on File, 1998.

Purvis, Hoyt H. *The Presidency and the Press.* Austin: LBJ School of Public Affairs, 1976.

Ragsdale, Lyn. *Vital Statistics on the Presidency: Washington to Clinton.* Rev. ed. Washington, D.C.: Congressional Quarterly, 1998.

Raskin, Marcus G. *Presidential Disrespect: From Thomas Paine to Rush Limbaugh.* New York: Carol Publishing, 1996.

Rejai, Mostafa, and Kay Phillips. *Demythologizing an Elite: American Presidents in Empirical, Comparative, and Historical Perspective.* Westport, Conn.: Praeger, 1993.

Ridings, William J., Jr., and Stuart B. McIver. *Rating the Presidents: A Ranking of U.S. Leaders, from the Great and Honorable to the Dishonest and Incompetent.* New York: Carol Publishing, 1996.

Rivals for Power: Presidential-Congressional Relations. Ed. James A. Thurber. Washington, D.C.: CQ Press, 1996.

Ryan, Halford R., ed. *U.S. Presidents as Orators: A Bio-Critical Sourcebook.* Westport, Conn.: Greenwood Press, 1995.

Seale, William. *The President's House: A History.* New York: Abrams, 1986.

Smith, Richard, and Timothy Walch. *Farewell to the Chief: Former Presidents in American Life.* Glendo, Wyo.: High Plains Press, 1990.

Sullivan, Michael J. *Presidential Passions: The Love Affairs of American Presidents.* New York: Sure Seller, 1992.

Watson, Richard A. *Presidential Vetoes and Public Policy.* Lawrence: University Press of Kansas, 1993.

Whitney, David C., and Robin V. Whitney. *The American Presidents: Biographies of the Chief Executives from Washington through Clinton.* New York: Doubleday, 1996.

V
CAMPAIGNS AND ELECTIONS

IN GENERAL

Q 377. Who was the first dark-horse candidate to win the presidency?

A When the Democratic national convention deadlocked in 1844 over the two leading candidates' opposition to slavery, James K. Polk emerged as a compromise candidate who had not even been considered at the outset. A classic dark-horse candidate—that is, one who comes out of obscurity to win the nomination—Polk won the 1844 Democratic nomination on the ninth ballot and went on to become the first dark horse to win the presidency. Even though he was not initially considered a candidate for the nomination, Polk was by no means a complete unknown. He had been Speaker of the House for four years (and became the first and only Speaker elected president).

Other dark-horse candidates who became president were Franklin Pierce, Rutherford B. Hayes, Warren G. Harding, and Jimmy Carter. Carter began as a dark-horse candidate in 1976 and gained the Democratic nomination by winning enough primary races.

Q 378. What goes into a candidate's decision to run?

A Prospective presidential candidates must answer many questions before they commit themselves to the race. For example, they must decide whether they have the necessary experience in public office, the ability to raise millions of dollars to meet campaign expenses, and the immense amount of time it takes to mount a successful campaign. Technical questions abound as well. Can they develop a winning media image? Where will they find top-notch campaign staffers? What party and state election rules must be met to get on the ballot? How will their campaign strategy appeal to voting blocs in cities, states, and regions across the country? Then too, the campaign and four years in the White House will have an impact on their personal lives—how will they and their families handle the psychological pressures? Prospective candidates even have to consider what personal secrets might come out once the media begin their background probes.

Q 379. Is the economy a factor in presidential elections?

A Yes, a good economy tends to work in favor of the incumbent president and the president's party; a bad economy produces voter resentment that helps the challenger. The election of 1932 was a clear example of what a bad economy can do. Republican Herbert Hoover was in office during the 1929 stock market crash and the ensuing Great Depression. By 1932 voters were blaming him for the economic collapse and chose Democratic challenger Franklin D. Roosevelt for their next president by a wide margin.

Among the more recent elections in which the economy was an important factor were: 1960, the economy slumped in October, just before the election, and the Republican nominee, Vice President Richard M. Nixon, lost; 1980, inflation, a faltering economy, and high interest rates helped sink incumbent Jimmy Carter's reelection bid; 1992, voter reaction to a poor election year economy probably cost incumbent George Bush his chance at a second term; 1996, the strong economy helped win President Bill Clinton a second term, despite scandals and political missteps.

(See 197 How did presidents come to be regarded as the "Managers of Prosperity"? 198 When did presidents begin to try controlling the economy through taxing and spending decisions? 511 In what ways does the government influence the economy?)

Q 380. Do we elect the president and vice president directly?

A No, they are elected indirectly through the electoral college. Each vote cast in a presidential election goes toward electing a slate of electors—not the candidates themselves. Each state has as many slates as there are candidates, and electors on each slate are pledged to vote for a particular candidate. After the popular election, the winning slates of electors cast their votes for president and vice president.

The Framers of the Constitution devised this system as a compromise between election by direct popular vote, which many distrusted, and selection of the president by Congress. Originally, electors voted for two candidates for president; the candidate with the most votes became president and the runner-up, vice president. But the confusion caused by a tie vote for president and vice president in 1800 brought about the current system in which electors vote separately for each official.

(See 26 Which amendments to the Constitution deal with the presidency? 437 What went wrong in the presidential election of 1800?)

Q 381. How does the electoral college work?

A The electoral college exists only for a brief period at election time, and it never meets together as a body. Before the popular election in November, slates of electors are chosen in each state—one slate for each presidential ticket. The number of electors on the slate is equal to the number of representatives and senators the state has in Congress. When voters cast their ballots for the presidential and vice-presidential candidates in November, they are in fact voting for a slate of electors pledged to that candidate (see question above). Almost all states have a "winner-take-all" system, whereby the candidate with the most popular votes gets all the state's electoral votes.

The winning slates of electors meet in their respective state capitals in December to vote for the president and vice president. Congress receives statements recording their votes and on January 6 conducts a ceremonial count of the electoral votes. The winning candidate must have at least a majority of the electoral votes (270 out of a total of 538 were needed in 1996).

(See 437 What went wrong in the presidential election of 1800? 440 What deal was made to win Republican Rutherford B. Hayes the presidency in 1876?)

Q 382. Can electors vote for whomever they please?

A The Constitution allows electors to vote for anyone they want, but in fact few have ever broken their preelection pledge and cast a ballot for another candidate. The rare "faithless electors" have never affected the outcome of an election, and since 1789 only nine have broken their pledge. The first was in 1796, when a Federalist elector voted for Thomas Jefferson. The most recent was in 1988, when a Dukakis elector voted for Lloyd Bentsen, Gov. Michael Dukakis's running mate.

Q 383. Did the Constitution give everyone the vote?

A No. Because most states limited the vote to citizens who owned property or who met other requirements, only about half of the adult white males could vote when the Constitution was ratified in 1788. White male indentured servants, women, and black and Indian slaves could not vote. (Slaves then made up about 20 percent of the population.) By 1850 most states had eliminated restrictions on voting by white males, and after the Civil War, freed male slaves got the right to vote (by the Fifteenth Amendment, 1870). Women won voting rights much later (Nineteenth Amendment, 1920). More recently, the voting age was dropped from twenty-one years of age to eighteen (by the Twenty-sixth Amendment, 1971).

Q 384. About what percentage of voters casts ballots in presidential elections?

A Presidential elections usually attract the highest voter turnouts, but, as in congressional, state, and local elections, only a portion of the eligible voters actually votes. For example, only 49 percent of registered voters went to the polls in 1996, the lowest turnout since 1924. That was down from a high of 62.8 percent of voters in 1960, the peak turnout since World War I.

Q 385. Which incumbent presidents lost their reelection bids?

A Eleven sitting presidents who ran again lost their reelection bids, five of them in the twentieth century. The most recent five were William Howard Taft (defeated by Woodrow Wilson, 1912), Herbert Hoover (lost to Franklin D. Roosevelt, 1932), Gerald R. Ford (lost to Jimmy Carter, 1976), Jimmy Carter (defeated by Ronald Reagan, 1980), and George Bush (defeated by Bill Clinton, 1992).

The other six incumbent presidents were in office, and tried for reelection, in the 1800s. All served just one term, with the exception of Grover Cleveland, who lost his releection bid to Benjamin Harrison in 1888 and then won a second, nonconsecutive term later in 1892. The six were: John Adams, John Quincy Adams, Martin Van Buren, Millard Fillmore, Grover Cleveland, and Benjamin Harrison.

Q 386. Have any presidents decided not to run for another term?

A Fifteen presidents did not run again, even though they could have. Three others—Dwight D. Eisenhower, Ronald Reagan, and Bill Clinton—served two terms but were prohibited from running for a third term by the Twenty-second Amendment (1951). Twelve presidents served either two full terms or a partial term and a full term (because they succeeded to the presidency) and chose not to run again. They were George Washington, Thomas Jefferson, James Madison, James Monroe, Andrew Jackson, Ulysses S. Grant, Grover Cleveland, Theodore Roosevelt, Woodrow Wilson, Calvin Coolidge, Harry S. Truman, and Lyndon B. Johnson. (Roosevelt declined to run again after serving out McKinley's unfinished term and one of his own, but four years later, in 1912, he mounted an unsuccessful bid for another term.) Three other presidents—James K. Polk, James Buchanan, and Rutherford B. Hayes—each served one term and did not run again.

(See 178 Why was the two-term limit imposed on the presidency?)

Q **387. Has a president's party ever refused to nominate him for another term?**

A Five sitting presidents failed to get their parties' nod: John Tyler, Millard Fillmore, Franklin Pierce, Andrew Johnson, and Chester A. Arthur. Tyler, a Whig, angered Whig Party leaders in Congress when he pursued an independent course after succeeding to the presidency in 1841. President Fillmore lost his bid for the Whig nomination in 1852. In 1856 Democrats refused to renominate President Pierce because of his decision in 1854 to sign the Kansas-Nebraska Act. The measure led to a bloody battle between pro- and antislavery supporters in Kansas that turned antislavery northerners in the Democratic Party against Pierce. Andrew Johnson was a pro-Union southern Democrat whom Abraham Lincoln, a Republican, had chosen as his running mate to promote unity in the closing months of the Civil War. Republicans in Congress warred against Johnson while he was finishing out Lincoln's second term and nominated Ulysses S. Grant to replace him in 1868. President Arthur, who had succeeded to the presidency after James A. Garfield's assassination in 1881, was dumped in favor of James G. Blaine in 1884. Arthur had fought with the Stalwart Republicans, a powerful faction within the party.

Q **388. How many vice presidents have gone on to win the presidency?**

A Only five of the forty-five vice presidents have been elected president after serving out their terms. John Adams became the first in 1796, directly after serving as vice president under President George Washington. Thomas Jefferson (1800) and Martin Van Buren (1836) also went straight from the vice presidency to the presidency. That did not happen again until 1988, when George Bush was elected directly from the vice presidency to the presidency. President Richard M. Nixon narrowly missed doing so in 1960, but he eventually won the presidency—in 1968. In the 2000 presidential election, Vice President Al Gore is the Democratic challenger for the nation's highest office.

(See 222 How many vice presidents have succeeded to the presidency?)

POLITICAL PARTIES

Q **389. Have there always been two opposing parties?**

A Political parties are not mentioned in the Constitution; in fact, George Washington and the other Founders believed the country would be better off without them. Nevertheless, parties began to emerge several years after the Constitution was ratified, during President George Washington's second term.

At that time two parties came into being, representing the opposing sides of a fundamental disagreement over the nature of the government. The Democratic-Republicans, led by Thomas Jefferson and James Madison, opposed a strong federal government, supported states' rights, and called for greater popular control of government. The Federalists, led by Alexander Hamilton and John Adams, supported a strong federal government and a commitment to federal involvement in economic policy. The Federalists remained in power throughout the 1790s, but their party disintegrated in the years after Jefferson won the presidency (1800), and for a time the Democratic-Republicans were the only party.

Factions split the party during the 1820s, though, and the group led by Andrew Jackson evolved into the Democratic Party over that decade. Before long, a new party, the Whigs, rose in opposition to the Democrats and managed to capture the White House for two terms during the 1840s and early 1850s. The slavery issue broke up the Whig Party in the mid-1850s, just prior to the founding of the Republican Party.

Q 390. When were the Democratic and Republican Parties founded?

A The Democratic Party is the older of the two major parties, having evolved in the 1820s from a faction of the Democratic-Republican Party led by Andrew Jackson. Jackson's group appropriated the name Democratic-Republican and used it until 1830, when they shortened it to Democratic Party.

The Republican Party came into being in 1854, when opponents of slavery began organizing around the country to oppose the new doctrine of popular sovereignty (it allowed the territories to adopt slavery, if voters approved). Opponents of slavery in Ripon, Wisconsin, held the first organizational meeting in March 1854, and the new party adopted the name Republican that same year. John C. Fremont became the party's first presidential candidate in 1856, and Abraham Lincoln was the first Republican to win the office.

Q 391. Who created the Democratic donkey and Republican elephant symbols?

A *Harper's Weekly* cartoonist Thomas Nast popularized these familiar party symbols during the late 1800s. Nast, a Republican, began drawing the Democratic donkey in his cartoons in 1870. Four years later he introduced the Republican elephant.

Q **392. What has been the longest string of consecutive presidencies for a party?**

A In the twentieth century, Democrats had the longest unbroken string, a total of five terms between 1933 and 1953. President Franklin D. Roosevelt was in office for three of those terms and part of the fourth. Harry S. Truman served out Roosevelt's fourth term and one of his own. The Republicans' longest series of consecutive administrations was six, from 1861 to 1885: Abraham Lincoln, Andrew Johnson, Ulysses S. Grant, Rutherford B. Hayes, and James A. Garfield/Chester A. Arthur. Johnson, a Democrat elected on a Republican ticket with Lincoln, served out Lincoln's unfinished term.

The all-time record for the most consecutive administrations belongs to the long-defunct Democratic-Republican Party—seven straight administrations from 1801 to 1829. Three Democratic-Republican presidents served two terms each—Thomas Jefferson, James Madison, and James Monroe—and one, John Quincy Adams, was in office for one term. Monroe's two terms (1817–1825) became known as the "Era of Good Feeling" because of the relative political tranquility during his administration (in part because the Democratic-Republicans were the only surviving political party at that time).

(See 348 When did the presidents and vice presidents serve? 389 Have there always been two opposing parties?)

Q **393. Which major party named the first woman as chairperson? The first black?**

A Democrats named Jean Westwood the first national committee chairwoman in 1972. A decade and a half later they also installed the first African American, Ronald Brown, as chairman of a major party. Brown served from 1989 to 1993, when he became secretary of commerce in the Clinton administration.

Republicans named their first national committee chairwoman in 1974—Mary Louise Smith.

Q **394. What is the oldest existing third party?**

A Formed in 1869, the Prohibition Party is the oldest. An outgrowth of the nineteenth-century temperance movement, it continues to nominate candidates for the presidency and has broadened its party platform to include other issues—such as religious freedom and opposition to abortion—besides prohibition of the sale of liquor. Prohibition's most successful candidate was John Bidwell, who won 2.2 percent of the popular vote in 1892. The party was only one of various temperance groups responsible for ratification of the Eighteenth Amendment in 1919. The amendment, which was repealed in 1933, authorized Congress to prohibit the manufacture, sale, and transportation of liquor.

(See 441 Which third party presidential candidate polled the most votes in an election?)

Q 395. What obstacles confront third parties?

A The biggest problem third parties face is the traditional loyalty of voters to the two major parties. While third parties have taken advantage of short-term conflicts within the Democratic or Republican Parties to bolster their ranks, that advantage has lasted only so long as the major party has refused to adjust its stand. Third parties also must contend with complex rules governing ballot access and campaign financing, which vary from state to state, and can expect only a tiny fraction of the media exposure major party candidates get. Both third party organizations and their presidential candidates are often less experienced as well. That and the popular notion of votes being "wasted" on a third party candidate (because of the assumption that the candidate cannot possibly win) further reduce the chances of a third party's success at the polls.

(See 441 Which third party presidential candidate polled the most votes in an election?)

PRIMARIES, NOMINATIONS, AND CONVENTIONS

Q 396. How are presidential candidates chosen?

A Potential candidates begin the process themselves by "throwing their hats into the ring"—that is, by announcing their candidacy, usually at least a year before election. Then, by setting up a political action committee (PAC), they start the all-important process of fund-raising for the campaign. Meanwhile, their exploratory committees begin the work of assessing the prospects for victory, creating the campaign organization, developing campaign strategies, and writing position papers and speeches.

As the primary season approaches, candidates must make sure they have complied with the complicated rules for entering their party's primaries and caucuses. When voters cast ballots for one of the candidates in a primary, they are actually voting for delegates to the national party convention who are committed to the particular candidate. By winning enough primaries, the candidate eventually amasses enough delegates to ensure getting the nomination at the convention.

Usually held in July or August, the conventions today are essentially a formality. The candidate who has won the primaries gets the party nomination after the delegates have voted. What may not be known until after the convention begins, however, is who the nominee will pick for a vice-presidential running mate.

Q **397. When did the practice of ticket balancing start?**

A Political parties usually balance their tickets by nominating vice presidents who are sure to appeal to the region, voting bloc, or faction of the political party most upset by their presidential nominees. The practice began in the early 1800s and produced many different pairings, including North-South and New York–Virginia. Republican President Abraham Lincoln balanced his ticket in 1860 by naming Hannibal Hamlin, from the southern border state of Kentucky, as his vice president. In 1864 he chose Andrew Johnson, an antisecession Democrat from Tennessee, in another effort to promote national unity. Ticket balancing is still practiced today, and among the more famous combinations in modern times was the Kennedy-Johnson ticket of 1960. Senator John F. Kennedy, a northern liberal from Massachusetts, chose Texan Lyndon B. Johnson to placate southern Democrats and increase the ticket's appeal in the South.

▶ *Has any sitting president ever been denied his party's nomination? See 387 Has a president's party ever refused to nominate him for another term?*

Q **398. What are the basic strategies for winning primaries?**

A Presidential candidates have used six basic strategies, or combinations of them, over the years, though not all are effective today. With the *insider strategy,* for example, the candidate relies mainly on party resources and endorsements of party leaders to win the nomination. But the increased importance of winning primaries in the nomination process has reduced the effectiveness of relying on the party power structure alone. The *outsider strategy* pits the candidate against the political establishment, offering dissatisfied voters an alternative (as did Jimmy Carter in 1976). The *early knockout* strategy depends on winning a series of quick primary victories to force the other contenders to drop out early. In the *trench warfare* strategy, one candidate hopes to outlast one or more strong rivals in a no-holds-barred primary fight, but the victory comes at a cost. The bitter primary fight often leaves the winner weakened and at a disadvantage in the general election. Both the *slow buildup* and *wait-and-see* strategies have been rendered obsolete by the current primary system, in which nominations can be won with a series of wins early in the primary season. The two obsolete tactics were designed to keep the candidate out of the early primary fighting so he or she could arrive late in the game and play the role of party savior.

Q 399. Which party was first to nominate a Catholic as its presidential candidate?

A The Democratic Party nominated the first Catholic candidate to run for president, Alfred E. Smith, in 1928. Smith was the grandson of Irish immigrants. Republican Herbert Hoover won the election by a wide margin, however, and a Catholic president would not finally take office until John F. Kennedy, another Irish Catholic, won the presidency in 1960.

Q 400. Has an African American ever been nominated for president or vice president by a major party? An Orthodox Jew?

A No, but on a few occasions black Americans have been included in the running for either nomination. The first was Sen. Blanche Kelso Bruce, a Mississippi Republican, who won eleven votes for vice president at the Republican nominating convention in 1880. Chester A. Arthur won the nomination. Neither major party proposed a black candidate for president until 1968, however, when Democrats considered the Reverend Channing E. Phillips. In 1972 Rep. Shirley Chisholm, a Democrat from New York, became the first black woman to mount a serious primary challenge for the Democratic nomination. But civil rights activist and minister Jesse Jackson has made the strongest primary showings to date for the Democratic presidential nomination—in 1984 and 1988. In 1988 he won Democratic primaries in ten states, as well as Puerto Rico, the Virgin Islands, and the District of Columbia.

In 2000 Democrats chose the first Orthodox Jew as their vice-presidential candidate Senator Joe Lieberman.

Q 401. What happens if a party's presidential candidate dies before the election?

A The two major parties have rules for replacing a presidential or vice-presidential nominee who dies or resigns before the election. If the candidate is a Democrat, by rules established in 1984 the party's elected and organizational officials (the party's so-called "super-delegates") meet to choose a successor. Before that, the Democratic National Committee made the selection and did so once, in 1972, when it replaced vice-presidential nominee Thomas F. Eagleton after he withdrew from the race. For Republican candidates, the party's national committee names the successor.

The Twentieth Amendment (1933) provides for situations that may arise after the election. If the president-elect, dies, resigns, or has not been chosen by inauguration day, the vice president-elect serves as acting president until a president is selected. If there is no vice president, the Speaker of the House becomes acting president.

(See 26 Which amendments to the Constitution deal with the presidency?)

Q 402. When was the first presidential primary?

A Florida enacted the first presidential primary law in 1901 as part of the movement to give voters, rather than party bosses and business leaders, the power to select candidates. The primary system then spread, and by 1916 twenty-six states were holding them. Enthusiasm for primaries had dropped off by the 1930s, however, because primary winners too often failed to get the nomination at the party's national convention. Primaries did not come back into fashion until after World War II.

Q 403. When do states hold presidential primaries and caucuses?

A The primary season begins in February of the election year and runs through early June. Traditionally, the Iowa caucus and New Hampshire primary—held in January and February—have led off the primary season, but in recent years other states have moved up the dates of their primaries and caucuses in order to have a greater impact on the selection of the presidential nominee. Both Republicans and Democrats have enacted rules changes to encourage state parties to hold primaries later in the season, so that candidates cannot lock up their nominations within the first weeks. But that has not stopped Super Tuesday and Junior Tuesday, in which several states hold their primaries on or about the same day in March—in the early weeks of the primary season.

(See 405 Which presidential campaign sparked new interest in primaries? 407 What are Super Tuesday and Junior Tuesday?)

Q 404. What is the difference between closed and open primaries?

A Primaries can be set up as closed, modified, or open. In *closed primaries,* voters must be registered members of the party holding the primary. Only registered Democrats, for example, can participate in a closed Democratic primary. About half the state primaries are closed. *Modified primaries* are basically closed primaries that allow independent voters to participate, but not members of the opposition party. *Open pri-*

maries allow any registered voter to participate, including members of the opposition party. Thus if enough Democrats and independents vote in an open Republican primary, they can influence the choice of the Republican nominee. That happened during some of the early primaries in the 2000 presidential election. A few states hold *blanket primaries* in which all candidates are listed on the same ballot.

Q 405. Which presidential campaign sparked new interest in primaries?

A Sen. John F. Kennedy, a Roman Catholic, battled his way through a series of consecutive wins in the 1960 Democratic presidential primaries and so showed party leaders that he could in fact be elected. His successful uphill battle for the nomination popularized the primary route for future presidential hopefuls of both parties. Among them were Republican Richard M. Nixon, who in 1968 shed his image as a loser by winning Republican primaries, and Democrat George S. McGovern, who overcame objections to his liberal views through Democratic primary wins in 1972. Years later, two southern Democrats, Jimmy Carter and Bill Clinton, came out of relative obscurity to win Democratic presidential nominations in 1976 and 1992, respectively, thanks to strong showings in the primaries.

Q 406. Can a candidate become president despite losing in the New Hampshire primary?

A Winning in New Hampshire has been a good bellwether for presidential hopefuls, but it is no guarantee. Since 1952 no candidate who has lost the New Hampshire primary has gone on to win the presidency—except for Bill Clinton, who lost there in 1992.

In fact, emerging victorious from the New Hampshire primary does not ensure the candidate will win his party's nomination. For example, in 1964 Henry Cabot Lodge won New Hampshire but lost the GOP nomination, and in 2000 Republican candidate John McCain, the victor in New Hampshire, failed to get the GOP nod. If Republican presidential nominee George Bush wins the election in 2000, he will join President Clinton in defying the New Hampshire primary rule.

Q 407. What are Super Tuesday and Junior Tuesday?

A Beginning in 1988 several southern states moved their primaries to the same Tuesday early in the primary season, creating what is called Super Tuesday. The idea was to give the southern states more clout in the primaries and to provide more support for candidates acceptable to their voters. On the first Super Tuesday (March 8, 1988), fourteen southern and border states participated, along with two New England states. That dropped to eight states in 1992 and 1996.

The first Junior Tuesday was held in March 1996. Six New England states (all except New Hampshire), plus Georgia and Maryland, created this new primary grouping when they decided to hold their primaries (or caucuses) in the week of March 2–9.

Q 408. When was the first national nominating convention held?

A The Anti-Masonic Party held the first national nominating convention in September 1831. Meeting in Baltimore, Maryland, the 116 delegates to the convention nominated William Wirt for president. The National Republicans, an offshoot of the Democratic-Republican Party, held their convention in December 1831 and nominated Henry Clay. Following suit, the Democrats held their first convention in May 1832 and nominated incumbent president Andrew Jackson. President Jackson won the election in 1832.

Q 409. How were candidates chosen before the conventions?

A The candidate selection process underwent several changes before parties adopted the convention system. In the first years of the Republic, members of the electoral college simply voted for the candidate of their choice. There were no official nominees and the candidate with the most votes became president. By the end of President George Washington's second administration, however, political parties began to emerge and the system of selecting candidates by congressional caucus came into being. By President James Monroe's election in 1816, the caucus system had become so strong that nomination by the so-called "King Caucus" all but guaranteed the nominee's election. The King Caucus system disappeared along with the Democratic-Republican Party in 1824, replaced by various decentralized nominating systems, including state party conventions and mass meetings. These gave way to the national nominating conventions established during the 1832 election cycle (*see question above*).

Q 410. What purpose do the national party conventions serve now?

A National conventions (and the party bosses who used to control them) once handled the presidential nominating process, but the increasing popularity of primaries since World War II has handed voters most of the control. Now the names of the nominees are all but certain long before the conventions, eliminating much of the drama that once surrounded these mass party gatherings. But even with their diminished role, conventions still provide the parties with an opportunity to showcase their nominees before millions of television viewers, to write and publicize their platforms, and to handle other business. Conventions may also give invaluable national exposure to up and coming party hopefuls, especially those who deliver a convention's keynote address.

(See 396 How are presidential candidates chosen? 402 When was the first presidential primary? 408 When was the first national nominating convention held?)

Q 411. What was the longest convention on record?

A The Democrats' seventeen-day convention in the 1924 campaign season was the longest. Held in New York City, the convention went through 103 roll call votes before choosing John W. Davis as the Democratic presidential nominee. Davis lost to Republican Calvin Coolidge, who won the 1924 election by a landslide.

Q 412. Which convention produced the longest party platform?

A The Democratic Party platform in 1984 ran over 45,000 words, the longest ever put forward by either party. Democrats also hold the distinction of having produced the first party platform—now the traditional statement of party principles—for the election of 1840. It ran less than 1,000 words.

Q 413. Who was the first woman contender for the presidential nomination of a major party?

A The Republican Party was the first major party to propose a woman presidential nominee. Sen. Margaret Chase Smith of Maine was put up for nomination at the 1964 convention, but fellow senator Barry Goldwater of Arizona ultimately became the Republican candidate.

The first woman to run for president was Victoria Claflin Woodhull, who ran as the People's (Equal Rights) Party nominee in 1872. The party ran women candidates in 1884 and 1888 as well, even though women did not have the right to vote at that time.

Q 414. Who was the first woman vice-presidential candidate of a major party?

A A three-term member of the House of Representatives, Geraldine Ferraro of New York, became the first in 1984, when Democratic presidential candidate Walter F.

Mondale chose her as his running mate. Mondale and Ferraro faced a strong Republican ticket, however—incumbents Ronald Reagan and George Bush, who went on to win the 1984 election by a landslide. Ferraro's candidacy was hampered by, among other things, her lack of experience, her position on abortion, and a controversy over her husband's business dealings.

Q **415. Which candidate broke tradition by accepting his nomination for president in person?**

A Franklin D. Roosevelt made the first personal appearance by a major party's nominee in 1932 at the Democratic convention in Chicago. Prior to that, candidates of major parties had accepted their party's nomination at a special ceremony held several weeks after the convention. The advent of radio coverage in 1924 helped to bring about the change—the acceptance speech added a dramatic high point to the convention.

Roosevelt went on to break another long-standing tradition by running for a third (and fourth) term as president, something no other president has done.

(See 178 Why was the two-term limit imposed on the presidency? 444 When did presidential candidates first give speeches in their own behalf?)

Q **416. When was the first televised convention?**

A Republicans held the first televised convention in 1940, when they nominated Wendell Willkie for president. Television was still in its infancy, however, and the viewing audience was quite tiny in comparison with today's convention broadcasts. Willkie lost the election to incumbent Democrat Franklin D. Roosevelt, who won his third term in 1940.

THE CAMPAIGNS

Q **417. What famous slogans have campaigns produced?**

A Catchy phrases have long been a staple of election campaigns—they grab voters' attention with wit, rhyme, alliteration, or emotional appeal. Slogans can tout a candidate, push a policy, or dump on an opponent, but in modern times at least, they have always been short enough to fit on a bumper sticker, placard, or campaign button. Every presidential campaign season has produced its share of slogans, and most are forgotten soon after the president takes office. A sampler of the more memorable campaign slogans are listed below:

Tippecanoe and Tyler Too. 1840 campaign. Memorable rhyming slogan for Whig candidates William Henry Harrison (hero of the 1811 Battle of Tippecanoe) and John Tyler.

Fifty-four Forty or Fight! 1844 campaign. Democrat James K. Polk's slogan, which called for setting the northwest boundary between the United States and Canada at latitude 54 degrees, 40 minutes. As president, Polk settled for a line extending along latitude 49 degrees.

Don't Change Horses in Mid-stream. 1864 campaign. Incumbent president Abraham Lincoln's slogan.

A Chicken in Every Pot, a Car in Every Garage. 1932 campaign during the height of the Great Depression. Attributed to Republican Herbert Hoover, who denied he ever said it.

Keep Cool with Coolidge. 1924 campaign. A bit of election year alliteration used by incumbent president Calvin Coolidge.

Don't Be a Third Termite. 1940 campaign. Republican Wendell L. Willkie's reminder that President Franklin D. Roosevelt was running for an unprecedented third term (thus the term-ite).

Give 'em Hell, Harry. 1948 campaign. Incumbent president Harry S. Truman's unofficial slogan, a reference to his outspoken style.

I Like Ike. 1952 and 1956 campaigns. One of Dwight D. Eisenhower's slogans, modeled on his nickname, Ike.

All the Way with LBJ. 1964 campaign. Incumbent president Lyndon B. Johnson's slogan.

Four More Years. 1972 campaign. Incumbent President Richard M. Nixon's slogan.

Are You Better Off than You Were Four Years Ago? 1976 and 1980 campaigns. Democrat Jimmy Carter used this slogan to successfully attack his opponent, incumbent president Gerald Ford. Carter's opponent in 1980, Republican Ronald Reagan, turned it against him.

Read My Lips, No New Taxes! 1988 campaign. Republican George Bush's slogan came back to haunt him in 1992, after he agreed to raise taxes.

It's the Economy, Stupid. 1992 campaign. Originally a reminder posted for the benefit of Democrat Bill Clinton's campaign workers, it became a campaign mantra. Candidate Clinton made the sluggish economy a key campaign issue, and after his election victory "It's the economy, stupid" survived as one of his campaign's more memorable slogans.

Q 418. Which presidents ran without opposition?

A Only two presidents have been elected without facing an opponent—George Washington and James Monroe. Washington's election as the first president under the Constitution was all but a foregone conclusion. He was, after all, the commander who won the Revolutionary War and the country's foremost national hero. Washington was unopposed in elections to his first and second terms (1789 and 1792).

James Monroe, a Democratic-Republican, did face a Federalist Party opponent in 1816 when he ran for his first term. But by 1820 the Federalist Party had disintegrated, and Monroe won reelection to a second term without opposition.

(See 292 Who became president without having been elected to the office?)

Q 419. Which president championed political parties?

A Martin Van Buren believed in the political party system of government and did much to promote party politics in the federal government during his terms as vice president under Andrew Jackson and as president. Van Buren later described the advantages of political parties in his book, *An Inquiry into the Origin and Course of Political Parties in the United States* (1867). Unlike George Washington and some other early leaders, Van Buren believed that the pursuit of selfish ends by individual parties ultimately would work to the benefit of all. Furthermore, presidents working within a party structure would tend to rely on building coalitions and on using the politics of consensus. Van Buren thought the personal politics of an independent president posed greater risks, notably that of polarizing the electorate.

Q 420. Why was the Log Cabin campaign of 1840 a success?

A One of the most colorful in American history, the Log Cabin campaign for the presidency was a tour de force of image making in electoral politics. William Henry Harrison was a war hero and Indian fighter from Ohio who had slipped into obscurity when the Whig Party ran him as its candidate in 1840. Party strategists decided to completely avoid any issues for the 1840 campaign; instead they built a remarkably successful campaign around Harrison's image as a pioneering folk hero and man of the people—the log cabin image. Harrison, a descendant of a prominent Virginia family, was portrayed as a hard-cider drinking general born in a log cabin. By contrast, Incumbent president Martin Van Buren was painted as a wine-drinking aristocrat with fancy tastes and an expensive mansion (Van Buren actually was a tavern keeper's son).

The Whigs' skillfully run campaign took advantage of the flourishing "penny press" newspapers—over 200 dailies were in operation then—by distributing campaign sheets that could be inserted in them. Horace Greeley's weekly *Log Cabin* insert was the most famous. The emotional appeal generated by the Log Cabin campaign worked wonders. Harrison and his running mate, John Tyler ("Tippecanoe and Tyler Too"), unseated an incumbent president and vice president for the first time and became the first Whigs to occupy the offices of president and vice president.

(See 68 Were any presidents actually born in log cabins?)

Q 421. What issue won Polk the presidency?

A When Texas won its independence from Mexico in 1836, it immediately asked to enter the Union as a state. But Presidents Andrew Jackson and Martin Van Buren both put off making a decision on statehood for two important reasons. For one thing, it would likely spark a war with Mexico, which refused to recognize Texas's independence. For another, adding a new state would raise the bitterly divisive issue of slavery—the South wanted slavery allowed in Texas, and northern abolitionists were dead set against it.

The issue of Texas statehood finally came to a head in the election of 1844. James K. Polk, former Speaker of the House of Representatives and governor of Tennessee, won the Democratic nomination that year because he supported Texas statehood. Democrats made statehood the central issue of the campaign, even forcing Polk's opponent, Whig Henry Clay, to reverse his opposition to it in a last-ditch effort to salvage the election. But Polk won a narrow victory, and by the time he took office in 1845, Texas had been annexed (President John Tyler issued the order in the last days of his administration).

(See 310 Who preached peace while waging war? 377 Who was the first dark-horse candidate to win the presidency?)

Q 422. Which presidential candidate made use of torchlight parades?

A Abraham Lincoln's campaign for president in 1860 featured displays by Republican marching clubs, called Wide Awakes. Sometimes numbering in the thousands, they put on impressive displays by marching through towns at night carrying torches and singing campaign songs.

The idea for the clubs began in February 1860, when a group of Republicans offered to escort Republican abolitionist and politician Cassius M. Clay from the train station to his lodgings in Hartford, Connecticut, prior to his speaking engagement. The small torchlight parade proved such a success that Wide Awake clubs began springing up throughout the North. Eventually 400,000 Republican marchers joined the clubs.

Q 423. When did the modern campaign button first appear?

A The presidential campaign of 1896 saw the first campaign buttons, made of celluloid attached to a metal holder and a device for fastening it to clothing. Celluloid plastics had been invented in 1868, and two experimental versions of buttons appeared some years later. But it was not until a New Jersey company, Whitehead and Hoag, acquired the patent for what became the modern campaign button in 1896 that buttons suddenly flooded the political landscape. For the 1896 campaign, over a thousand different buttons were manufactured, and in the years that followed they became a staple of political campaigns.

Q 424. Why did candidate McKinley adopt the slogan "In Gold We Trust"?

A One of many pro-gold slogans used by William McKinley's campaign in 1896, it was meant to counter the remarkably effective campaign for silver money advanced by populist Democrat William Jennings Bryan. Bryan touted free coinage of silver—effectively abandoning the gold standard—as a way to make more money available to struggling farmers and workingmen. They were being hurt by an economic depression, which had begun in 1893. At the Democratic national convention, Bryan delivered a stirring address, his "Cross of Gold" speech, in which he denounced the gold standard as the means by which business interests kept workers from getting ahead.

McKinley, a conservative Republican backed by big business and the eastern establishment, opposed the idea of expanding the money supply through silver coinage. He feared it would cause ruinous inflation and instead favored protecting American jobs by raising tariffs on foreign imports. While Bryan barnstormed the country speaking to thousands of voters, McKinley conducted a "front porch" campaign in which large groups of voters came by train to hear him speak from his home in Ohio. McKinley eventually won the election in 1896 with his pro-gold stand and a promise that prosperity was on the way.

▶ *Why did Teddy Roosevelt form the Bull Moose Party? See 441 Which third party presidential candidate polled the most votes in an election?*

Q **425. When did FDR introduce his New Deal concept?**

A Franklin D. Roosevelt made the first reference to a "new deal" for Americans during his acceptance speech before the Democratic national convention in 1932. But he did not make it a major theme until after he won the election and began instituting his program of economic and social reforms to counter the Great Depression. Roosevelt's "Hundred Days" in office saw a burst of legislative activity; the president pushed New Deal bills through Congress to create public works and relief agencies, reform the banking system, reorganize farm credit programs, and establish the Tennessee Valley Authority.

As impressive as Roosevelt's Hundred Days were, his New Deal did not stop there. Over the next years he established the Social Security system and other programs that committed the federal government to playing an active role in solving the country's social and economic problems. To accomplish that, however, Roosevelt vastly expanded the size, scope, and powers of the federal government and the presidency.

(See 319 What did President Roosevelt mean when he said, "The only thing we have to fear is fear itself"?)

Q 426. Who won the presidency with a "whistle-stop" campaign?

A President Harry S. Truman, facing an uphill battle for election to a new term in 1948, took his campaign to the people by riding the nation's railroads and speaking at towns and cities across the country. He had little choice; FDR's old New Deal coalition was breaking up. Southern Democrats were in open revolt against Truman's backing for civil rights (South Carolina governor Strom Thurmond became the candidate of States' Rights Democrats), while left-wing Democrats had formed another splinter group, the Progressive Party, with former vice president Henry A. Wallace as their candidate.

Against all odds Truman managed to make the whistle-stop campaign work—he won the biggest upset victory in U.S. history by beating his Republican rival, Thomas E. Dewey, by over two million votes. Thurmond won only four Deep South states. Dewey had been considered the easy winner throughout the campaign.

Truman himself gave us the name "whistle-stop" campaign. When his train arrived in Los Angeles, he joked that it was the biggest whistle-stop on his tour. From that comment came the expression that is now part of the campaign vocabulary. Truman was not the first candidate to use the railroad for campaigning, however. William Jennings Bryan spoke at six hundred railroad stops around the country during his unsuccessful presidential bid in 1896.

Q **427. Which candidate was dubbed an "egghead"?**

A Illinois governor Adlai E. Stevenson, the Democratic presidential nominee in 1952, had a reputation as a well-spoken liberal intellectual, but Republicans managed to turn that against him by labeling the governor an "egghead." The implication was that Stevenson was out of touch with the world of average Americans because he was an intellectual. Republican presidential candidate Dwight D. Eisenhower, by contrast, was hailed as a national hero, who had led Allied troops to victory in Europe during World War II.

Republicans made the first extensive use of television in the 1952 campaign, and it probably contributed to the drubbing of Stevenson at the polls that year. Eisenhower received 55.1 percent of the popular vote to Stevenson's 44.4 percent.

▶ *Why was Nixon forced to give his "Checkers speech"? See 345 What was Nixon's "Checkers speech" about?*

Q **428. Which first lady pioneered the role of political campaign surrogate for the president during election campaigns?**

A President Lyndon B. Johnson's wife, Lady Bird Johnson, was the first to act as a surrogate campaigner. During the 1964 presidential elections, Lady Bird frequently campaigned alone on her husband's behalf, spearheading an effort to win over southern voters who resented his support for civil rights legislation. Since then, other first ladies have followed in her footsteps, actively campaigning for their husbands' election.

(See 126 How did Eleanor Roosevelt reshape the role of first lady? 180 What does the first lady do?)

Q 429. Which candidates debated on television?

A The first four televised debates by presidential candidates took place in 1960 between Richard M. Nixon and John F. Kennedy. Nixon did not come across well on television (Kennedy did) and many believed he lost the election because of it. That may be one reason why there were no further presidential debates until 1976, when President Gerald R. Ford and his Democratic challenger, Jimmy Carter, went before television cameras three times. Since then, every election year has featured a debate between the major presidential contenders (Ronald Reagan and Jimmy Carter, 1980; Reagan and Walter F. Mondale, 1984; George Bush and Michael S. Dukakis, 1988; Bill Clinton, Bush, and Ross Perot, 1992; Clinton and Bob Dole, 1996).

The first vice-presidential candidates to debate were Walter F. Mondale and Bob Dole in 1976. George Bush debated Geraldine Ferraro in 1984, and since then there have been vice-presidential debates before each election (Dan Quayle and Lloyd Bentsen Jr., 1988; Quayle, Al Gore, and James Stockdale, 1992; Gore and Jack Kemp, 1996).

Q 430. When did preelection public opinion surveys come into being?

A Newspapers began taking preelection straw polls early in the 1800s by sending reporters out to ask train or steamship passengers which candidate they preferred. By the 1930s, however, these informal polls had given way to more formal operations in which newspapers mailed out sample ballots to thousands of readers. But even these polls were inaccurate at best; no effort was made to use scientific sampling techniques until the Gallup Organization was formed in the 1930s. Gallup's preelection polls successfully predicted President Franklin D. Roosevelt's victory over Republican challenger Alf Landon in 1936. Despite a major setback in 1948 (pollsters missed a late surge for Harry S. Truman, who scored a major upset victory over Republican challenger Thomas E. Dewey), preelection polling developed into a key component in presidential campaigns. President George Bush even went so far as to name a pollster, Robert M. Teeter, as his campaign manager—the first president to do so.

(See 426 Who won the presidency with a "whistle-stop" campaign?)

Q 431. Can pollsters correctly predict the winning candidate?

A Polls taken close to election day tend to be more accurate than those reported earlier in the campaign season. In recent years the eleventh-hour preelection polls have routinely come within a couple of percentage points of the actual outcome, but those taken as late as the close of the nominating conventions—only about two months from the elections—can be very inaccurate. President Lyndon B. Johnson, for example, was shown leading by 36 percentage points in the summer of 1964, but finally won the election by 23 percentage points. In the seesaw race between President George Bush and challenger Bill Clinton in 1992, polls showed Bush leading early on and then had him trailing by as much as 20 percent of the vote. The race ended with Clinton winning 43 percent, Bush 38 percent, and Ross Perot 19 percent.

The biggest miss for the polls came in the 1948 elections, when President Harry S. Truman won the biggest upset in political history. Pollsters took their last surveys in September and October and so missed Truman's late comeback rally. Supposedly trailing Republican challenger Thomas E. Dewey by 11 percent, Truman won the election by 4.5 percent of the popular vote.

ELECTING THE PRESIDENT AND VICE PRESIDENT

Q **432. Which presidents have won by the biggest and smallest vote margins?**

A Few presidents have won by a landslide—by 60 percent or more of the popular vote—and among these big winners Democrat Lyndon B. Johnson holds the record. In 1964 Johnson received 61.1 percent of the vote (about 43.1 million votes), crushing Republican Barry Goldwater, who finished with 38.5 percent of the vote.

The other biggest winners were Republican Warren G. Harding in 1920, Democrat Franklin D. Roosevelt in 1936, and Republican Richard M. Nixon in 1972. Nixon won by the biggest popular vote margin, 17.9 million votes, though his 60.7 percent of the total vote was shy of Johnson's mark.

The closest presidential election of all time was President James A. Garfield's hair's-breadth victory in 1880. Garfield beat Democratic challenger Winfield Scott Hancock by just 1,898 votes, or one-tenth of a percent. Four other election victories also were decided by 1 percent of the popular vote or less: Grover Cleveland in 1884, Benjamin Harrison in 1888, John F. Kennedy in 1960, and Richard M. Nixon in 1968.

(See 434 What is a minority president?)

Q **433. What were the popular and electoral vote counts in each of the presidential elections?**

A Forty-two presidents and forty-five vice presidents have held office. President Grover Cleveland is counted twice because he served nonconsecutive terms, the only president to do so. No vice president has served nonconsecutive terms, but two have served under different presidents.

In the table below, popular vote counts are not listed for the 1789–1820 elections because reliable figures are not available. For elections between 1789 and 1800, votes for president and vice president were not separate. The candidate with the most electoral votes became president; the one with the second highest total became vice president. For the Twentieth Century, the table includes major third party candidates who received electoral votes. (Abbreviations for political parties are: AI–American Independent, D–Democratic, DR–Democratic-Republican, F–Federalist, NR–National Republican, P–Progressive, R–Republican, SRD–States Rights Democrat, W–Whig.)

Year	Candidate party	Popular Vote	Percent of Total Popular Vote	Electoral Vote
1789	George Washington (F)	—	—	69
	John Adams (F)	—	—	34
1792	George Washington (F)	—	—	132
	John Adams (F)	—	—	77
1796	John Adams (F)	—	—	71
	Thomas Jefferson (DR)	—	—	68
1800	Thomas Jefferson (DR)	—	—	73
	Aaron Burr (DR)	—	—	73
	John Adams (F)	—	—	65
	Charles Cotesworth Pinckney (F)	—	—	64
1804	Thomas Jefferson (DR)	—	—	162
	Charles Cotesworth Pinckney (F)	—	—	14
1808	James Madison (DR)	—	—	122
	Charles Cotesworth Pinckney (F)	—	—	47
1812	James Madison (DR)	—	—	128
	George Clinton (F)	—	—	89
1816	James Monroe (DR)	—	—	183
	Rufus King (F)	—	—	34
1820	James Monroe (DR)	—	—	231
	John Adams (F)			1

Year	Candidate party	Popular Vote	Percent of Total Popular Vote	Electoral Vote
1824	John Quincy Adams (DR)	113,122	30.9	84
	Andrew Jackson (DR)	151,271	41.3	99
1828	Andrew Jackson (D)	642,553	56.0	178
	John Quincy Adams (NR)	500,897	43.6	83
1832	Andrew Jackson (D)	701,780	54.2	219
	Henry Clay (NR)	484,205	37.4	49
1836	Martin Van Buren (D)	764,176	50.8	170
	William Henry Harrison (W)	550,816	36.6	73
1840	William Henry Harrison (W)	1,275,390	52.9	234
	Martin Van Buren (D)	1,128,854	46.8	60
1844	James K. Polk (D)	1,339,494	49.5	170
	Henry Clay (W)	1,300,004	48.1	105
1848	Zachary Taylor (W)	1,361,393	47.3	163
	Lewis Cass (D)	1,223,460	42.5	127
1852	Franklin Pierce (D)	1,607,510	50.8	254
	Winfield Scott (W)	1,386,942	43.9	42
1856	James Buchanan (D)	1,836,072	45.3	174
	John C. Fremont (R)	1,342,345	33.1	114
1860	Abraham Lincoln (R)	1,865,908	39.9	180
	Stephen A. Douglas (D)	1,380,202	29.5	12
1864	Abraham Lincoln (R)	2,218,388	55.0	212
	George B. McClellan (D)	1,812,807	45.0	21
1868	Ulysses S. Grant (R)	3,013,650	52.7	214
	Horatio Seymour (D)	2,708,744	47.3	80
1872	Ulysses S. Grant (R)	3,598,235	55.6	286
	Horace Greeley (D)	2,834,761	43.8	(died after election)
1876	Rutherford B. Hayes (R)	4,034,311	48.0	185
	Samuel J. Tilden (D)	4,288,546	51.0	184

Year	Candidate party	Popular Vote	Percent of Total Popular Vote	Electoral Vote
1880	James A. Garfield (R)	4,446,158	48.3	214
	Winfield S. Hancock (D)	4,444,260	48.3	155
1884	Grover Cleveland (D)	4,874,621	48.5	219
	James G. Blaine (R)	4,848,936	48.2	182
1888	Benjamin Harrison (R)	5,443,892	47.8	233
	Grover Cleveland (D)	5,534,488	48.6	168
1892	Grover Cleveland (D)	5,551,883	46.1	277
	Benjamin Harrison (R)	5,179,244	43.0	145
1896	William McKinley (R)	7,108,480	51.0	271
	William J. Bryan (D)	6,511,495	46.7	176
1900	William McKinley (R)	7,218,039	51.7	292
	William J. Bryan (D)	6,538,345	45.5	155
1904	Theodore Roosevelt (R)	7,626,593	56.4	336
	Alton B. Parker (D)	5,082,898	37.6	140
1908	William Howard Taft (R)	7,676,258	51.6	321
	William J. Bryan (D)	6,406,801	43.0	162
1912	Woodrow Wilson (D)	6,293,152	41.8	435
	Theodore Roosevelt (P)	4,119,207	27.4	88
	William Howard Taft (R)	3,486,333	23.2	8
1916	Woodrow Wilson (D)	9,126,300	49.2	277
	Charles E. Hughes (R)	8,546,789	46.1	254
1920	Warren G. Harding (R)	16,153,115	60.3	404
	James M. Cox (D)	9,133,092	34.1	127
1924	Calvin Coolidge (R)	15,719,921	54.0	382
	John W. Davis (D)	8,386,704	28.8	136
	Robert M. LaFollette (P)	4,832,532	16.6	13
1928	Herbert Hoover (R)	21,437,277	58.2	444
	Alfred E. Smith (D)	15,007,698	40.8	87
1932	Franklin D. Roosevelt (D)	22,829,501	57.4	472
	Herbert Hoover (R)	15,760,684	39.6	59

Year	Candidate party	Popular Vote	Percent of Total Popular Vote	Electoral Vote
1936	Franklin D. Roosevelt (D)	27,757,333	60.8	523
	Alfred M. Landon (R)	16,684,231	36.5	8
1940	Franklin D. Roosevelt (D)	27,313,041	54.7	449
	Wendell L. Willkie (R)	22,348,480	44.8	82
1944	Franklin D. Roosevelt (D)	25,612,610	53.4	432
	Thomas E. Dewey (R)	22,017,617	45.9	99
1948	Harry S. Truman (D)	24,179,345	49.6	303
	Thomas E. Dewey (R)	21,991,291	45.1	189
	J. Strom Thurmond (SRD)	1,176,125	2.4	39
1952	Dwight D. Eisenhower (R)	33,936,234	55.1	442
	Adlai E. Stevenson (D)	27,314,992	44.4	89
1956	Dwight D. Eisenhower (R)	35,590,472	57.4	457
	Adlai E. Stevenson (D)	26,022,752	42.0	73
1960	John F. Kennedy (D)	34,226,731	49.7	303
	Richard M. Nixon (R)	34,108,157	49.5	219
1964	Lyndon B. Johnson (D)	43,129,566	61.1	486
	Barry Goldwater (R)	27,178,188	38.5	52
1968	Richard M. Nixon (R)	31,785,480	43.4	301
	Hubert H. Humphrey (D)	31,275,166	42.7	191
	George C. Wallace (AI)	9,906,473	13.5	46
1972	Richard M. Nixon (R)	47,169,911	60.7	520
	George McGovern (D)	29,170,383	37.5	17
1976	Jimmy Carter (D)	40,830,763	50.1	297
	Gerald R. Ford (R)	39,147,793	48.0	240
1980	Ronald Reagan (R)	43,904,153	50.7	489
	Jimmy Carter (D)	35,483,883	41.0	49
1984	Ronald Reagan (R)	54,455,075	58.8	525
	Walter F. Mondale (D)	37,577,185	40.6	13
1988	George Bush (R)	48,886,097	53.4	426
	Michael S. Dukakis (D)	41,809,074	45.6	111

Year	Candidate party	Popular Vote	Percent of Total Popular Vote	Electoral Vote
1992	Bill Clinton (D)	44,909,326	43.0	370
	George Bush (R)	39,103,882	37.4	168
1996	Bill Clinton (D)	47,402,357	49.2	379
	Bob Dole (R)	39,198,755	40.7	159

▶ *Which incumbent presidents lost their reelection bids? See 385.*

▶ *How often have vice presidents been elected president? See 388 How many vice presidents have gone on to win the presidency?*

Q **434. What is a minority president?**

A In seventeen elections, presidential candidates have won the presidency without getting a majority of the votes cast, making them "minority presidents." Three of the candidates—John Quincy Adams (1824), Rutherford B. Hayes (1876), and Benjamin Harrison (1888)—got fewer votes than their rivals but won anyway. The House decided the elections of Adams and Hayes, while Harrison wound up winning more electoral votes. The fourteen minority presidents and the seventeen elections in which they failed to gain a majority were:

Year	Candidate	Percent of Popular Vote
1824	John Quincy Adams*	30.9
1844	James K. Polk	49.6
1848	Zachary Taylor	47.3
1856	James Buchanan	45.3
1860	Abraham Lincoln	39.8
1876	Rutherford B. Hayes*	48.0
1880	James A. Garfield	48.3
1884	Grover Cleveland	48.5
1888	Benjamin Harrison*	47.8
1892	Grover Cleveland	46.1
1912	Woodrow Wilson	41.8
1916	Woodrow Wilson	49.2

Year	Candidate	Percent of Popular Vote
1948	Harry S. Truman	49.6
1960	John F. Kennedy	49.7
1968	Richard M. Nixon	43.4
1992	Bill Clinton	43.0
1996	Bill Clinton	49.2

*Candidate won the presidency even though he had fewer popular votes than his opponent.

(See 438 How many presidential elections have been decided by the House? 440 What deal was made to win Republican Rutherford B. Hayes the presidency in 1876?)

Q 435. What does it mean when a president is said to have "long coattails"?

A Presidential candidates with long coattails are so popular that they also help members of their party get elected to Congress or to state governorships. President Ronald Reagan, for example, proved so popular with voters in 1980 that Republican Senate candidates were swept into office with him. For the first time since 1952 Republicans achieved a majority in the Senate. Unpopular presidents can have the reverse effect. Voters blamed President Herbert Hoover for the Great Depression, and in 1932 they turned both Hoover and many Republicans in Congress out of office, giving Democrats control of the presidency and both houses of Congress.

A president's popularity, however, does not always help other candidates in the party. President Bill Clinton personally maintained high approval ratings, but during his administration Republicans gained control of the House for the first time since 1952 and held majorities in both houses of Congress for most of his two terms in office.

Q 436. What is a plurality?

A When two or more candidates run, the margin the top vote-getter wins by is called the winner's plurality. In most U.S. elections, candidates need only a plurality—that is, more votes than the other candidate—to win. But in the electoral college presidential candidates must have an absolute majority—270 votes or more—of the 538 votes cast to win the presidency. The House of Representatives decides the election if no candidate polls a majority of electoral votes. Some state primaries also require an absolute majority instead of the winner-by-plurality system.

(See 381 How does the electoral college work? 438 How many presidential elections have been decided by the House?)

Q **437. What went wrong in the presidential election of 1800?**

A The Constitution created a potential problem by requiring electors to vote for the president and vice president on the same ballot. By this system, a tie vote for the president and vice president in the electoral college was possible, throwing the election into the House of Representatives.

That is exactly what happened in the election of 1800. Thomas Jefferson was the intended presidential candidate for the Democratic-Republicans and Aaron Burr was the vice-presidential candidate. But when the electoral votes were counted, both candidates had received seventy-three. It was then up to the House, controlled by the Federalists, to choose who would become president. Some House members wanted to name Burr president because he was politically less threatening to the Federalist Party, but Federalist Party leader Alexander Hamilton threw his support behind Jefferson. Jefferson finally won on the thirty-sixth ballot in the House.

The Twelfth Amendment to the Constitution was passed in 1804 to eliminate the electoral defect. It changed the system so that electors voted separately for the president and vice president.

(See 26 Which amendments to the Constitution deal with the presidency?)

Q **438. How many presidential elections have been decided by the House?**

A The House of Representatives has been called on to decide two elections, in 1800 and 1824. In 1800 it broke a tie vote in the electoral college between Thomas Jefferson, the presidential candidate, and his vice-presidential running mate, Aaron Burr *(see question above)*. The House eventually named Jefferson president.

In the 1824 election, divisions within the Democratic-Republican Party resulted in four candidates running for the presidency—John Quincy Adams, Andrew Jackson, Henry Clay, and William H. Crawford. Jackson won the most popular votes and electoral votes, but because he did not win a majority of electoral votes the House had to decide the election. Henry Clay, Speaker of the House, threw his support behind Adams, who won the vote in the House. (Adams then named Clay his secretary of state.)

The election of 1876 was not decided by the House alone, but some of its members sat on the commission that did.

(See 440 What deal was made to win Republican Rutherford B. Hayes the presidency in 1876?)

Q 439. Why did the Senate have to decide the vice-presidential election of 1837?

A Democrat Richard M. Johnson, Martin Van Buren's running mate in the 1837 election, just missed gaining the necessary electoral majority by one vote. A protest by twenty-three electors from Virginia caused the shortfall. They cast their ballots for Van Buren but refused to vote for Johnson, citing his affairs with slave mistresses. With that, the election was thrown into the Senate, the only time that body has been called on to decide an election. A vote along party lines gave Johnson the vice presidency.

Q 440. What deal was made to win Republican Rutherford B. Hayes the presidency in 1876?

A In the 1876 election, Republican Rutherford B. Hayes appeared to have lost both the popular and electoral votes to Democrat Samuel J. Tilden by a narrow margin, but Tilden had failed to gain the necessary electoral majority by one vote and a number of electoral votes were in dispute. The political wranglers that followed finally resulted in what is sometimes called either the Compromise of 1877 or the Stolen election.

The dispute revolved around challenged vote counts in Florida, Louisiana, and South Carolina—enough votes to give Hayes a one-vote electoral victory. Democratic and Republican machines in these states sent conflicting sets of electoral votes to the Republican-controlled Senate, which set up a commission made up of members of the House, Senate, and Supreme Court to decide the challenge. In the commission, Republicans had a one-vote advantage. Meeting in early 1877, the commission voted on each states contested election results, and eventually awarded Hayes all twenty disputed electoral votes, enough to win the election. But voting was strictly along party lines, and without Democratic support for the commission findings, a serious political crisis could have resulted. Even as the commission was voting, a faction in the Democratic-controlled House threatened a filibuster to block approval of the electoral vote until after the March 4 inauguration day. Meanwhile both sides worked behind the scenes to negotiate and end to the standoff.

Just two days before the inauguration, Republicans and Democrats struck a deal, however. In return for the Democrats' support for the commission findings, Republicans agreed to withdraw federal troops that had been stationed in southern states since the Civil War. That effectively ended the Reconstruction era in the South. Without the federal presence, white southern Democrats were able to impose the strict segregationist policies that continued in the South until the 1960s.

Q **441. Which third party presidential candidate polled the most votes in an election?**

A Former president Theodore Roosevelt, running as the Progressive Party candidate in the 1912 presidential election, received 27.4 percent of the popular vote and 88 electoral votes—the best showing by a third party candidate. Roosevelt, a Republican, had stepped down after serving one partial term (after William McKinley's death) and one full term as president. But he became dissatisfied with William Howard Taft's administration and unsuccessfully tried to wrest the Republican nomination from him at the 1912 convention. When that failed, he formed the Progressive (nicknamed Bull Moose) Party. His third party candidacy drew off enough votes to defeat Taft and throw the election to the Democratic challenger, Woodrow Wilson.

Ex-president Millard Fillmore polled the next best third party vote in 1856. He ran as the American Know-Nothing Party standard bearer and captured 21.5 percent of the popular vote. Independent candidate Ross Perot and his Reform Party won 18.9 percent of the popular vote in 1992, but the party's showing in 1996 dropped to 8.4 percent. Other notable third party bids included Strom Thurmond's 1948 challenge as the States Rights' Democratic (Dixiecrat) candidate (he carried three states) and George Wallace's 1968 presidential bid (he carried two states and won 13.5 percent of the popular vote).

(See 394 What is the oldest existing third party? 395 What obstacles confront third parties?)

FOR THE RECORD

Q **442. Who holds the record for running for president the most times?**

A When Harold Stassen, Minnesota's Republican governor, entered his first presidential race in 1948, he began what became an epic but otherwise fruitless pursuit of the office. Between 1948 and 1992 Stassen ran for president ten times and never polled more than a fraction of a percent of the popular vote. He skipped only two elections—1956 and 1972—when Republican presidents Dwight D. Eisenhower and Richard M. Nixon ran for their second terms.

Two other frequent candidates earlier in the century were socialists Norman Thomas (six elections beginning in 1928) and Eugene Debs (five elections beginning in 1900). Debs won nearly a million votes in his last effort in 1920, despite being in prison at the time for protests against World War I. President Warren G. Harding ordered Debs released in 1921.

443. How many losing candidates have run again and won?

A Six presidential candidates have ignored earlier defeats and gone on to win the presidency. The first was Thomas Jefferson, who became vice president after finishing second in the 1796 race for the presidency. He won the presidency on his second try in 1800. The most recent was Richard M. Nixon, who lost by a narrow margin to John F. Kennedy in 1960. Eight years later he won the presidency by defeating the Democratic challenger, Hubert H. Humphrey. The losing candidates who went on to win were:

Candidate	Lost Election	Won Election
Thomas Jefferson	1796	1800
James Monroe	1808	1816
Andrew Jackson	1824	1828
William Henry Harrison	1836	1840
Grover Cleveland*	1888	1892
Richard M. Nixon	1960	1968

  *Cleveland, who served his first term from 1885 to 1889, was the only president to win a second, nonconsecutive term.

Q **444. When did presidential candidates first give speeches in their own behalf?**

A Whig Party candidate William Henry Harrison became the first to give his own campaign speeches when he ran for president in 1840. He delivered twenty-three of them during the course of the campaign, none of which (deliberately) focused on specific issues. Nevertheless they were reprinted in newspapers and pamphlets to help advance his candidacy.

Prior to 1840 and for many years after, presidential candidates refrained from speaking, allowing surrogates to address campaign rallies for them. Harrison also used surrogate speakers during his 1840 campaign, including Abraham Lincoln and Daniel Webster.

(See 420 Why was the Log Cabin campaign of 1840 a success?)

Q 445. Who was the first vice president to campaign actively nationwide?

A Theodore Roosevelt, campaigning as President William McKinley's running mate in the 1900 election, was one of the first active campaigners and the first vice president to do so. President McKinley's campaign strategy, like those of other presidential candidates before him, was to remain aloof from the fight while surrogates campaigned for him. Roosevelt ultimately gave 673 speeches in twenty-four states. The exposure earned him a national reputation and helped him to make the transition to the presidency after McKinley was assassinated in 1901.

The only other member of a national party ticket to campaign nationwide before Roosevelt was William Jennings Bryan, the Democratic presidential nominee in 1896.

(See 426 Who won the presidency with a "whistle-stop" campaign?)

Q 446. Who won two terms as vice president and two as president?

A Two-term vice president Richard M. Nixon, whose political career seemed finished after his loss in the 1960 presidential race, went on to win two terms as president. He had served as vice president under Dwight D. Eisenhower from 1953 to 1961 before losing the presidential election of 1960 to John F. Kennedy by a razor-thin margin. His bitter comment after losing his 1962 bid for governor of California—"You won't have Nixon to kick around any more"—marked a low point in his political fortunes. In 1968, however, with Democrats deeply divided over the Vietnam War, Nixon managed to eke out a victory over Democratic challenger Hubert H. Humphrey. President Nixon won reelection to a second term in 1972, but the Watergate scandal forced him to resign after serving only part of the term.

Two other presidents served two terms as vice president before entering the White House—John Adams and George Bush. Both served only one term as president, however.

Q 447. What city has hosted the most conventions?

A Chicago has held twenty-five major party national nominating conventions, more than double the total for any other city. Democrats held eleven of their conventions there, Republicans fourteen. Baltimore, Maryland, has hosted ten national conventions, all but one Democratic. Philadelphia has hosted eight conventions, six of them Republican. Eighteen other cities have provided the site for anywhere from one to five national conventions. Republicans held their 2000 convention in Philadelphia, the Democrats in Los Angeles.

Q 448. Who was the first "baby boomer" to become president?

A Bill Clinton was the first president born after 1945, the beginning of the "baby boom" generation. His predecessor, Republican George Bush, was born in 1924; he served in World War II. Bush's vice president, Dan Quayle, earned the distinction of being the first baby boomer to hold the vice presidency. Both the Republican and Democratic candidates for president in 2000 were boomers born after 1945.

FINANCING ELECTIONS

Q 449. How much have candidates spent in past elections?

A Spending on presidential campaigns began rising significantly during the 1950s, thanks in part to the advent of television advertising. Republican candidate Dwight D. Eisenhower spent $6.6 million in his successful run for the presidency in 1952. Richard M. Nixon shelled out a record $25.4 million in 1968, and more than doubled that for what was then a new record of $61.4 million in 1972. Despite campaign finance laws and public funding for presidential candidates, spending continued rising in the 1980s and 1990s. In 1992 the two parties spent a combined total of about $550 million on the presidential race. In 1996 total spending reached $700 million.

Q 450. What are PACs?

A Political action committees, called PACs, receive and distribute millions of dollars in campaign contributions from special interest groups and private individuals. They have proliferated in recent years, but in terms of total dollars contributed PACs are far more important to congressional races than to presidential elections. However, presidential hopefuls do form PACs early in their run for the nomination, mainly to raise money for primary races.

(See 396 How are presidential candidates chosen?)

Q 451. Why was the Federal Election Commission organized?

A Numerous attempts to reform questionable and corrupt campaign finance practices during the twentieth century culminated in the creation of the Federal Election Commission (FEC) in 1975. Campaign finance abuses revealed in the Watergate scandal provided the final impetus for the reform.

The FEC monitors and enforces compliance with campaign finance laws and reviews the financial disclosure statements it collects from candidates, campaign committees, and political action committees. It investigates suspected abuses and may impose fines or seek prosecution for violations. The FEC also administers the Presidential Election Campaign Fund, which distributes about $135 million in public funds to offset the costs of presidential primaries, national conventions, and general election expenses for presidential candidates.

Q 452. How do "hard" and "soft" money differ?

A *Hard money* is the familiar term for campaign funds that are regulated by the Federal Election Commission (FEC). It includes money candidates receive from contributors and money they spend for direct campaign expenses, such as travel, mailing lists and postage, and radio and television ads. The FEC limits both how much "hard" money contributors can give (see question 454 below) and how much of it candidates can spend.

Soft money is not regulated by the FEC. It is money donated to a political party and spent for party building and other general political activities, such as issue ads and voter registration drives. It must not be spent directly on a particular candidate's election. Because there are no limits on soft money contributions, they have become an important source of funding for the Democratic and Republican Parties. Democrats raised $122.3 million in soft money for the 1996 elections, Republicans $141.2 million.

Q 453. What campaign finance rules did the Clinton-Gore campaign allegedly break during the 1996 presidential race?

A Critics have charged the Clinton-Gore fund-raising effort with various campaign finance rule violations, some of which have led to criminal prosecutions. The allegations continued to dog Vice President Al Gore well into the 2000 presidential campaign season and thereby threatened to become an important campaign issue. One serious problem with Democratic fund-raising revolved around illegal contributions by foreign nationals, notably Chinese and other Asians, who are not allowed to make campaign contributions. Questions also arose about the Chinese communist government's alleged scheme to influence the U.S. elections by illegally donating money to the Clinton-Gore campaign. Eventually, the Democratic National Committee was forced to return about $3 million in illegal contributions from various sources, including foreigners. (Republicans had to return some questionable donations too).

President Clinton also was criticized for using White House coffees and overnight stays in the Lincoln Bedroom to raise campaign funds. Both Clinton and Gore came under fire for soliciting campaign contributions while in White House offices, a violation of federal laws. In another incident, Vice President Gore fended off criticism for his part in a fund-raising event at a Buddhist temple by saying he did not know it was a fund-raiser. Later he claimed the funds raised were unregulated "soft money," but notes on memos reportedly showed he knew some of it was being used as hard money, in violation of election laws. Neither Clinton nor Gore has been charged with any crimes relating to the 1996 Democratic fund-raising campaign, but other high-level fund-raisers were charged and convicted.

Q 454. What limits on campaign contributions are there?

A The size of campaign donations are limited in two ways: by the size of donations to specific candidates and groups and by the overall amount contributors give in a year. Individuals are allowed to give no more than $1,000 to a candidate each year per election (primary, runoff, general election) and can contribute a maximum of $20,000 annually to a political party. Contributions to a political action committee cannot exceed $5,000. The annual limit on an individual's contribution is $25,000.

No limits have been placed on the yearly campaign contributions of political action committees. They can donate up to $5,000 to a specific candidate, $5,000 to a PAC, and $15,000 to a party organization.

FOR FURTHER INFORMATION

Books on presidential elections range from anecdotal treatments and topical analyses to sources of historical and statistical information. Paul F. Boller's *Presidential Campaigns* is a very readable history of election campaigns with many colorful anecdotes. Two helpful reference books on election history and statistics should be available at most libraries— John L. Moore's *Elections A to Z* and *Congressional Quarterly's Guide to U.S. Elections.*

Air Wars: Television Advertising in Election Campaigns, 1952–1996 by Darrell West studies the impact of television on presidential campaigns, and Roger A. Fischer's *Tippecanoe and Trinkets Too: The Material Culture of American Presidential Campaigns, 1828–1984* takes an informative look at campaign paraphernalia. Biographies of individual presidents usually also offer some coverage of their campaigns. Various Internet sites, including one maintained by the Federal Election Commission (www.fec.gov), provide current information on election statistics.

America at the Polls, 1920–1956: A Handbook of American Presidential Election Statistics. Compiled by Alice V. McGillivray and Richard M. Scammon. Washington, D.C.: Congressional Quarterly, 1994.

America at the Polls, 1960–1996: A Handbook of American Presidential Election Statistics. Compiled by Alice V. McGillivray, Richard M. Scammon, and Rhodes Cook. Washington, D.C.: Congressional Quarterly, 1998.

America Votes: A Handbook of Contemporary American Election Statistics. Compiled by Richard M. Scammon, Alice V. McGillivray, and Rhodes Cook. Washington, D.C.: CQ Press, biennial.

Boller, Paul F. *Presidential Campaigns.* New York: Oxford University Press, 1996.

Byrne, Gary C., and Paul Marx. *The Great American Convention: A Political History of Presidential Elections.* Palo Alto, Calif.: Pacific Books, 1977.

Congressional Quarterly's Federal PACs Directory, 1998–1999. Washington, D.C.: Congressional Quarterly, 1998.

Connolly, Thomas, and Michael Senegal. *Almanac of the American Presidents.* New York: Facts on File, 1991.

Cook, Rhodes. *United States Presidential Primary Election, 1968–1996: A Handbook of Election Statistics.* Washington, D.C.: CQ Press, 2000.

Cook, Rhodes, and Alice V. McGillivray. *U.S. Primary Elections, 1997–1998.* Washington, D.C.: Congressional Quarterly, biennial.

Cunningham, Noble E. *Popular Images of the Presidency: From Washington to Lincoln.* Columbia: University of Missouri Press, 1991.

Dallek, Robert. *Hail to the Chief: The Making and Unmaking of American Presidents.* Westport, Conn.: Hyperion, 1996.

Davis, James W. *U.S. Presidential Primaries and the Caucus-Convention System: A Sourcebook.* Westport, Conn.: Greenwood, 1997.

Dover, E. D. *Presidential Elections in the Television Age.* Westport, Conn.: Greenwood, 1994.

Fields, Wayne. *Union of Words: A History of Presidential Eloquence.* New York: Free Press, 1995.

Fischer, Roger A. *Tippecanoe and Trinkets Too: The Material Culture of American Presidential Campaigns, 1828–1984.* Urbana: University of Illinois Press, 1988.

Frost-Knappman, Elizabeth. *The World Almanac of Presidential Quotations*. New York: Pharos Books, 1993.

Gardner, Gerald. *Campaign Comedy: Political Humor from Clinton to Kennedy*. Detroit: Wayne State University Press, 1994.

Gelderman, Carol. *All the Presidents' Words: The Bully Pulpit and Creation of the Virtual Presidency*. New York: Walker and Co., 1997.

Graff, Henry F. *The Presidents: A Reference History*. New York: Macmillan, 1996.

Guide to U.S. Elections. 3d ed. Washington, D.C.: Congressional Quarterly, 1994.

Israel, Fred L. *Student's Atlas of American Presidential Elections, 1789–1996*. Washington, D.C.: Congressional Quarterly, 1997.

Langston, Thomas S. *With Reverence and Contempt: How Americans Think about Their President*. Baltimore: Johns Hopkins University Press, 1995.

Levy, Leonard W., and Louis Fisher. *Encyclopedia of the American Presidency*. New York: Simon and Shuster, 1993.

Moore, John L. *Elections A to Z*. Washington, D.C.: Congressional Quarterly, 1999.

National Party Conventions, 1831–1996. Washington, D.C.: Congressional Quarterly, 1997.

Nelson, Michael, ed. *Congressional Quarterly's Guide to the Presidency*. 2d ed. 2 vols. Washington, D.C.: Congressional Quarterly, 1996.

The Presidency A to Z. 2d ed. Washington, D.C.: Congressional Quarterly, 1998.

The President, the Public, and the Parties. 2d ed. Washington, D.C.: Congressional Quarterly, 1997.

Presidential Elections, 1789–1996. Washington, D.C.: Congressional Quarterly, 1997.

Presidential Polls and the News Media. Boulder: Westview Press, 1996.

Ragsdale, Lyn. *Vital Statistics on the Presidency: Washington to Clinton*. Rev. ed. Washington, D.C.: Congressional Quarterly, 1998.

Rozell, Mark J., and Clyde Wilcox. *Interest Groups in American Campaigns: The New Face of Electioneering*. Washington, D.C.: CQ Press, 1999.

West, Darrell M. *Air Wars: Television Advertising in Election Campaigns, 1952–1996*. 2d ed. Washington, D.C.: Congressional Quarterly, 1997.

VI
THE EXECUTIVE BRANCH AT WORK

THE WHITE HOUSE OFFICE

Q 455. How is the White House staff organized?

A Staffers in the White House Office (WHO) serve the president exclusively, providing him with information and advice and following up on presidential directives to make sure they are carried out. The office is under the president's complete control, and its staffers serve entirely at the president's discretion—appointment to the staff is not subject to Senate approval.

Presidents can reorganize the White House Office as they see fit. However, today's presidents would find it very difficult to do without a chief of staff, a press secretary, and certain other key advisers. Among the other staffers prominent in recent administrations were the national security adviser, domestic policy adviser, and the special counsel—the president's private lawyer. Because presidents can and do reorganize the White House Office, its major divisions vary considerably over time. The Clinton White House Office comprised the following offices:

Office of the Chief of Staff
Office of the Staff Secretary
Office of the General Counsel
Office of Cabinet Affairs
Office of Intergovernmental Affairs
Office of Political Affairs
Office of Public Liaison
Foreign Intelligence Advisory Board
President's Council on Sustainable Development
President's Crime Prevention Council
Office of Management and Administration
Office of Scheduling and Advance

Office of Presidential Personnel
Office of the Press Secretary
Office of Legislative Affairs
Office of Communications
Office of Outreach
Office of Research
Office of Speechwriting
Office of the First Lady
White House Military Office

Q 456. Who has served as chief of staff?

A The president's chief gatekeeper, the chief of staff, manages access to the president by reviewing and rerouting reports to ease the president's workload and by controlling face-to-face meetings with the president. The chief of staff ensures that the White House staff functions smoothly, acts as a shield for the president when need be, and often plays an advisory role as well.

The chief of staff position is a fairly new innovation. In 1946 President Harry S. Truman created a post for an aide who would act as a liaison with the federal agencies, but it was Dwight D. Eisenhower who had the first full-fledged chief of staff, Sherman Adams. The next president to have a chief of staff was Richard M. Nixon—H. R. Haldeman ran the Nixon White House with ruthless efficiency. President Carter tried to eliminate the post, but found himself overwhelmed without someone to act as gatekeeper. Every president since has had a chief of staff.

Chief of Staff	President Served	Years
Sherman Adams	Eisenhower	1953–1958
Wilton Persons	Eisenhower	1958–1961
—	Kennedy	—
—	Johnson	—
H. R. Haldeman	Nixon	1969–1973
Alexander M. Haig	Nixon	1973–1974
Donald Rumsfeld	Ford	1974–1975
Richard M. Cheney	Ford	1975–1977
Hamilton Jordan	Carter	1979–1980
Jack Watson	Carter	1980–1981
James A. Baker III	Reagan	1981–1985

Chief of Staff	President Served	Years
Donald T. Regan	Reagan	1985–1987
Howard H. Baker Jr.	Reagan	1987–1988
Kenneth Duberstein	Reagan	1988–1989
John H. Sununu	Bush	1989–1991
Samuel Skinner	Bush	1991–1992
James A. Baker III	Bush	1992–1993
Thomas F. MacLarty III	Clinton	1993–1994
Leon Panetta	Clinton	1994–1996
Erskine Bowles	Clinton	1997–1998
John Podesta	Clinton	1998–

Q 457. What are the two basic patterns for organizing White House staffers?

A Although presidents are free to arrange the White House staff any way they want, they tend to choose one of two organizational systems: circular or pyramidal. In the circular system, the president occupies the central position, like the hub of a wheel, and serves as his own chief of staff. All his trusted advisers (the spokes) have direct access to the president and receive assignments directly from him. Presidents Franklin D. Roosevelt and John F. Kennedy used the circular system, but it places heavy demands on the president's time and can lead to counterproductive friction among staffers.

In the pyramidal system, the president occupies the top position in a hierarchical structure. The chief of staff and a few trusted staffers have direct access to the president, while the rest of the White House staffers are ranked in order of descending importance. The lower ranks are more numerous than those at the top, giving the organizational structure a pyramid shape. The chief of staff screens and digests information routed from lower-ranking staffers for the president's attention, limits access to the president, hands out assignments, and follows up on presidential directives, so that the president has more time for important work. The danger with the pyramidal approach is that the president can become too isolated and that, by restricting the flow of information, the staff winds up controlling the president instead of the opposite.

▶ *How has the president's staff grown? See 30.*

▶ *What does the press secretary do? See 261 How do the media and the president interact?*

▶ *How does the White House deal with interest groups? See 274 What does the White House Office of Public Liaison do?*

Q 458. What is detailing?

A The practice of borrowing personnel from executive departments for work in the White House is called detailing. Presidents have frequently resorted to this method of supplementing their White House staffs by requisitioning military personnel from the Defense Department, for example. Presidents sometimes also have appointed trusted advisers to posts in the executive departments and then have detailed them for White House duties as needed. This gambit has allowed presidents to circumvent limits on the size of their White House staff and budgets.

Q 459. Which president expanded staff responsibility at the expense of the cabinet departments?

A President John F. Kennedy continued the trend toward larger and larger White House staffs, but with an important difference. Under Kennedy the White House staff began taking the task of policy making away from the cabinet departments, effectively concentrating that power in the White House and greatly increasing the White House staff's influence. Presidents Lyndon B. Johnson and Richard M. Nixon both continued to increase the power of the president's staff. In fact, the concentration of power in the White House staff during the Nixon administration was believed to be at least part of the reason why the abuses in the Watergate affair took place.

EXECUTIVE OFFICE OF THE PRESIDENT

Q 460. What does the Executive Office of the President do?

A Directly responsible to the president, the Executive Office of the President (EOP) helps him carry out his duties as the chief executive. The thousands of staffers who work at EOP provide the advice and information needed to formulate policy, and also make it possible for presidents to monitor the activities of the multitude of federal agencies and departments, to promote his priorities, to draft legislation and lobby Congress on behalf of administration bills, and write their annual proposed budget.

The Executive Office of the President is actually composed of offices and agencies that report only to the president. The president's closest advisers make up the most important of these offices, the White House Office (WHO). Other key EOP agencies include the National Security Council, Office of Management and Budget, Council of Economic Advisers, and Office of Policy Development. With the exception of members of the White House Office, key appointees in the EOP must be confirmed by the Senate. During President Bill Clinton's second term, the EOP consisted of the following agencies:

White House Office
Office of Management and Budget
National Security Council
Office of Policy Development
Council of Economic Advisers
Office of the U.S. Trade Representative
Office of Science and Technology Policy
Council on Environmental Quality
Office of National Drug Control Policy
Office of the Vice President
Office of Administration
Domestic Policy Council
National Economic Council
National Partnership Council
Office of National AIDS Policy
Office of Special Representative for Trade Negotiations

(See 189 Who advises the president on policy matters? 455 How is the White House staff organized? 464 What does the president's cabinet do?)

Q 461. What legislative role does the Office of Management and Budget play?

A The Office of Management and Budget (OMB) routinely reviews and analyzes legislation the administration plans to propose to Congress and bills Congress has passed in order to assess their impact on the federal budget. OMB also is responsible for preparing various economic forecasts and reports the president is required to submit to Congress, for assessing the performance of federal programs, and for evaluating management and organizational effectiveness within the executive branch.

The first budget bureau was established in 1921 to help the president control federal spending, to prepare a proposed federal budget each year, and to act as the administration's legislative clearinghouse. In 1939 the agency became formally incorporated into the new Executive Office of the President as the Bureau of the Budget, but did not receive its present-day name, Office of Management and Budget, until 1970 during the Nixon administration.

Q 462. Why was the National Security Council formed?

A Congress created the National Security Council (NSC) in 1947 to help the president coordinate military and foreign policy. Because the United States had emerged from World War II as a leading military power and because the cold war was just beginning, the government put a new emphasis on coordinating U.S. policy abroad. An advisory body, the NSC has seen its influence wax and wane from one president to the next, depending on the president's own preferences. President Richard M. Nixon, for example, gave the NSC the power to make and execute foreign policy.

The NSC has four members: the president, the vice president, and the secretaries of state and defense. The chairman of the Joint Chiefs of Staff and the director of the Central Intelligence Agency act as advisers to the NSC. Under the Clinton administration, the secretary of the Treasury, director of the Office of Management and Budget, the permanent representative to the United Nations, and the president's chief of staff and assistants for national security affairs and for economic policy were invited to all NSC meetings. The NSC staff, headed by the president's national security adviser, has become an important tool for promoting the president's foreign policies.

Q 463. Who advises the president on economic matters?

A The first presidents relied on the secretary of the Treasury for advice on economic and financial matters, but today's presidents have other advisers as well. While the secretary of the Treasury continues to be an important economic adviser, the director of the Office of Management and Budget and the chairman of the Council of Economic Advisers, for example, also sometimes play a major role in formulating the president's economic policy. In addition, political advisers on the White House staff and other cabinet secretaries may have an influence on the president's economic and fiscal policies.

The Council of Economic Advisers was created in 1946 to prepare the president's annual economic report to Congress and to provide advice on economic matters.

THE CABINET AND DEPARTMENTS

Q 464. What does the president's cabinet do?

A Made up of the president, vice president, and the heads of the fourteen executive departments, the cabinet was originally intended to act as an advisory body that would provide the president with information and policy recommendations. Individual cabinet members have been influential advisers—especially those who hold key cabinet posts, such as the secretaries of state, defense, and Treasury, and the attorney general (the so-called inner cabinet). But the cabinet as a whole has seldom functioned successfully as a policy-making or advisory body and, in recent administrations especially, policy-making functions have been concentrated in the White House staff at the expense of individual cabinet departments.

Dwight D. Eisenhower was the most recent president to try to make use of cabinet meetings for policy making. But competition among cabinet secretaries, a normal tendency for secretaries to become advocates for their own departments, and concerns that a strong cabinet with decision-making powers might jeopardize the president's control of the executive have helped defeat such efforts.

The cabinet departments do, however, play an important role in the government. By elevating an agency to a cabinet department, the federal government is expressing its commitment to the area of concern—be it veterans affairs, energy, or defense—and is establishing an institutional framework for providing aid and solving problems over the long term. The fourteen cabinet departments are: Agriculture, Commerce, Defense, Education, Energy, Health and Human Services, Housing and Urban Development, Interior, Justice, Labor, State, Transportation, Treasury, and Veterans Affairs.

(See 32 How has the cabinet grown since President Washington's administration? 40 What are the major parts of the executive branch? 189 Who advises the president on policy matters? 191 How much control over federal departments and agencies does the president actually have? 459 Which president expanded staff responsibility at the expense of the cabinet departments? 460 What does the Executive Office of the President do?)

Q 465. How many people work for the executive departments?

A As of 1999 the fourteen executive departments had just under 1.77 million paid civilian employees. That was almost 327,000 fewer employees than in 1993, largely a result of the military cutbacks at the end of the cold war and the Clinton administration's efforts to downsize the government. The 1999 employment levels of the departments are as follows (note that the figures are rounded):

Department	Number of Civilian Employees
Agriculture	95,500
Commerce	47,300
Defense	681,000
Education	4,500
Energy	15,900
Health and Human Services	58,900
Housing and Urban Development	10,000
Interior	67,000
Justice	121,300
Labor	16,300
State	29,400
Transportation	63,700
Treasury	143,700
Veterans Affairs	205,500
Total	1,778,400

(See 506 Which agencies and government corporations are the largest?)

▶ *What is the oldest cabinet department? See 32 How has the cabinet grown since President Washington's administration?*

Q 466. Why was the "Bobby Kennedy" law passed?

A President John F. Kennedy's decision to appoint his brother Robert F. "Bobby" Kennedy to a cabinet post as attorney general provided the president with a trusted adviser. At that time the appointment broke no laws, but it did leave the president open to criticism for nepotism. In fact, it generated enough concern that in 1967 Congress passed the so-called "Bobby Kennedy" law, making it illegal for presidents to give family members government jobs.

Presidents can still seek unpaid advice from family members, however. President Bill Clinton, for example, named First Lady Hillary Rodham Clinton to a nonpaying advisory post as head of the administration's health care reform task force.

Q 467. Which presidents once served as cabinet members?

A Six presidents served as secretary of state before becoming president, three as secretary of war, and one as secretary of commerce. James Monroe held two cabinet posts—secretary of state and secretary of war. Ulysses S. Grant served briefly as war secretary in 1867–1868, but Congress, then battling President Andrew Johnson, declared the appointment illegal and forced Grant's resignation.

Presidents who served as secretary of state

Thomas Jefferson, 1790–1793
James Madison, 1801–1809
James Monroe, 1811–1814, 1815–1817
John Quincy Adams, 1817–1825
Martin Van Buren, 1829–1831
James Buchanan, 1845–1849

Presidents who served as secretary of war

James Monroe, 1814–1815
Ulysses S. Grant, 1867–1868
William Howard Taft, 1904–1908

President who served as secretary of commerce

Herbert Hoover, 1921–1928

Q 468. When were the first minority and women members of the cabinet appointed?

A The first woman to become a cabinet secretary was Frances Perkins, President Franklin D. Roosevelt's secretary of labor. Perkins held the post from 1933 to 1945. President Lyndon B. Johnson appointed the first black cabinet member, Robert C. Weaver, in 1966. Weaver served as secretary of housing and urban development until 1968. A decade later, President Jimmy Carter appointed the first black woman as cabinet secretary. Patricia Roberts Harris served as his secretary of health, education, and welfare from 1979 to 1981 (her department was reorganized as Health and Human Services in 1980). President Ronald Reagan appointed the first Hispanic cabinet member, Lauro F. Cavazos, naming him education secretary. Cavazos remained in office from 1988 to 1990, serving under both Presidents Reagan and George Bush.

(See 484 Which secretary helped bring the Labor Department into its own?)

Q **469. What are Treasury's primary responsibilities?**

A The Treasury Department takes care of the nation's finances and manages its money, and the Treasury secretary is usually among the president's most influential advisers. The department collects federal taxes and tariffs from organizations, businesses, and individuals; writes the checks to pay the government's bills; and reports the government's financial transactions. But that is not all. It also conducts economic research, regulates the national banks, prints money and mints coins, investigates counterfeiting cases, and provides protection for the president, vice president, and their families through the U.S. Secret Service.

Q **470. Why was Alexander Hamilton's work as Treasury secretary so important?**

A As the first Treasury secretary, Alexander Hamilton played a major role in setting the new federal government on a sound financial footing. He was President George Washington's most influential adviser and a leading proponent of a strong central government led by a powerful chief executive. But his most enduring accomplishment was the financial system he established. To help provide the new nation with a sound economy, he proposed a series of measures that President Washington supported and Congress enacted, despite stiff opposition from agrarian interests. He called for the federal government to assume the states' Revolutionary War debts and to establish its credit by guaranteeing repayment of all federal debt. He also pushed for the enactment of tariffs and excise taxes to provide revenue for operating the government and repaying the debt. And, to control the economy, he convinced Congress to establish a national bank.

Q **471. Why was the Secret Service created?**

A President Abraham Lincoln set up the Secret Service within the Treasury Department in 1865 to investigate counterfeiting, which then was a serious problem. Eventually, Secret Service agents also investigated other crimes and handled intelligence work for the government as well. The creation of the Federal Bureau of Investigation in 1908 and Central Intelligence Agency in 1947 left the Secret Service with its original mission of catching counterfeiters and one new responsibility—protecting the president (*see next question*).

Q 472. When did the Secret Service become responsible for protecting the president and the White House?

A The general public had virtually free access to the White House grounds, and often the White House itself, until President John Tyler's administration. Soon after taking office in 1841 Tyler, the first vice president to succeed to the presidency, enraged leaders of his own Whig Party by vetoing a key bill reestablishing the Bank of the United States. That evening a mob of angry Whig supporters gathered outside the White House gates, burned Tyler in effigy, threw rocks, and fired guns in what remains the most violent demonstration ever outside the executive mansion. Soon after, Congress provided funds for the first White House security force (four police guards), at Tyler's request.

The White House guard was increased (and supplemented by soldiers) during wartime, but it remained more or less fixed at three policemen for the better part of the 1800s. By the mid-1890s, however, President Grover Cleveland was receiving so many death threats that the number of policemen assigned to the White House was increased to twenty-seven. A few Secret Service agents also provided protection, but the Secret Service was not formally charged with protecting the president until 1906, five years after President William McKinley's assassination.

In 1922 the White House Police Force was created as a separate entity to protect the grounds. After a curious sightseer walked undeterred into the White House and interrupted President Herbert Hoover's dinner in 1930, the Secret Service became responsible for all White House security. Since then, Congress has expanded the Secret Service's protective duties to include all first family members, presidential candidates, former presidents and first ladies, vice presidents and their families, etc.). About 1,200 agents are currently assigned to the White House and other protective duties.

(See 299 Who was the first president to have a bodyguard?)

Q 473. What does the State Department do for the president?

A The president's main channel for negotiating with foreign countries is through the State Department's network of embassies in countries around the world. State also provides the president with information on foreign governments, expert advice, and foreign policy recommendations. But State is not the only government agency involved in foreign policy matters these days. For example, the Central Intelligence Agency and military intelligence agencies gather and analyze information on foreign countries that State could not possibly provide. Or, if presidents so choose, they can circumvent the State Department altogether and use their National Security Council staff to handle delicate negotiations.

The State Department is considerably larger than it was in 1789 when Thomas Jefferson became the first secretary of state under the Constitution. Besides Jefferson, there was only a part-time French translator, five clerks, and two messengers. Today, State has about 29,000 employees, many of whom are stationed abroad. The secretary of state is fourth in the line of succession to the presidency.

Q 474. Does the United States have relations with every country in the world?

A The United States maintains diplomatic ties with over 160 nations—nearly ever country in the world. It does not maintain embassies in all of them, however. For some small countries, diplomatic communications are handled through the United Nations or via U.S. embassies in neighboring countries. The U.S. ambassador in each country acts as the personal representative of the president and is responsible for implementing U.S. policy within the country.

Q 475. What is the largest cabinet department?

A The Defense Department ranks first among the departments in both size and budget (defense spending is second only to that for Social Security, which is administered by an independent agency, the Social Security Administration, not a cabinet department). At its most recent peak in the 1980s, defense employed over 1 million civilians and had over 2.2 million soldiers and sailors in uniform. The next largest department, Veterans Affairs, had only about 251,000 employees.

Since the end of the cold war in the 1990s, the number of defense employees and military personnel has been reduced, and the department's budget has been cut back. But defense spending, which in the past has accounted for over 25 percent of federal spending, remains a big budget item. In fiscal 1999, $261.3 billion, or 15.3 percent of the federal budget, went for defense.

(See 33 How has American military power grown over the years? 465 How many people work for the executive departments?)

Q 476. When was the Defense Department created?

A Congress created the War Department in 1789 and the separate Navy Department almost ten years later, in 1798. The two cabinet departments operated independently under the president's command until the National Security Act of 1947 reorganized the military into three separate branches (army, air force, and navy/marines) within a single cabinet department, the Department of Defense. The defense secretary was the nominal head of the department, but the secretaries of the three military branches were more or less autonomous. The Department of Defense Reorganization Act of 1958 took the final step toward unification of the department by subordinating the secretaries of the service branches to the secretary of defense.

Q 477. What do the Joint Chiefs of Staff do?

A Made up of the Defense Department's top five military officers, the Joint Chiefs of Staff (JCS) plan overall military strategy and provide the president with advice on military matters. The chief of naval operations, the army and air force chiefs of staff, and the Marine Corps commandant all are members of the JCS. In addition, the president appoints another top officer (with Senate confirmation) to serve as JCS chairman for a two-year term.

Q 478. How would the military respond to a nuclear attack?

A A surprise nuclear missile attack on the United States could cause tremendous destruction within a half hour of its launch. For that reason, the military has set up procedures for detecting and notifying the president quickly in the event of an attack.

The first line of defense is the North American Aerospace Defense Command (NORAD), which uses satellites and radar stations to detect an incoming attack by intercontinental ballistic missiles. If NORAD were to detect and confirm an attack in progress, it would immediately alert the president. The president would then consider the nuclear counterattack options outlined in a top-secret document called the Single Integrated Operational Plan (SIOP). If the president decides to order a counterattack, he would retrieve the launch codes from the "football," a black bag carried by a military officer who is always near the president, and then send the launch codes to the missile silos or nuclear subs to authorize the actual firing of the retaliatory missiles.

(See 209 Are there limits on the president's power to order a nuclear attack?)

Q 479. Which came first, the Justice Department or the attorney general?

A The attorney general. In fact, the attorney general's post, created by the Judiciary Act of 1789, was one of the first Congress established. The first attorney general, Edmund Randolph, had no department—his staff consisted of one clerk—but he held cabinet rank as the nation's chief legal officer. The Department of Justice was created almost a century later in 1870, with the attorney general as its top officer.

Q 480. How does the Justice Department carry out its law enforcement duties?

A As head of the Justice Department, the attorney general has access to a wide array of law enforcement resources, including the department's some five thousand lawyers who specialize in areas such as civil rights and antitrust, tax, environmental, civil, and criminal law. The Federal Bureau of Investigation (FBI) is the department's chief investigative agency; its Drug Enforcement Administration (DEA) specializes in cases involving the smuggling and distribution of illegal drugs. The U.S. Marshals Service provides police protection and support for federal courts, and the Immigration and Naturalization Service identifies and deports illegal aliens. And for those convicted of the federal crimes, the Justice Department's Bureau of Prisons operates a nationwide network of federal prisons.

Q 481. Why is the solicitor general sometimes called the Supreme Court's "tenth justice"?

A Among the top officials in the Justice Department, the solicitor general decides which cases the federal government will bring before the Supreme Court. Because government-related cases make up about two-thirds of the Court's caseload each year, the solicitor general wields considerable influence on the Court's docket, a fact that has given rise to the appellation "tenth justice." Ultimately, though, it is the justices who decide which cases to hear.

Q 482. Which future president tried to make the Commerce Department the most powerful cabinet department?

A Herbert Hoover, who served as secretary of commerce during the Harding and Coolidge administrations (1921–1928), actively sought to expand the department's powers. Under his stewardship, the department helped bolster U.S. exports, developed industry and transportation safety codes, took over the administration of the Patent Office, and added various other new divisions. The department's role was cut back sharply during the Great Depression, however, and under President Franklin D. Roosevelt it was almost disbanded. But during World War II the department's National Bureau of Standards (renamed the National Institute of Standards and Technology in 1988) proved an important asset—it helped to ensure weapons parts were interchangeable. Moreover, both its Civil Aeronautics Board (the forerunner of today's Federal Aviation Administration) and transportation divisions gained in importance, giving Commerce a new lease on life.

Ⓠ 483. What role does the Commerce Department play today?

Ⓐ Originally established as the Department of Commerce and Labor in 1903, Commerce became a department unto itself in 1913. Today it has a wide array of missions; it promotes trade and tourism, works to increase economic growth and greater competitiveness of U.S. products overseas, develops statistical and scientific research information, and helps businesses take advantage of scientific and technological advances. The department's National Oceanic and Atmospheric Administration conducts research in the earth sciences and provides weather forecasts. The Patent and Trademark Office registers and protects intellectual properties. The Census Bureau conducts the national census every ten years and produces many statistical studies in the years in between.

Ⓠ 484. Which secretary helped bring the Labor Department into its own?

Ⓐ Although the Labor Department was created as a separate executive department in 1913, opposition from the business community and conservatives in Congress resulted in undersized budgets and little influence for the department. During the Roosevelt administration, however, the Labor Department and labor generally won greater influence because of New Deal programs then being enacted to ease the suffering of unemployed workers and the working poor. Roosevelt's secretary of labor, Frances Perkins—the first woman ever named a cabinet secretary—had much to do with the department's growth in authority during the Roosevelt years. During her long tenure from 1933 to 1945, she saw the department take on new responsibilities and helped bring it into its own as a full-fledged member of the executive branch.

Ⓠ 485. How do Labor Department programs affect workers?

Ⓐ The department's unemployment compensation program, employment services, and job-training programs are among those with the most direct effect on workers. Unemployment insurance, for example, provides a safety net for millions of workers that was unheard of in the United States before the insurance was established during the Great Depression. But programs run by other divisions within the Labor Department also have an impact on workers. For example, the Occupational Safety and Health Administration sets safety standards and monitors workplaces nationwide to prevent accidents and injuries. The Employment Standards Administration handles standards for the minimum wage, overtime, and equal opportunity employment by federal contractors. And the Pension and Welfare Benefits Administration helps ensure the security of millions of workers' retirement funds.

Q 486. Who created the Department of Health, Education and Welfare?

A President Dwight D. Eisenhower created the Department of Health, Education and Welfare (HEW) in 1953 as part of his cabinet reorganization. He formed the cabinet-level department from the Federal Security Agency, which President Franklin D. Roosevelt established in 1939 to oversee the Office of Education, Public Health Service, Social Security Board, Food and Drug Administration, and other agencies.

HEW grew into one of the biggest federal bureaucracies during the 1960s as a result of President Lyndon B. Johnson's Great Society programs (notably Medicaid, Medicare, and programs providing federal aid to education). Under President Jimmy Carter, HEW was split in 1979 into a Department of Education and a Department of Health and Human Services (HHS).

Q 487. How is the current Department of Health and Human Services organized?

A The Department of Health and Human Services (HHS) has three major operating divisions. The Administration for Children and Families handles programs for the elderly, the disabled, Native Americans, family assistance, community services, refugee resettlement, and others. Another division, the Public Health Service, operates programs aimed at protecting the public's health, including the Centers for Disease Control, National Institutes of Health, and Food and Drug Administration. Finally, the Health Care Financing Administration is responsible for the Medicare and Medicaid programs.

The Social Security Administration was a fourth operating division of HHS until 1995, when it became an independent agency within the executive branch.

Q 488. Why are the Medicare and Medicaid programs so important?

A These health care programs are important for two reasons—they provide millions of Americans with medical care, and their cost has been soaring in recent years. Medicare, which is administered as part of the Social Security program, pays for the medical care of some 33 million elderly and disabled persons. Medicaid, a program shared with the states, supplies medical care to about 38 million needy persons.

Both Medicare and Medicaid are tremendously popular and do considerable good, but their cost has been rising sharply for years—elevenfold in the past twenty years. Whereas federal spending on health care was just 2.1 percent of the entire federal budget in 1962, it topped 21 percent in 1999. With more and more people getting older and becoming eligible for these programs, the cost is only expected to rise further.

Q 489. What limits did Congress impose on the transportation secretary's powers?

A When Congress created the Department of Transportation (DOT) in 1966, it brought together for the first time the federal agencies regulating all the diverse forms of transportation—highways, railroads, aviation, mass transit, waterways, and oil and gas pipelines. President Lyndon B. Johnson's idea for creating the department was to facilitate a coordinated national transportation system. Instead, the bill Congress passed established decentralized control—that is, each of the department's subdivisions has control over the transportation sector within its domain. Meanwhile, the transportation secretary had the authority to develop coordinated transportation policies, but not to control matters within the sectors.

Q 490. How does the Federal Highway Administration control the interstate highway system?

A The federal government itself did not build the 45,000 plus miles of the interstate highway system or the other 800,000 miles of roads under the jurisdiction of the Federal Highway Administration. Instead, its part of building and maintaining roads was (and is) to issue federal grants to the states where the roadways are located. As part of its job of overseeing the highway grant program, however, the Federal Highway Administration does attach various requirements to the money grants, including specifications for constructing the highways and the speed limit on the interstates. If a state does not want to adhere to a particular set of requirements, the Federal Highway Administration could refuse to make the grant.

Q 491. What percentage of the U.S. land area does the Interior Department control?

A Interior administers about 30 percent of the country's land area, amounting to over 600 million acres of public lands (except for the nation's forests, which are the responsibility of the Department of Agriculture). Interior's Bureau of Land Management administers about 270 million acres of public lands in the west and Alaska; the Bureau of Reclamation seeks to restore arid lands in the west through irrigation; the Bureau of Indian Affairs provides services to Native Americans and holds about 56 million acres of Indian lands in trust for them; and the National Park Service runs the National Park System's 367 parks and historic sites. Among Interior's other divisions are the U.S. Geological Survey, the Minerals Management Service, and the U.S. Fish and Wildlife Service.

Q 492. What does the Agriculture Department do?

A Created in 1862 and made a cabinet department in 1889, the U.S. Department of Agriculture (USDA) aids farmers, sets food quality standards, and administers programs for distributing food to the needy. It helps farmers by providing credit, rural development loans, and subsidies, as well as by conducting agricultural research and administering conservation programs. In addition to setting food quality standards, USDA also inspects meat and other commodities to be sure they are safe to consume. Among the food distribution services it provides are the food stamp, school lunch, and food-for-the-needy programs.

▶ *Which president created the Education Department? See 486 Who created the Department of Health, Education and Welfare?*

Q 493. Does the Education Department actually run our schools?

A No, the federal government does not have direct control over schools; that is exercised by local government. Instead, the Education Department distributes federal grant money to states, which then distribute the funds to local schools. The grants can be earmarked for any number of specific purposes, such as improving preschool, elementary, or secondary school education or helping with the costs of educating disadvantaged children. The federal government can and does impose strict guidelines on how the money is to be spent, however, and accepting the grant may mean local schools have to comply with various federal standards.

Q 494. What sparked efforts to create the Energy Department?

A The Arab oil embargo of 1973–1974 forced the federal government to begin formulating a comprehensive energy policy and to organize new approaches to the energy problem. President Richard M. Nixon took the first step in 1974 by centralizing energy-related programs from various agencies into the Federal Energy Administration and the Energy Research and Development Administration. Just before leaving office in 1977, President Gerald R. Ford sent Congress a plan for organizing a Department of Energy, which would add further cohesion to energy policy making. President Jimmy Carter submitted a similar plan when he took office, and later in 1977 Congress officially established the department.

The Department of Energy coordinates energy policy making and oversees various federal programs related to energy, including those dealing with energy regulations, energy conservation, marketing of federal power, energy research, and energy data collection and analysis.

Q 495. How does the Department of Housing and Urban Development help meet the nation's housing needs?

A Programs operated by the Department of Housing and Urban Development (HUD) address specific housing problems. The Federal Housing Administration (FHA), for example, provides rent subsidies for low-income families, promotes rehabilitation of rental apartments, and provides mortgage insurance for qualifying homeowners. Other programs within HUD investigate housing discrimination cases, protect home buyers against fraud, and assist neighborhood development and preservation projects. The Government National Mortgage Association (Ginnie Mae) is a government corporation within HUD that works to increase the funds available for home mortgages.

Q 496. What programs does the Department of Veterans Affairs (VA) administer?

A The VA oversees a wide range of programs established to help veterans and their families. For example, it manages a network of VA hospitals and other medical facilities that provide veterans with medical care *(see next question)*. The department also administers programs for rehabilitation, disability compensation, education, and pensions for veterans. The VA home loan program offers veterans home loans with little or no down payment. Another division of the VA runs the national cemeteries.

Q 497. How big is the Department of Veterans Affairs health system?

A The Veterans Affairs Department (VA) presides over a nationwide network of hospitals and other facilities that serve injured and disabled war veterans. Tens of thousands of doctors, nurses, and other staffers work in the medical facilities. As of 1998 the VA operated 173 hospitals and 376 outpatient clinics. The VA also runs 39 facilities for patients needing temporary nursing care and 131 nursing homes. Another 205 outreach centers serve Vietnam War veterans.

THE PRESIDENT AND THE BUREAUCRACY

Q 498. What have presidents said about the bureaucracy?

A Few things frustrate presidents more than the bureaucracy. The sheer size and complexity of it make getting things done difficult enough, but presidents also must contend with bureaucratic inertia—a systemic tendency to resist change. Part of the problem is, of course, that presidents have only four to eight years to put their policies into action; government employees will still be at their desks long after any one president is gone.

Presidential comments on the bureaucracy range from patient understanding to sheer frustration. Those listed below offer a sampling of presidents' words on the subject of the bureaucracy.

Harry S. Truman: "I thought I was the president, but when it comes to these bureaucracies I can't make 'em do a damn thing."

John F. Kennedy: "[Working with bureaucrats] is like trying to nail jelly to the wall."

Jimmy Carter: "Before I became president, I realized and was warned that dealing with the federal bureaucracy would be one of the worst problems I would have to face. It has been worse than I anticipated."

Ronald Reagan: "Bureaucracy does not take kindly to being assailed and isn't above using a few low blows and a knee to the groin when it fights back."

▶ *Does the president control the bureaucracy? See 191 How much control over federal departments and agencies does the president actually have?*

Q 499. What does the civil service system do?

A The civil service governs the hiring of government employees, provides guidelines for classification of government jobs, and maintains rules for pay scales, promotions, and other personnel matters. The cornerstone of the civil service is the merit system— based on an individual's job skills, education, performance on the civil service test, and similar factors—for hiring and promoting civil service employees. About 90 percent of all federal workers are covered by the merit system; the rest are in the excepted service category, about 3 percent of which are the president's political appointees.

Before the civil service system, hiring for federal jobs was done on the basis of political favoritism (the spoils system). The president and party bosses rewarded political supporters with federal jobs regardless of their qualifications. The corruption and inefficiency this created led to calls for reform that went unheeded until the late 1800s. The assassination of President James A. Garfield by a rejected office-seeker finally led to passage of the Pendleton Act of 1883, which created the merit-based civil service system. Initially only about 10 percent of federal jobs came under the system, but over the years the merit system was expanded to include almost all government employees.

(See 306 Which president introduced the "spoils system"?)

Q 500. What was the National Performance Review all about?

A The fruit of President Bill Clinton's campaign promise to "reinvent" government, the National Performance Review sought to cut bureaucratic red tape, reduce spending, decentralize authority, and improve efficiency. Vice President Al Gore managed the six-month study that reviewed and evaluated every federal program in 1993 and recommended whether they should be reorganized, downsized, or cut altogether. Gore's final report, delivered September 7, 1993, concluded that the government needed streamlining by eliminating 252,000 jobs. The report estimated $108 billion would be saved over five years.

(See 46 Did the Clinton administration succeed in cutting the size of government?)

Q 501. When did the move toward declassifying government secrets begin?

A The first step came in 1966, when Congress approved the Freedom of Information Act, which allowed citizens to petition for the release of certain unpublished government documents. A decade later, President Jimmy Carter set up a program to promote the review and disclosure of classified material, the Information Security Oversight Office, but it failed because many government workers ignored the program and the Reagan administration reversed it. President Bill Clinton renewed the drive for declassifying documents, and soon after taking office in 1993 he ordered that all documents pertaining to Vietnam and Korean War soldiers missing in action be declassified.

FEDERAL AGENCIES AND GOVERNMENT CORPORATIONS

Q 502. What is an independent agency?

A Independent agencies—such as the Securities and Exchange Commission—operate to protect the public interest and are outside the direct control of the president, Congress, and the judiciary. Usually they are set up to regulate business and industry.

A bipartisan commission generally heads an independent agency, and its members serve fixed terms of between four and seven years. Commission members are appointed by the president, subject to confirmation by the Senate, but the president cannot remove them from office. Nor do the commissioners report directly to the president or Congress.

The agencies operate by issuing rules that businesses in a particular industry, such as the airline industry, must obey, by issuing licenses for various types of activities, and by monitoring compliance with agency rules. Among the independent regulatory agencies are the Securities and Exchange Commission, Nuclear Regulatory Commission, Federal Communications Commission, Federal Trade Commission, and the Federal Reserve System.

(See 190 Can the president fire any government official? 193 Are there any agencies the president cannot control? 506 Which agencies and government corporations are the largest?)

Q 503. When was the first regulatory agency created?

A Congress did not set up an independent regulatory agency in its modern form until 1887. That year the Interstate Commerce Commission (ICC, now defunct) was established to control ruthless and corrupt business practices in the railroad industry. The progressive reform movement of the early 1900s also brought about the creation of federal agencies designed to regulate business and the economy. Then, in the 1930s, President Franklin D. Roosevelt's New Deal programs sparked the rapid expansion of the federal government's regulatory control, a trend that reached its height with the government's commitment to social regulation in the 1960s (such as civil rights and health care).

The government has established two basic types of regulatory agencies—independent and semi-independent. Independent regulatory agencies are run by bipartisan boards of commissioners who are outside the president's control *(see previous question)*. Semi-independent agencies are under the president's control, and the president has the power to remove their directors. Usually semi-independent agencies are located within cabinet departments—for example, the Food and Drug Administration is part of the Department of Health and Human Services and the Occupational Safety and Health Administration is a division of the Department of Labor. A hybrid form, the independent executive agency, exists outside of any executive department. For example, the Environmental Protection Agency is not part of any department, but because it is only semi-independent the president can fire its director.

(See 190 Can the president fire any government official? 193 Are there any agencies the president cannot control?)

Q 504. Which industries have been deregulated?

A Begun during the Carter administration and continued by Presidents Ronald Reagan, George Bush, and Bill Clinton, the federal government has eased federal regulation in a number of industries to foster greater efficiency of the businesses and lower prices to consumers. In the process, some or most federal regulations have been lifted from the airline, truck, bus, railroad, television, and cable industries, although with varying degrees of success. Increased competition (which regulations had prevented) lowered airline ticket prices, for example, but the public outcry over rising cable rates forced Congress to reregulate the cable industry in 1992. In the finance sector, banking deregulation during the 1980s aggravated existing problems for the savings and loan banks, bringing on the costly savings and loan crisis.

Q 505. What is a government corporation?

A The federal government sets up government corporations to provide public services that private enterprise has been unable or unwilling to do on a for-profit basis. Among the better-known government corporations are the U.S. Postal Service (reorganized from a cabinet department to a government corporation in 1970), Tennessee Valley Authority (TVA), Federal Deposit and Insurance Corporation (FDIC), and National Railroad Passenger Corporation (Amtrak).

Unlike federal agencies, government corporations have greater freedom to operate. They act in the name of the corporation, not the federal government; they can buy, develop, and sell property; they can make a profit like an ordinary business; and they can sue and be sued. Government corporations are usually run by a chief executive officer and a board of directors, all of whom are appointed by the president and confirmed by the Senate.

Q **506. Which agencies and government corporations are the largest?**

A The U.S. Postal Service has long been one of the federal government's biggest employers, and among the agencies and government corporations, it ranks first in size with 852,000 employees. The Social Security Administration, which employs about 66,000 workers, is a distant second. After that come the National Aeronautics and Space Administration, the Environmental Protection Agency, and the government's watchdog, the General Services Administration.

Independent Federal Agencies and Government Corporations

Agency	Paid Civilian Employees, 1996
American Battle Monuments Commission	371
Board of Governors, Federal Reserve System	1,740
Environmental Protection Agency	17,160
Equal Employment Opportunity Commission	2,655
Export-Import Bank	426
Farm Credit Administration	332
Federal Communications Commission	2,069
Federal Deposit Insurance Corporation	10,008
Federal Emergency Management Agency	6,569
Federal Labor Relations Authority	232
Federal Mediation and Conciliation Service	293
Federal Trade Commission	941
General Services Administration	15,654
International Trade Commission	391
National Aeronautics and Space Administration	21,006
National Endowment for the Arts	337
National Labor Relations Board	1,970
National Science Foundation	1,249
National Transportation Safety Board	370
Nuclear Regulatory Commission	3,148
Office of Personnel Management	3,524
Panama Canal Commission	9,355
Railroad Retirement Board	1,440
Securities and Exchange Commission	2,838
Selective Service System	221
Small Business Administration	4,839
Smithsonian Institution	5,188

Independent Federal Agencies and Government Corporations

Agency	Paid Civilian Employees, 1996
Social Security Administration	66,314
Tennessee Valley Authority	16,022
U.S. Postal Service	852,285
All other	21,298
Total	1,070,245

(See 475 What is the largest cabinet department?)

(See 475 What is the largest cabinet department?)

Q 507. Which president established the forerunner of the FBI?

A Theodore Roosevelt set up the Bureau of Investigation within the Justice Department in 1908. Reorganized and vastly expanded, that agency was officially renamed the Federal Bureau of Investigation in 1935.

In 1908 Roosevelt had asked Congress for approval to expand the mandate of the Secret Service to investigate crimes other than just counterfeiting. But fearing establishment of a national police force (and expansion of the president's powers), Congress refused. Roosevelt rightly foresaw that the Justice Department needed an investigative arm to enforce laws enacted by Congress, however, and used his powers to quietly set up the Bureau of Investigation within the Justice Department. Abuses of the bureau's powers during the Harding administration led to the appointment of a new director, J. Edgar Hoover, in 1924 and his remarkably successful reorganization of the bureau. Hoover, who served as director from 1924 until 1972, was not without his critics, but he molded the FBI into an efficient and highly regarded crime-fighting organization. Because of his longevity and high-profile position, Hoover has been called the most famous bureaucrat.

Q 508. How does the Federal Reserve affect the economy?

A The nation's central bank, the Federal Reserve (the "Fed"), controls the economy indirectly through the banking system, mainly by increasing or decreasing the growth of the money supply. If the Fed's board of governors decides to increase the money supply to stimulate the economy, for example, banks will have more money to lend and interest rates will decline. As loans become less costly, businesses borrow more to build new factories and purchase equipment, among other things, which in turn improves economic growth.

The Fed can increase or decrease the growth of the money supply in various ways, but most often it does so by buying or selling government securities. When it buys securities from the banks, they have more money to lend to businesses and individuals. When it sells securities at attractive rates, banks buy them up and have less money to lend. The Fed also can change the money supply by raising or lowering the discount rate—that is, the interest the Fed charges for loans to commercial banks. When the rate goes up, banks cannot borrow as much and so have less money to lend customers.

The Fed uses a network of twelve regional Federal Reserve banks and twenty-five branches to effect its monetary policies. The board of governors, which controls the Federal Reserve and sets monetary policy, is made up of seven members who are appointed by the president and confirmed by the Senate. Governors serve a single fourteen-year term and so are insulated from political pressures.

(See 201 Do presidents control the Federal Reserve System?)

Q 509. When was the Postal Service established as a government corporation?

A Prodded by President Richard M. Nixon, Congress removed the Post Office from the president's cabinet in 1970 and reorganized it as an independent government corporation called the United States Postal Service. The move was designed to improve the efficiency of the Postal Service and end the massive government subsidies needed to keep it running.

The forerunner of the U.S. Post Office was established in 1775 during the American Revolution, and after adoption of the Constitution, it became part of the Treasury Department. President Andrew Jackson gave the postmaster general cabinet rank in 1829, and as the nation expanded westward, the post office grew with it. Until World War II, when the size of the U.S. defense establishment mushroomed, the Post Office was the government's largest employer. Today, some 850,000 employees work for the U.S. Postal Service.

(See 371 What was the Star Route scandal about?)

Q 510. When was the CIA created?

A The Central Intelligence Agency (CIA) was established in 1947, essentially by expanding the World War II spy agency, the Office of Strategic Services (OSS). Up to that time, the United States had gathered intelligence information through various channels, including reports from U.S. ambassadors, the army and navy, and after Pearl Harbor, the OSS as well. Because these reports were often contradictory and confusing, President Harry S. Truman asked Congress to create an agency to gather and assess the information. Congress obliged by creating the CIA and giving it the power to gather intelligence and to conduct covert operations overseas in the national interest.

ECONOMY, BUDGETING AND FINANCE

Q 511. In what ways does the government influence the economy?

A Because federal spending amounts to about $1.7 trillion—some 19 percent of the country's entire gross domestic product—the government cannot help but affect the economy. Even a modest rise in federal spending can give it a boost, and a cutback can help cool it off when it is overheated. But the government has other ways of influencing the economy as well. Through the Federal Reserve System, for example, it controls the money supply and can raise or lower certain interest rates, changes that affect the cost of borrowing money. It also has the power to regulate many economic activities, which may increase costs to the consumer but can eliminate unfair or unsafe business practices. Through its redistribution of wealth, the government influences the economy as well—the taxes paid by business and rich citizens are used to finance programs that help the poor.

Q 512. What has the current emphasis on monetary policy done for the economy?

A Economists generally credit the Federal Reserve's emphasis on controlling the growth of the money supply with having brought the high inflation of the 1970s and early 1980s under control. That is because the amount of money circulating in the economy is now believed to have an effect on economic activity: when the amount of money available is increased, interest rates tend to fall (because banks have more money to lend) and economic activity heats up. Decreasing the growth rate of the money supply does the opposite. Interest rates rise (because banks have less money to lend) and the economy slows. That reduces demand for goods and services and so helps cut inflation.

Q 513. What is the president's role in preparing the federal budget?

A The president is a key player in the budget writing process. Each year he proposes a budget that includes revenue and spending estimates for the hundreds of agencies and departments within the government. Congress then votes to accept, reject, or modify the president's figures.

The budget process begins with the federal agencies, which submit their annual budget requests to the Office of Management and Budget (OMB). Applying the policy goals outlined by the president, OMB works with the agency requests to prepare a proposed budget, which the president sends to Congress in early February. At this point the beginning of the fiscal year, October 1, is still eight months away.

Congress then begins its work, which includes passing a budget resolution to set spending guidelines for the upcoming fiscal year. The House and then the Senate appropriations committees begin the work of writing and passing the thirteen major appropriations bills that must be enacted to complete the budget for the upcoming year.

Although Congress now has control of the budget process, the president does not sit idly by on the sidelines. White House staffers, lobbyists, and members of the president's party in Congress fight to keep as much of the president's proposed budget intact as possible. Tradeoffs are inevitable, but the president can and does use his veto to reject individual spending bills, usually to force Congress to reconsider unacceptable spending cuts or remove wasteful spending projects. Ideally, Congress will have passed, and the president will have signed, all thirteen appropriations bills by October 1, the start of the fiscal year. But conflicts over spending priorities can delay passage of some for months, forcing Congress to pass interim spending measures called continuing resolutions.

Q **514. How do interest groups affect the budget process?**

A Labor unions, business and industry groups, senior citizens, doctors, lawyers, environmentalists, farmers, minorities, and other groups all have lobbyists who represent their interests in Washington and help them pressure Congress and the president for passage of legislation. These special interest groups have a stake in how the budget is written, because a tax break or a spending increase can mean millions of dollars in new benefits. On the other hand, a spending cut or benefit eliminated can hurt millions of other voters. With this kind of competition among special interest groups for available federal money, Congress and presidents have found it difficult to impossible in years past to keep spending in line with revenues. They often simply cannot resist the pressure from large blocs of voters to make difficult budget cuts or set workable budget priorities.

Q 515. When did income taxes become the largest source of federal revenue?

A For many years the government did not collect an income tax; instead it taxed imported foreign goods to raise the revenue it needed. The first income tax was levied in 1862 to help pay for the Civil War, and the government let it expire ten years later. After ratification of the Sixteenth Amendment in 1913, which empowered Congress to levy an income tax, the federal government imposed a 1 percent tax on incomes. That low tax rate did not last long, though. Increases to pay for World War I pushed up income tax revenues sixfold, and during the 1920s total revenue from income taxes continued to rise. It made up more than half of all federal revenue for the first time in 1930, and every year since 1941 income tax revenues have provided the lion's share of funds the government has taken in.

Q 516. Has the government ever run out of money?

A Technically, yes, but, using a bit of fancy financial footwork, the Treasury Department was able to avert an actual shortfall. The problem revolved around battles between the White House and Congress over the federal budget. The government routinely borrows money when it is needed, but only up to the "debt ceiling" set by Congress. Congress must pass legislation to raise that limit, yet during budget standoffs in 1984 and 1985, the Treasury Department found itself at the end of its borrowing authority. Treasury Secretary James A. Baker III had to resort to drastic measures both times to deal with the crises. His temporary solution was to disinvest (take back) billions in government securities held by Social Security and other retirement funds. That step technically reduced the government's indebtedness, allowing Treasury to borrow billions more. After Congress raised the debt limit in the 1984 and 1985 crises, Baker returned the disinvested securities, with interest.

FOR FURTHER INFORMATION

Readers who are simply looking for information on how to contact specific agencies will find books such as the *Federal Staff Directory* and *Congressional Quarterly's Washington Information Directory* most helpful. For details about the responsibilities and history of the many government departments and agencies, encyclopedic works such as *Congressional Quarterly's Guide to the Presidency* and the *Encyclopedia of the American Presidency* will answer most questions. Some of the other works listed below will help answer questions about specific topics, such as the budget or the position of chief of staff. Too numerous to list here are books on specific agencies, such as the Treasury and the Federal Bureau of Investigation.

Arnold, Peri E. *Making the Managerial Presidency: Comprehensive Reorganization and Planning, 1905–1980.* Princeton: Princeton University Press, 1986.

Bennett, Anthony J. *The American President's Cabinet: From Kennedy to Bush.* New York: St. Martin's Press, 1996.

Burke, John P. *The Institutional Presidency.* Baltimore: Johns Hopkins University Press, 1992.

Cronin, Thomas E., and Sanford E. Greenberg, eds. *The Presidential Advisory System.* New York: Harper and Row, 1969.

Edwards, George C., III, and Stephen J. Wayne. *Presidential Leadership.* 3d ed. New York: St. Martin's Press, 1994.

Federal Regulatory Directory. 9th ed. Washington, D.C.: Congressional Quarterly, biennial.

Federal Staff Directory. Washington, D.C.: CQ Press, three issues per year.

Fesler, James W., and Donald F. Kettl. *The Politics of the Administrative Process.* Chatham, N.J.: Chatham House, 1996.

Hess, Stephen. *Organizing the Presidency.* Washington, D.C.: Brookings, 1988.

Kernell, Samuel, and Samuel L. Popkin, eds. *Chief of Staff: Twenty-five Years of Managing the Presidency.* Berkeley: University of California Press, 1986.

King, Anthony, ed. *Both Ends of the Avenue: The Presidency, the Executive Branch, and Congress in the 1980s.* Washington, D.C.: American Enterprise Institute, 1983.

King, Gary, and Lyn Ragsdale. *The Elusive Executive: Discovering Statistical Patterns in the Presidency.* Washington, D.C.: CQ Press, 1988.

Kurtz, Howard. *Spin Cycle: Inside the Clinton Propaganda Machine.* New York: Free Press, 1998.

Levy, Leonard W., and Louis Fisher. *Encyclopedia of the American Presidency.* New York: Simon and Shuster, 1993.

Mackenzie, G. Calvin. *The In-and-Outers: Presidential Appointees and Transient Government in Washington.* Baltimore: Johns Hopkins University Press, 1987.

Macy, John W., Bruce Adams, and J. Jackson Walter. *America's Unelected Government: Appointing the President's Team.* Cambridge: Ballinger, 1983.

Milkis, Sidney M., and Michael Nelson. *The American Presidency: Origins and Development, 1776–1998.* Washington, D.C.: CQ Press, 1999.

Nelson, Michael, ed. *Congressional Quarterly's Guide to the Presidency.* 2d ed. 2 vols. Washington, D.C.: Congressional Quarterly, 1996.

———, ed. *The Evolving Presidency: Addresses, Cases, Essays, Letters, Reports, Resolutions, Transcripts, and Other Landmark Documents, 1787–1998.* Washington, D.C.: CQ Press, 1998.

The Politics of the U.S. Cabinet: Representation in the Executive Branch, 1789–1984. Pittsburgh: University of Pittsburgh Press, 1988.

Powers of the Presidency. 2d ed. Washington, D.C.: Congressional Quarterly, 1997.

The Presidency A to Z. 2d ed. Washington, D.C.: Congressional Quarterly, 1998.

Ragsdale, Lyn. *Vital Statistics on the Presidency: Washington to Clinton.* Rev. ed. Washington, D.C.: Congressional Quarterly, 1998.

Sabato, Larry J. *The Rise of Political Consultants.* New York: Basic Books, 1981.

Schick, Allen. *The Federal Budget: Politics, Policy, Process.* Washington, D.C.: Brookings, 1995.

Schlesinger, Arthur M., Jr. *The Imperial Presidency.* Boston: Houghton Mifflin, 1991.

Small, Norman J. *Some Presidential Interpretations of the Presidency.* New York: Da Capo Press, 1970.

Stein, Herbert. *Presidential Economics: The Making of Economic Policy from Roosevelt to Reagan and Beyond.* Washington, D.C.: American Enterprise Institute, 1988.

Warshaw, Shirley Anne. *The Domestic Presidency: Policy Making in the White House.* Boston: Allyn and Bacon, 1997.

———. *Powersharing: White House-Cabinet Relations in the Modern Presidency.* Albany: State University of New York Press, 1996.

Washington Information Directory. Washington, D.C.: CQ Press, annual.

Weko, Thomas J. *The Politicizing Presidency: The White House Personnel Office.* Lawrence: University Press of Kansas, 1995.

Wetterau, Bruce. *Congressional Quarterly's Desk Reference on American Government.* 2d ed. Washington, D.C: CQ Press, 2000.

———. *Congressional Quarterly's Desk Reference on the Federal Budget.* Washington, D.C.: Congressional Quarterly, 1998.

INDEX

References in the index correspond to question numbers in the text.

References in the index correspond to question numbers in the text.

References in the index correspond to question numbers in the text.

Cabinet Committee on Price
Stability for Economic Growth,
282
Cable deregulation, 504
Calhoun, John C.
born into wealthy family, 138
children, 140
dates, as VP, 348
death, 173
first VP to resign, 343
member of Congress, 142
resigned as VP, 59, 60, 307
rift with Jackson, 307
served two presidents, 343
spoils system and, 306
tie-breaking votes, 225
Camp David, 183
Camp David accords, 362
Campaign buttons
first, 423
Campaign financing. *See* Elections
and campaigns
Campaigns. *See* Elections and
campaigns; Primaries
Cancer
Grant and, 168
Capitalism
Kitchen debate and, 359
Capitol
crypt in, 171, 174
first inauguration in, 47
president's funeral and, 170
Carlucci, Frank, 192
Caroline Fillmore
death, 135
marriage, 116, 118, 119
Carter, Jimmy
bills vetoed, 230
birthday, 80
Camp David and, 362
campaign slogan, 417
children, 130
classified material review, 501
college and, 106
Congress, party control, 291
created Energy Department, 494
dark-horse candidate, 377
dates, presidency, 348
debates, 429
Democrats control Congress, 239
deregulation, 504
election of 1976, 331, 377, 385,
398, 405, 429

election of 1980, 331, 379, 385,
417, 429
election, votes won, 433
first black woman cabinet
member, 468
first political office, 102
Iranian hostage crisis, 363
marriage, 116, 119
military interventions, 364
military service, 109
new cabinet departments, 486
no Court appointments, 248
occupation, 105
oldest child, 83
outsider approach, 331
pardons and, 206
party infighting and, 236
presidential library, 166
primaries and, 405
quote on bureaucracy, 498
religion, 107
served as governor, 103
shortened name, 91
sports, 97
staff chief and, 456
summit, 1979, 357
walks inaugural parade route, 49
work routine, 341
writings, 93
Carter, Rosalynn
causes supported, 128
children, 130
marriage, 116, 119
occupation, 127
reputation of, 115
Case Act (1972), 259
Cass, Lewis
election, votes won, 433
Cavazos, Lauro F., 468
Cemetery Ridge, 312
Census Bureau, 483
Centers for Disease Control, 487
Central Intelligence Agency, 462,
471
origins of, 510
Cermonial duties. *See* Chief of state
Cermak, Anton J., 297
Chance for Peace, 323
Checkers speech, 345
Checks and balances, 22
Cheney, Richard M., 456
Chicago
holds most party conventions,
447

Chief executive
president's duties as, 176
Chief of staff
National Security Council, 462
role of, 456
staff chiefs listed, 456
Chief of state
president's duties, 176, 196
China
Clinton campaign contributions,
451
Korean War end, 358
Nixon's policy on, 361
Chisholm, Shirley, 400
Churchill, Winston
summits and, 357
Circular system, 457
Civil Aeronautics Board, 482
Civil rights, 480
1877 compromise and, 440
Great Society and, 325
Johnson on riots, 327
regulatory agencies and, 503
Civil Service
limits appointments, 181
Pendleton Act, 306
role of, 499
Civil War, 245
Cemetery Ridge, 312
censorship, 265
Confederates pardoned, 206
Davis on, 311
Emancipation Proclamation, 311
emergency powers, 247
Gettysburg Address, 312
income tax and, 515
Lincoln on, 311
Lincoln's emergency powers, 212
Lincoln's war powers expanded,
211
martial law and, 214
VP Breckinridge and, 344
Classified material
declassification, 501
Clay, Henry, 408, 421
election of 1824, 438
Roorback forgery, 367
Clemency. *See* Pardon power
Cleveland, Frances
children, 130
death, 135
education, 124
marriage, 119, 350
outlived husband, 134

References in the index correspond to question numbers in the text.

popularity of, 115
White House childbirth, 129
White House wedding, 350
Cleveland, Grover
bills vetoed, 230
birthday, 80
cancer and, 155
changed name, 91
children, 129, 130
close election, 1884, 432
dates, presidency, 348
death, 173
election of 1884, 85, 286, 432, 434
election of 1888, 286, 385, 432
election of 1892, 132, 286, 385, 394, 434, 443
election, votes won, 433
fathered illegitimate child, 85, 365
first political office, 102
marriage, 84, 119
minority president, 434
nonconsecutive terms, 286
numbering of presidents and, 9
occupation, 105
Pullman strike and, 21
ranked near great, 340
refused renomination, 286
religion, 107
served as governor, 103
served two terms, 275, 386
sports, 97
stature, 146
White House security and, 472
White House wedding, 350
Clinton, Bill
big government quote, 333
bills vetoed, 230
birthday, 80
campaign finance scandal, 453
campaign slogan, 417
children, 130
college and, 106
Comprehensive Test Ban Treaty, 258
Congressional majority and, 435
dates, as governor, 103
dates, presidency, 348
debates, 429
declassification, 501
Democrats control Congress, 239
deregulation, 504
effective communicator, 262
election of 1992, 379, 385, 405, 406, 417, 429, 431, 434, 441, 449

election of 1996, 375, 379, 384, 429, 449, 452, 453
election, votes won, 433
father died, 77
first baby boomer president, 448
first political office, 102
first woman press secretary, 269
foreign travel, 354
government shutdowns, 239
health care reform, 283, 466
impeachment described, 65
inaugural balls, 51
lefthanded, 92
Lewinsky scandal, 376
line-item veto and, 229
marriage, 119
military interventions, 364
minority president, 434
musical talent, 95
National Performance Review, 500
numbering of presidents, 9
occupation, 105, 110
only child, 79
parade costs, 49
pardons, 206
polls and, 431
practiced law, 100
primaries and, 405
public appearances, 29
religion, 107
served two terms, 275
sexual affairs, 365
sports, 97
staff size, 30
stature, 146
Whitewater scandal, 375
work routine, 341
workforce cuts, 46
Clinton, George
birth, 137
Continental Congress member, 142
dates, as VP, 348
death, 60, 173
election, votes won, 433
first VP to die in office, 343
second oldest VP, 145
served two presidents, 343
tie-breaking votes, 225
Clinton, Hillary Rodham
causes supported, 128
children, 130
education, 124

health care reform commission, 283, 466
marriage, 119
occupation, 127
reputation of, 115
Whitewater scandal, 375
Closed primaries, 404
Coins
presidents' images on, 14
Cold war. *See also* Soviet Union; Summits
brushfire wars, 358
containing communism, 356
Defense downsizing, 46, 475
Kitchen debate, 359
Nixon's China card, 361
summit conferences, 357
Truman Doctrine, 356
war powers and, 211
Colfax, Schuyler, 369
birth, 137
Crédit Mobilier scandal, 66
dates, as VP, 348
death, 173
member of Congress, 142
tie-breaking votes, 225
Commander in chief. *See also* War powers
president's duties, 176
Commerce Department
date created, 32
employment, 465
Hoover's influence on, 482
president's who headed, 467
role of, 483
Commerce and Labor, 483
Commissions. *See* Presidential commissions
Committee to Preserve the White House, 284
Communism
Kitchen debate and, 359
Compilation of the Messages and Papers of the Presidents, 1789–1897, 288
Comprehensive Test Ban Treaty, 258
Compromise of 1877, 440
Confederacy
Cemetery Ridge, 312
Davis on Civil War, 311
Stone Mountain, 175
VP became general, 344
Congress and the presidency

References in the index correspond to question numbers in the text.

References in the index correspond to question numbers in the text.

References in the index correspond to question numbers in the text.

Early, Stephen T., 36
Eastern Europe
    summit on, 1989, 357
Eaton, John
    Eaton affair, 123
Eaton, Peggy
    Eaton affair, 123
Economy
    economic crises, 213
    economic summits, 357
    emergency controls on, 213
    Federal Reserve and, 201
    federal spending and, 198
    government influence over, 511
    Great Depression, 336
    Hamilton and, 470
    monetary policy and, 512
    presidential elections and, 379
    presidents and, 197
    president's approval rating and,
        338
    president's economic advisers,
        463
    spending increases and, 45
    Vietnam War and, 326
Eden, Anthony, 357
Education, of presidents, 106
Education Department, 493
    date created, 32
    employment, 465
    first Hispanic heads, 468
Egghead label, 427
Egypt, 362
    signs peace treaty with Israel, 362
Eighteenth Amendment, 394
Eisenhower, Dwight D.
    bills vetoed, 230
    birthday, 80
    cabinet and, 464
    campaign slogan, 417
    campaign spending, 449
    changed name, 91
    childhood lesson on temper, 72
    children, 130
    coins term executive privilege,
        203
    college and, 106
    Congress, party control, 291
    dates, presidency, 348
    death, 173
    election of 1952, 345, 406, 417,
        427, 449
    election of 1956, 160, 417
    election, votes won, 433

first multiple inaugural balls, 51
first political office, 102
first staff chief, 456
first televised press conferences,
    280
football and, 94
foreign travel, 354
Health, Education and Welfare,
    486
Little Rock and, 21
major speeches, 29
marriage, 117, 119
massive retaliation policy, 358
military interventions, 364
military service, 108, 109
military-industrial complex and,
    163
names first VP to head
    commission, 219
never elected before, 101
Nixon's Checkers speech, 345
nuclear peace and, 323
occupation, 105
Open Skies plan, 323
presidential library, 166
press secretary and, 36
religion, 107
rumored sexual liasion, 365
served two terms, 275
sports, 97
summits, 357
war hero, 101
Warren nomination, 246
work routine, 341
Eisenhower, Mamie
    children, 130
    death, 135
    marriage, 116, 117, 119
El Salvador, 374
Elections and campaigns. See also
    Electoral college; Primaries
    baby boomers and, 448
    basic primary strategies, 398
    campaign buttons, 423
    campaign contribution limits, 454
    campaign funding, 452
    campaign spending, 449
    candidate selection, 396, 409, 410
    candidates stump, 444
    candidates, PACs and, 450
    dark-horse candidates, 377
    direct election of president, 27
    economy a factor in, 379
    election, closest, 432

election of 1796, 443
election of 1800, 26, 264, 380,
    437, 438
election of 1804, 218
election of 1808, 443
election of 1816, 409, 418, 443
election of 1820, 418
election of 1824, 434, 438
election of 1828, 343
election of 1832, 366
election of 1836, 439
election of 1840, 412, 420, 444
election of 1844, 421
election of 1848, 131, 217, 433,
    434
election of 1852, 342, 387, 433
election of 1856, 441
election of 1860, 311, 422
election of 1864, 397, 433
election of 1868, 387, 433
election of 1872, 413, 433
election of 1876, 434, 438, 440
election of 1880, 432
election of 1884, 85, 131, 286,
    387, 413, 432, 434
election of 1888, 286, 434
election of 1892, 132, 295, 385,
    394, 433
election of 1896, 423, 424, 445
election of 1900, 445
election of 1904, 433
election of 1908, 178, 433
election of 1912, 441
election of 1916, 402, 433
election of 1920, 442
election of 1924, 411
election of 1928, 399, 433
election of 1932, 379, 435
election of 1936, 430, 432, 433
election of 1940, 416
election of 1944, 178, 433
election of 1948, 426, 441
election of 1952, 345, 427
election of 1956, 417, 433
election of 1960, 384, 429, 443
election of 1964, 428, 431, 432
election of 1968, 388, 400, 405,
    432 441, 443, 446, 449
election of 1972, 58, 373, 400,
    401, 405, 417, 432, 446, 449
election of 1976, 331
election of 1980, 331, 332, 435
election of 1984, 412, 414

References in the index correspond to question numbers in the text.

References in the index correspond to question numbers in the text.

References in the index correspond to question numbers in the text.

References in the index correspond to question numbers in the text.

---

marriage, 116, 119
occupation, 127
Harding, Warren G.
   appointed Taft justice, 151
   bills vetoed, 230
   birthday, 80
   college and, 106
   dark-horse candidate, 377
   dates, in Congress, 104
   dates, presidency, 348
   death, 55, 158, 168, 173
   election of 1920, 432
   election, votes won, 433
   fathered illegitimate child, 85,
      365
   first political office, 102
   first president on radio, 149
   historians' ranking, 340
   hobbies, 96
   marriage, 116, 118, 119
   musical talent, 95
   occupation, 105
   oldest child, 83
   ordered Debs released, 442
   prepares first proposed budget,
      37
   religion, 107
   sports, 97
   studied law, 100
   survived by father, 81
   Teapot Dome scandal, 317, 372
   twenty-year jinx, 294
   wins by big margin, 432
Harris, Patricia Roberts, 468
Harrison, Anna, 350
   children, 130
   death, 135
   marriage, 119
Harrison, Benjamin
   bills vetoed, 230
   birthday, 80
   children, 130
   college and, 106
   dates, in Congress, 104
   dates, presidency, 348
   death, 173
   election of 1888, 432
   election of 1892, 385
   first political office, 102
   had wealthy parents, 77
   marriage, 116, 119
   military service, 108, 109
   minority president, 434
   most siblings, 79

occupation, 105
religion, 107
sports, 97
stature, 146
W. H. Harrison's grandson, 78
work routine, 341
Harrison, Caroline
   children, 130
   death, 132, 135, 295
   marriage, 119
Harrison, John Scott
   declined run for presidency, 131
Harrison, Mary
   children, 130
   death, 135
   marriage, 118, 119
   outlived husband, 134
Harrison, William Henry
   Benjamin Harrison's
      grandfather, 78
   birthday, 80
   born in log cabin, 68
   children, 130
   college and, 106
   dates, presidency, 348
   death, 54, 55, 173, 295
   election of 1840, 420
   election, votes won, 433
   first political office, 102
   first stump speeches, 444
   foreign service, 111
   last president born before
      indpendence, 73
   log cabin campaign and, 68
   longest inaugural speech, 53
   lost both parents, 80
   marriage, 119
   military service, 108
   no bills vetoed, 230
   occupation, 105
   religion, 107
   second oldest president, 145
   served shortest term, 285
   Tippiecanoe slogan, 417
   tried again and won, 443
   twenty-year jinx, 294
   youngest child, 83
Havana, Cuba
   Maine explodes, 313
Hayes, Lucy
   called first lady, 113
   children, 130
   college grad, 124
   death, 135

education, 124
marriage, 119
Hayes, Rutherford B.
   bills vetoed, 230
   birthday, 80
   born after father's death, 81
   children, 130
   college and, 106
   dark-horse candidate, 377
   dates, as governor, 103
   dates, in Congress, 104
   dates, presidency, 348
   death, 173
   did not run again, 386
   election of 1876, 440
   election, votes won, 433
   first political office, 102
   marriage, 119
   military service, 108, 109
   minority president, 434
   occupation, 105
   presidential library, 166
   presidential seal, 5
   religion, 107
   Spiegel Grove, 112
   youngest child, 83
Health and Human Services
   Department, 204, 468
   date created, 32
   employment, 44, 465
   organization of, 487
Health Care Financing
   Administration, 487
Health, Education and Welfare
   Department
   history of, 486
Health of presidents. See Medical
   problems of presidents
Hemings, Sally
   Jefferson and, 365
Hendricks, Thomas A.
   dates, VP term, 348
   died, 60, 173
   member of Congress, 142
   tie-breaking votes, 225
Henry Clay, Henry
   election, votes won, 433
Hermitage, 112
Highways, 490
Hinckley, John W. Jr., 162, 297
Hispanics
   first cabinet member, 468
Historians' ratings of presidents,
   340

References in the index correspond to question numbers in the text.

Hobart, Garret A.
  dates, VP term, 348
  death, 173
  tie-breaking votes, 225
Honduras
  Marines sent, 355
Hoover Commissions, 284
Hoover, Herbert
  A Chicken in every pot slogan, 417
  appeared on experimental TV, 149
  appointed first press secretary, 36
  bills vetoed, 230
  birthday, 80
  born west of Mississippi, 73
  children, 130
  college and, 106
  comment on presidency, 293
  Congress, party control, 291
  dates, presidency, 348
  dates, Secretary of Commerce, 467, 482
  death, 173
  election of 1928, 399
  election of 1932, 379, 385
  election, votes won, 433
  executive orders, 195
  first political office, 102
  Great Depression and, 318
  hobbies, 96
  Hoovervilles, 318
  inaugural filmed, 47
  long lived, 172
  lost both parents, 81
  marriage, 116, 119
  never elected before, 101
  occupation, 105
  presidential library, 166
  presidential security, 472
  religion, 107
  sports, 97
  staff size, 30
  war relief work, 101
  writings, 93
Hoover, J. Edgar, 507
Hoover, Lou
  children, 130
  death, 135
  education, 124
  marriage, 116, 119
  occupation, 127
Hopkins, Harry, 189

Hostage crisis. *See* Iranian hostage crisis
House of Representatives. *See also* Congress and the presidency
  election of 1800, 437
  election of 1876, 438
  impeachment process, 62
House, Col. Edward, 189
Housing, 495
Housing and Urban Development Department
  black named secretary, 468
  date created, 32
  employment, 465
  role of, 495
Howe, Louis, 189
Hughes, Charles E.
  election, votes won, 433
Hughes, Sarah Tilghman, 13
Human rights, 357
Humphrey, Hubert H.
  dates, presidency, 348
  death, 173
  election of 1968, 446
  election, votes won, 433
  member of Congress, 142
  tie-breaking votes, 225
Humphrey's Executor v. United States
  removal power limited, 190
Hundred Days, 425
  president's expanded legislative powers, 238

"I Like Ike," 417
Immigration and Naturalization Service, 204, 480
Immunity, presidential, 187
Impeachment
  as check on president's power, 22
  Clinton's described, 65
  impeachable offenses, 61
  Nixon escapes by resigning, 58
  presidents impeached, 63
  process, 62
Impressment, 302
"In Gold We Trust," 424
Inauguration
  day, 177
  date moved to Jan. 20, 26, 52
  firsts, 47, 49
  Harrison's long address, 285

Jackson's raucous inaugural, 50
  longest speech, 53
  outgoing presidents and, 48
  parade costs, 49
  VP/VP-elect dies before, 401
Independent agencies, 503
  described, 502
  employees, 506
  in executive branch, 40
Independent regulatory agencies
  independence of, 205
  outside president's control, 193
  president's removal power limited, 190
Inflation
  money supply and, 512
Information Security Oversight Office, 501
Integration
  president's enforcement of, 24
Intelligence community
  origins of, 510
Interest groups and the presidency
  budget process and, 514
  cabinet and, 273
  expansion of, 270
  how presidents sidestep, 335
  number of, 270
  Office of Public Liaison, 274
  PACs, 450
  party supported, 272
  president and, 271
  Washington warns against, 163
Interest rates
  Federal Reserve and, 511
  money supply and, 512
Interior Department
  date created, 32
  employment, 465
  role of, 491
Intermediate Nuclear Force (INF) Treaty, 357
Internal Revenue Service, 204
International Trade Commission
  employees, 506
Interstate Commerce Commission, 314, 503
Iowa caucus, 403
Iran-contra scandal, 374
Iranian hostage crisis, 363
"It's the Economy, Stupid," 417

Jackson, Andrew
  among greatest presidents, 340

Johnson, Lyndon B., 112
  balanced ticket, 397
  biggest winning margin, 432
  bills vetoed, 230
  birthday, 80
  campaign slogan, 417
  children, 130
  college and, 106
  comment on presidency, 293
  Congress, party control, 291
  Congress, success with, 237
  dates, presidency, 348
  death, 173
  election of 1964, 428, 431, 432
  election, votes won, 433
  first black cabinet member, 468
  first political office, 102
  Great Society program
    announced, 240
    described, 325
  Health, Education and Welfare
    Department, 486
  high approval rating, 339
  marriage, 119
  member of Congress, 142
  memorial grove, 174
  military interventions, 364
  military service, 109
  new cabinet department, 489
  occupation, 105, 110
  oldest child, 83
  ordered minority hiring, 194
  polls and, 337, 431
  pollster on staff, 337
  presidential library, 166
  race riots and, 213, 327
  religion and, 107
  served in Congress, 104
  sexual affairs, 365
  sports, 97
  staff powers, 459
  stature, 146
  succeeded Kennedy, 55, 222
  summit (1967), 357
  sworn in by a woman, 13
  television and, 235
  tie-breaking votes, 225
  Vietnam War and, 326
  wife campaigns, 428
  work routine, 341
Johnson, Richard M.
  children, 140
  dates, VP term, 348
  death, 173

election of 1837, 439
  member of Congress, 142
  tie-breaking votes, 225
Joint Chiefs of Staff, 462. *See also*
  Defense Department
  role, 477
Jones, Paula, 376
  Clinton lawsuit leads to
    impeachment, 65
Jordon, Hamilton, 456
Judiciary Act of 1789, 479
Judiciary Act of 1925, 151
Junior Tuesday, 403
  described, 407
Justice Department, 205
  date created, 32
  employment, 44, 465
  FBI created, 507
  law enforcement duties, 480
  law enforcement role, 204
  lower court appointments, 249
  origins, 479
  solicitor general, 481
  Whitewater, 375

Kansas-Nebraska Act, 387
Kemp, Jack, 429
Kennedy, Jacqueline, 296
  buried at Arlington, 171
  causes supported, 128
  children, 130
  death, 135
  education, 124
  marriage, 119
  occupation, 127
  outlived husband, 134
  popularity of, 115
  son dies, 133
Kennedy, John F.
  Addison's disease and, 161
  advised by brother Robert, 189
  "Ask not" quote, 324
  assassination described, 296
  Berlin Wall speech, 360
  bills vetoed, 230
  birthday, 80
  buried at Arlington, 171
  children, 130
  college and, 106
  comment on presidency, 293
  Congress, party control, 291
  created Presidential Medal of
    Freedom, 186
  Cuban missile crisis, 358

dates, in Congress, 104
dates, presidency, 348
death, 172, 173
debates, 429
election of 1960, 432
election, votes won, 433
expanded staff powers, 459
first Catholic president, 99, 399
first political office, 102
had wealthy parents, 77
live TV news conferences, 280
marriage, 119
military interventions, 364
military service, 109
minority president, 434
New Frontier program, 324
only president survived by both
  parents, 81
ordered public housing
  integrated, 194
presidential library, 166
primaries and, 405
quote on bureaucracy, 498
religion, 107
second-youngest president, 145
sexual affairs, 365
shot, 55
son dies, 133
sports, 97
staff, 457
summit, 357
television and, 235, 262
twenty-year jinx, 294
VP Johnson balanced ticket,
  397
wins Pulitzer Prize, 93
work routine, 341
Kennedy, Robert F., 189, 466
Khomeini, Ayatollah Ruholla, 363
Khrushchev, Nikita, 357
  Cuban missile crisis, 358
  debate with Nixon, 359
King, Edward B., 250
King, Martin Luther Jr., 327
  riots after assassination, 213
King, Rufus
  election, votes won, 433
King, William R.
  dates, presidency, 348
  death, 173
  member of Congress, 142
  served shortest term, 342
  tie-breaking votes, 225
King Caucus, 409

References in the index correspond to question numbers in the text.

References in the index correspond to question numbers in the text.

References in the index correspond to question numbers in the text.

first political office, 102
foreign service, 111
King Caucus and, 409
marriage, 119
military service, 109
Monroe Doctrine, 353
occupation, 105
oldest child, 83
ran unopposed, 418
religion, 107
served as governor, 103
served in Congress, 104
tried again and won, 443
two terms, 275, 386
Monroe, Maria, 350
Monticello, 112
sold at auction, 168
Montpelier, 112
Moore, Sara Jane, 297
Morgan, J. P., 314
Morris, Robert, 28
Morton, Levi P.
dates, presidency, 348
death, 173
long-lived, 172
member of Congress, 142
tie-breaking votes, 225
Most
bills vetoed, 230
cabinet rejections, 277
children by president, 130
consecutive presidencies, 392
conventions hosted by city, 447
Court appointments, 248
frequent presidential candidate,
442
presidents born in October, 80
presidents, success with
Congress, 237
press conferences held, 268
siblings of president, 79
third party votes, 441
veto overrides, 231
Mount Rushmore, 175
Mount Vernon, 112
Muckraking, 266
Myers v. United States
removal power upheld, 190
Myers, Dee Dee, 269

Nast, Thomas, 391
National Aeronautics and Space
Administration
employees, 506

National cemeteries, 496
National Commission on
Alcoholism and Alcohol-Related
Problems, 284
National Economic Council, 460
National Endowment for the Arts
employees, 506
National Guard, 204
National Institute of Standards and
Technology, 482
National Institutes of Health, 487
National Labor Relations Board
employees, 506
National Oceanic and Atmospheric
Administration, 483
National Park Service, 491
National Park System, 1, 491
National Partnership Council, 460
National party conventions. *See
also* Elections and campaigns;
Primaries
candidate selection, 409
city hosted the most, 447
convention, 1832, 408
convention, 1844, 377
convention, 1932, 415, 425
convention, 1964, 413
first, 408
first televised convention, 416
first woman VP candidate, 414
longest, 411
longest party platform, 412
nominee accepts in person, 415
procedures, 396
purpose of, 410
National Performance Review, 46,
500
National Railroad Passenger
Corporation (Amtrak), 505
National Republicans, 408
National Science Foundation
employees, 506
National Security Act of 1947, 476
National Security Council, 460
advisory role, 189
described, 462
origins, 462
staff, 374
VP attends, 215, 219
National Transportation Safety
Board
employees, 506
Native Americans, 487, 491
Navy. *See* Defense department

Nepotism
Bobby Kennedy law, 466
New Deal
Court appointees and, 247
Court rules against, 241
Court-packing and, 243
described, 425
effect of programs, 319
employment growth and, 43
fireside chats and, 336
interest groups and, 270
legislative powers and, 238
regulatory agencies expanded,
503
New Frontier program, 324
New Hampshire primary, 403, 406
New York City, 411
Nicaragua, 374
Marines sent, 355
Nineteenth Amendment, 383
Nixon v. Fitzgerald (1982)
presidential immunity and, 187
Nixon, Pat, 117
children, 130
death, 135
education, 124
marriage, 116, 199
occupation, 127
Nixon, Richard M.
Agnew resigned, 59
appointments influenced Court,
247
bills vetoed, 230
birthday, 80
campaign slogan, 417
campaign spending, 449
Checkers speech, 345
children, 130
China card, 361
China trip, 361
close election, 1968, 432
college and, 106
Congress, party control, 291
dates, in Congress, 142
dates, presidency, 348
daughter Tricia wed, 350
death, 173
debates, 359, 429
détente, 357
election of 1960, 379, 443, 446
election of 1968, 432, 443
election of 1972, 432, 446
election, votes won, 433
energy policy, 494

References in the index correspond to question numbers in the text.

References in the index correspond to question numbers in the text.

References in the index correspond to question numbers in the text.

References in the index correspond to question numbers in the text.

References in the index correspond to question numbers in the text.

References in the index correspond to question numbers in the text.

References in the index correspond to question numbers in the text.

References in the index correspond to question numbers in the text.

References in the index correspond to question numbers in the text.

References in the index correspond to question numbers in the text.

Warren, Earl, 247
Warren Commission, 284
Washington, Lucy Payne, 350
Washington Mall, 174
Washington Monument
  building of, 174
Washington Senators, 352
Washington, George
  a Founding Father, 4
  among greatest presidents, 340
  attended Congress session, 232
  bills vetoed, 230
  birthday, 80
  burial, 171
  cherry tree and, 69
  children, 120
  dates, presidency, 348
  death, 173
  elections, votes won, 433
  executive mansion name, 289
  executive privilege and, 203
  Farewell address, 163
  federal spending then, 42
  first appointee, 276
  first executive orders, 195
  first led troops in battle, 87
  first national holiday, 349
  first pardons, 206
  first patronage, 306
  first president, 10
  first presidential commission, 281
  first veto, 278
  image on stamps, 15
  inauguration, 47
  Jay Treaty, 302
  large family and, 79
  lobbying Congress and, 232
  marriage, 119
  military service, 108, 109
  most Court appointments, 248
  Mount Rushmore, 175
  Mount Vernon, 77, 112
  movies about, 150
  oath traditions and, 12
  occupation, 105
  official residences, 28
  opposed political parties, 389, 409, 419
  pardons, 301
  parties emerge, 409
  political opposition, 303
  portrait by Stuart, 305
  precedents set, 300

ran unopposed, 418
religion, 107
rumored sexual affair, 365
shortest inaugural speech, 53
sports, 97
staff, 31
state named after, 16
State of Union address, 240
stature, 146
tooth problems, 152
two terms, 275, 386
two-term tradition, 178
Washington Monument, 174
Whiskey Rebellion and, 301
  youngest to enter politics, 102
Washington, Martha
  child died, 120
  death, 135
  marriage, 118, 119
  missed first inauguration, 47
  outlived husband, 134
  residences as first lady, 28
  Revolutionary War and, 120
Watergate scandal, 373
  alienated voters, 331
  coverup, 330
  executive privilege and, 203
  FEC and, 451
  Nixon resigned, 58
Watson, Jack, 456
Weaver, Robert C., 468
Webster, Daniel
  refuses VP nomination, 217
  surrogate campaigner, 444
Weddings
  in White House, 350
Weems, Mason
  invents cherry tree myth, 69
West Berlin, 360
Westward expansion
  Louisiana Purchase, 287
  Manifest Destiny, 309
  Polk and, 310
Westwood, Jean, 393
Wheatland, 112
Wheeler, William A.
  birth, 137
  dates, presidency, 348
  death, 173
  member of Congress, 142
  tie-breaking votes, 225
Whig Party, 387, 444, 472
  described, 389
  election of 1840, 420

famous slogan, 417
Jackson and, 366
Whiskey Rebellion, 281
  described, 301
  pardons and, 206
Whiskey Ring scandal, 370
White House staffer and, 31
Whistle-stop campaign, 426
White House
  burned by British, 305
  childbirth in, 129
  first president to live in, 290
  funeral ceremonies, 170
  hostess, 122, 180
  Jackson's raucous inaugural, 50
  Jefferson introduced
    handshaking, 303
  name origin, 289
  operating costs, 183
  Oval Office history of, 8
  prayer, 290
  press corps, 263
  residences before the White
    House, 28
  Secret Service and, 472
  security, 472
  VP office, 216
  weddings, 350
White House coffees, 453
White House conferences
  described, 281
White House Military Office, 455
White House Office
  advisory role, 189
  cabinet and, 464
  detailing, 458
  economic policy and, 463
  Executive Office and, 460
  organization, 455
  staff powers expanded, 459
White House Office of Public
  Liaison, 274
White House Police Force, 472
White House press corps
  reporters in, number, 263
White House staff
  chief of staff, 456
  FDR gets more staff, 39
  history of, 31
  organizational strategies, 457
  size of, 30
Whitehead and Hoag, 423
Whitewater scandal, 375
Wide Awake clubs, 422

References in the index correspond to question numbers in the text.

References in the index correspond to question numbers in the text.